Book One for Your New Business Library

Packed with tips, information, examples, and insights on the way different types of people think, act, and react to you, *You're the Boss!* is a reference volume to read, reread, and keep to help you solve specific management problems as they arise. Written with humor and understanding and sprinkled with the author's original poems on work and life, this is the book no new supervisor should be without.

You're the Boss!

A Guide to Managing People with Understanding and Effectiveness

"I believe *You're The Boss!* speaks to the new supervisor better than any text I have seen."

—Rodney P. Tompkins, First Vice President,
Operations Group Manager,
American Savings & Loan Association

"A practical book on managing diversity. This book is a must for every first-time supervisor and for managers mentoring supervisors!"

—Buford Macklin, Ph.D.,
Director of Administrative Services,
Department of Housing and Urban Development,
Washington, D.C.

"...should be considered mandatory reading for all new managers."

—George J. Harris,
Director of Field Services (M.S.I. DATA)

"A very real world, practical survival text for managers new in their position..."

—Margaret H. Burns,
Coca Cola USA

Natasha Josefowitz, Ph.D., is a nationally known expert on management theories and techniques. An adjunct professor at San Diego State University, she is a ... er,
and frequent talk show guest. S ... r, a
best-selling book on career pl ... *Vas*
Going?, a book of poetry on the

YOU'RE THE BOSS!

A Guide to Managing People with Understanding and Effectiveness

Natasha Josefowitz, Ph.D.

A Warner Communications Company

Other books by the author
Paths to Power
Is This Where I Was Going?

Warner Books, Inc., 666 Fifth Avenue, New York, NY 10103

 A Warner Communications Company

Printed in the United States of America

First Printing: April 1985

10 9 8 7

Library of Congress Cataloging in Publication Data

Josefowitz, Natasha.
You're the boss!

Bibliography: p.
Includes index.
1. Supervision of employees. I. Title.
HF5549.J65 1985 658.3'02 84-15332
ISBN 0-446-37744-9

To My Son, Paul:
My Toughest Critic
and
My Greatest Supporter.
Thank You for Both.

ACKNOWLEDGMENTS

Many have been helpful. I want to acknowledge Dean Bruce Stewart of Mira Costa College, and Lois Stalsonburg and Yolanda Bareno of the North Island Naval Station of San Diego, all of whom supported my research on minority populations and work.

As I was writing this book, I asked my friends and colleagues for feedback. I want to thank them for being so generous with their time. Their suggestions are part of this book.

I am grateful to Buford Macklin, Ph.D., director of administrative services at the Department of Housing and Urban Development (HUD); Richard L. Hays, assistant to the planning director, city of San Diego; Len Goodstein, Ph.D., chairman of the board of University Associates and former editor of the *Journal of Applied Behavioral Sciences* (JABS); Allen E. Armstrong, Captain US Coastguard—retired; Edith Whitefield Seashore, consultant; and Marjorie Hansen Shaevitz, psychologist.

I also thank my Warner Books editor, Fredda Isaacson—my champion, my supporter, and my friend—with whom I could always test new ideas; Sue Berggren, for typing from my handwriting—a feat in itself; and my agent, Margaret McBride, for her creative problem-solving.

And finally it is Herman Gadon to whom I owe my largest debt of gratitude. He gave up seeing friends, going to the movies, and taking walks on the beach together because I was writing. He never faltered in his encouragement and love.

CONTENTS

NOTE

As you will notice throughout the book, I have written poems to illustrate specific concepts. They reflect either my own experiences or those shared with me by friends and colleagues.

INTRODUCTION

The new boss: challenge or anxiety, excitement or fear, competence or failure—which will it be? What will make the difference? Supervisors are only as good as the workers who work for them, so to be the best supervisor a worker ever had and the best supervisor a plant, office, or institution ever hired or promoted, we need to understand the workers' needs as well as the organization's goals. How do we know what workers need and want, how much to expect from them, how hard to push, or what rewards to give, especially if those workers are different from most people we have known? How do we supervise anyone? This book addresses the questions, worries, and issues of the newly hired supervisor, as well as of the supervisor who has been at it for a while and who wants to do an even better job. Many of the issues discussed apply to managers as well.

As a professor of management at the University of New Hampshire, I was asked by the then director of training, Bev Parker, to design and lead a series of workshops for the supervisors working on campus—the electricians, plumbers, grounds personnel, security guards, food service people, contractors, maintenance workers, audiovisual people, and all the administrators connected with the running of a university. We started a series of eight three-hour workshops, held once a week, dealing with the broad topic of supervision. The first series was so successful that we kept offering them, one after another, for several years. In order to train graduate students to lead these seminars, I devised a booklet to help them learn the methods I was using, including lectures, discussions, experiential exercises, simulations, and role plays.

At the same time, I was asked by several corporations to give courses for supervisors, and again I devised teaching methods to accomplish my objectives. As I worked in a variety of settings, I came to realize that whether I was dealing with blue-collar workers, engineers in high-tech organizations, or service employees, the problems of supervising others were very similar. This book is an outgrowth of those experiences.

It also grew out of discussions I had with my students, who

came from the Far East, the Near East, or just the East Coast—students whose parents spoke only Spanish or Vietnamese, whose different values gave them problems in their places of work. Because I teach both undergraduates and MBA's, usually during evening classes, most of my students work full-time, have families, and go to school. Some complain about their bosses, others about their workers. As I travel throughout the United States on lecture tours speaking to "displaced homemakers" and police chiefs, women in engineering and Rotarians, the Junior League and executives of corporations, I get many questions about "how to deal with that other person different from me, whom I just don't understand."

As more and more women and minority populations are entering the work force, they remain concentrated in lower-level positions, supervised by people who may not understand them. There are differences among people because of cultural heritage—race, sex, age, education, nationality, and religion. If you're just out of college, what do you know about older people or blue-collar workers? If you're an older person, how well do you understand today's youth? If you're black, do you understand the Mexican-Americans? If you're Asian, do you understand the American Indians? If you're a man, do you understand women? If you're a woman, do you understand other women?

It is impossible to avoid stereotyping people. For example, I fit into several categories and have many reactions that are typical for my gender: female; for my age: 58; for my education: an M.S.W. at age 40 and a Ph.D. at age 50; for my family background: born in Paris, France, a child of Russian immigrants; for my current work: teacher, lecturer, consultant, writer of management books, as well as poetry. I am also a mother and grandmother. Just knowing these things about me will give you clues as to how you might relate to me and what to expect from me.

Stereotyping is useful in the early phases of relationships. It becomes prejudice when individual differences are not acknowledged. The challenge is to be able to use generalizations yet recognize when they don't fit particular persons. This book is written to help you do that by providing opportunities to use the generalizations in order to understand individuals.

Because we all bring our differences and our distinctions to work, it is important for the supervisor to be sensitive to the issues of a work force that is already 20 percent nonwhite and over 40 percent female, 95 percent of whom are concentrated in the lower-level jobs. This is the population that needs to be valued and understood, on one hand, and taught to fit in, on the other.

The research for this book came from a variety of fields: counseling, psychology, sociology, anthropology, international management, business, industry, and nonprofit organizations.

I believe in doing serious research, but I also believe that research should be made available to the people who are the subjects of such work so that they can also become its users. The contents of this book are based on studies by other people as well as on my own research and observations. I wrote this book because I believe that there is nothing quite like it and that most people are usually not given enough training to become good bosses and handle their responsibilities effectively.

A supervisor can be demanding and compassionate, caring and in control. This book is for those of you who are on the first rungs of the ladder, with a close-up view of the places just below and a more distant view of the top. It begins with the news of a promotion and the initial reactions to it; it continues from the first day of the new position to the first week. It tells you how to handle your feelings, what actions you should take, what you should look out for, what important skills you should be acquiring, and what issues you will have to deal with as you get settled. The chapters are sequential and progress through your development as a new boss, whether you are managing workers, dealing with superiors, or coping with conflicts and stress.

This book is intended for the men and women who supervise others and who want to understand their workers in order to help them achieve top performance and provide better work climates.

Good bosses make better workers. If I can help you become a more effective boss, this book will have been worth writing.

Supervision is both a skill and an art. The skills can be taught—and this book teaches—but the art must be felt as you read through the pages. The art is reflected in an attitude toward people and toward work. People matter and work matters, and all we can do is to be aware of both and be the best boss anyone has ever had.

PART I

GETTING STARTED

1

YOU'VE JUST BEEN PROMOTED

Congratulations! You walk out of your boss's office. Your palms are sweaty, you feel cold, you're flushed, your head is pounding, your mouth is dry, your stomach feels queasy, your head is spinning, you're excited, happy, and scared out of your wits. What happened?

You've just been promoted!

You're going to be a boss! Who? Yes, you!

You got a handshake, a pat on the back, and a "We know you can make it." You go someplace to collect your wits to see what it feels like to be a "boss."

Don't panic—first things first. Whom do you tell, when and how?

If you did not discuss this with your supervisor, go back into his or her office and ask how this news is to be made known. It is best that your supervisor make the announcement to the people who will be reporting to you, as well as to your new peers—the other supervisors. Too often, there are misunderstandings as to who reports to whom. Insist on this being made very clear to all concerned so that the legitimacy of your authority is not challenged. Emphasize that many potential problems will be avoided if your authority is clear to everyone. Drop into people's offices informally, talk over coffee breaks, and make the news known to your peers. If your boss for some reason is unable or unwilling to announce it, arrange a meeting yourself and *formally* make the announcement to your subordinates. You may want to take that opportunity to talk about what the promotion means to you and to the people around you. This will be the last time that you'll be "one of them." That evening, after you have told your spouse or called your parents and friends, you'll have to begin preparing for your first day as boss. In the best of circumstances, you will have enough time to examine your objectives, to read this book, to get additional training, and to seek guidance from others who have "been there." If tomorrow is the day you start, what should you be thinking about on your first day as boss? How will you begin? You'll walk in and do what? Say what? To whom? Much will depend on how you were promoted: from the ranks as an old-timer, from the ranks as a new worker, from another department, or from outside the company. It depends on the four scenarios.

How You Got There

Let us look at these scenarios, because each one will make you feel differently about your promotion, and you will therefore act differently and will need different strategies.

Scenario 1

You have been at your job for what seems to be forever and finally, finally you have been given added responsibilities—you believe that "It's about time!" and somehow can't quite enjoy it because it's past due. The company took too long in recognizing your merits, and there is pleasure mixed with some bitterness at having been passed over so many times, at not yet being where you feel you ought to be, considering your age or the time you have been with the company.

You don't smile at the congratulations, you don't thank your boss, and you get down to the business of managing without a transition. After all, you've been there long enough to know the ropes. *Mistake*! Even though you know everything there is to know about your organization, your department, and your workers, today everything is different. You will now be perceived differently, you will be talked to differently, and your former colleagues will wait to see if you will change. Yes, you *will* change. If you do not, you will not be doing your job. Your relationships based on years of friendship and years of sharing daily events will not be the same. You are now in a position of power, and you can affect the lives of others. Some of those others will be political opportunists. They'll stay on your good side, and they'll try to use the friendship to their advantage. You'll get requests like the following:

> "You don't mind if I take Friday off, do you?"
> "You're going to report *that* after what we used to do?"
> "Oh, come on, let me leave a little earlier; what's with the new boss stuff?"
> "What's the matter with you? You've turned into a drill sergeant or something."

It will be difficult to establish your role because you can no longer indulge in old patterns of behavior: sharing secrets or gossiping about your supervisors, punching out for one another, or taking longer lunches with former peers who are now your workers, because you will then be seen as playing favorites.

You are not the person you were yesterday; you are a boss, and being a boss is a role. A role is a prescription for behavior, and you now have a new prescription. As soon as you step into your new job, you're in the role of a supervisor. This does not mean being phony. You bring who you are to the role of supervisor. You may not want to accept this: "Why do I need to change? Why do I have to give up the easy sociability?" If you don't revise your social behavior, you will have an impossible task when you need to refuse favors or have to reprimand, discipline, demote, or even fire people who are friends. It does not mean that you are not a friend but that you're a boss first. If you choose to remain "equal," you may be liked but not respected. If you choose to accept your dominant position, you may lose the pleasant camaraderie but will earn respect if you are a fair boss.

It is not an easy choice, but it must be made at the start. Your workers will be watching you closely to see what you do. Don't count on their making it easy for you; it is to their advantage to keep you at their level. There are exceptions: Where group work is effective without formal leadership or when workers can begin their jobs on their own and can control their own results, the supervisor may still be accountable to higher-ups but may be more of a team member than a leader.

So thank your boss and accept the congratulations. You are now part of the management team, and your support will come from them.

Let's look at an example. Nora had been on the assembly line for many years. She liked her job, the income it produced, and especially the friends she had there. Families would get together for picnics, couples went bowling, and the women baby-sat for each other. Company policy had been to promote from within, and even though she had seniority, managers in the plant had always been men. Nora was finally promoted. Of course, she was pleased; her boss assured her she would have no trouble because she knew the operation and the people so well. Nora's friends congratulated her, saying that finally "one of us made it." But was she still "one of them"? Nora received more invitations to come by for coffee and dessert in one week than she had in the previous six months, and Nancy, her closest friend, had already asked to be switched to another part of the line. What should she do?

If Nora is smart, she'll tell Nancy she can't play favorites, explaining that she would be seen as unfair by the others; and that if the opportunity arises where the switch will make sense, she'll remember her request. Nora is in for a difficult time when she'll have to make some tough choices between remaining a friend or being a fair boss. The change of role from worker to supervisor may be the most difficult adjustment in the workplace.

Scenario 2

You have recently been hired, haven't learned all you need to know about your job, and have already been promoted. Is it because you worked hard, because you are smart, or because of affirmative action? Did the company need to fill a slot or fulfill a quota? You don't feel prepared and are scared. The assumption many people make is that they're not ready, not "good enough," or that they'll be "found out." This assumption is made more often by women than by men. (Research indicates that college men with a C+ average think they can do graduate work, but college women with a B+ average think they cannot.[1])

I talked with a group of young women recently, all Ph.D. candidates, about their career plans. Each wanted to know what additional courses she ought to take, what seminars she should attend, what workshops would be useful, what books she should read. In other words, what other preparation should she have that she hadn't as yet acquired? Not one woman felt that she was ready. When I pointed this out to them, they recognized that their fears were based on not being willing to accept responsibilities. As long as you call yourself a learner, you don't hold yourself accountable for the mistakes you make. It takes courage to be willing to make mistakes. Most errors are reparable. The first few mistakes are part of training. It is only the fearful who do nothing and who don't make mistakes. You probably have higher expectations of yourself than anyone else has. What you don't know, you will learn on the job. Remember, if you do something wrong, *you* are not the mistake, and the mistake is only *a* mistake.

You have two points of view to consider: how you perceive yourself and how others perceive you. If you think of yourself as inadequate, not ready, too young, too new, too junior, you will project this image by the way you stand, sit, talk, and even dress. You can come across either as a "helpless young thing who doesn't know" or as a person who accepts responsibilities and who can ask for the needed information to perform effectively or can seek the necessary training.

Remember what it's like to be in charge of younger children? You know the score, and they don't. You are responsible for what happens. Get in touch with that "in charge" feeling and carry it to work with you. Don't wait until you think you've asked all the questions, mastered all the techniques, and done all the research. Begin having authority from Day One. First impressions last. In some organizations, if you give the impression that you are a learner, you will always be remembered as a learner and will have a hard time transcending that image. This brings us to a second problem: how others perceive you. When I have former students who become colleagues, I have a very hard time thinking of them as peers. They always remain "former students" as opposed to equals. I may admire their work and respect them as professionals, but I manifest parental pride in their achievements. Our children never catch up with us even if they overtake us.

Sometimes it is so difficult to stop being regarded as a learner that the only alternative is to leave the place of your beginnings and move somewhere else so that you can start out as a professional person.

If some people think you have been promoted "too quickly," you may be resented for quite a while: "Why you and not me?" If you're a man, some people may accuse you of having "pull" or using friendships to get ahead. If you're a woman, men who have been passed over will say you've benefited unfairly from affirmative action and will be angry at you for taking advantage of a political situation. Other women who may have less merit than you may attribute your promotion to the fact that you flirted with your boss. They may insinuate that you "slept" your way to the top. It is often comforting for the one who has been passed over to believe that someone has done well not because she's better but because of some unfair advantage she used for her own advancement, such as political or sexual manipulation. Seldom, if ever, will someone say, "She was more qualified than I and will do a better job than I could have." So much for human nature. What is important to remember is that it is human nature to protect one's ego.

This does not mean that some people might not be genuinely pleased for you and be ready to cooperate, but others will be competitive, difficult to work with, and may even try to sabotage you.

None of this should frighten you away; it is a "worst-case" scenario. If everything always went smoothly, there would be no need for this book.

Sandra had been working a short time as a researcher in the chemical lab of a large drug company when her boss called her in and asked her if she would like to be in charge of a seven-person lab, the present supervisor of which was being transferred. Sandra was surprised; she had only recently received her advanced degree, but she knew her work was exceptional. She worried what others would say, especially the two older men who were continually denigrating her. Her boss felt that she was the most creative of the team, in addition to being very meticulous and committed to doing well. She would often work late into the night rather than stopping in the middle of an experiment. When she mentioned her worry about her acceptance by her peers, her boss just shrugged his shoulders. Sandra asked him to make the announcement and to be very clear about her new responsibilities. Sandra was right to be uncomfortable; there was much grumbling, often within earshot. She decided to sit down with the members of the team and discuss the various projects they were working on, her expectations, their problems, and her willingness to be supportive. She was able to confront the more difficult men with their feelings of having a younger female in charge. It was Mike, the oldest member of the team, who gave her trouble. He talked disparagingly about women in general and was barely polite to her. She was afraid of a confrontation but felt one was necessary. She asked him to come to her office and asked her secretary, in front of Mike, to hold all calls. They had the following conversation:

> SANDRA: Mike, you seem particularly unhappy with my being in charge. Is it because of something I have done, because you worry I won't work out, or just because I'm a woman and you don't believe women should be in charge? (Notice that she gives him alternative explanations for his behavior.)
> MIKE: Well, I just don't understand why the boss thinks you're so great. We never had a woman doing this kind of work, and I don't know why we should start now.
> SANDRA: In other words, you're not sure I'm going to be good, and you're worried about the future of the lab. (She offers him a face-saving device.)
> MIKE: Right, you haven't proven yourself, and there is so much at stake.
> SANDRA: I appreciate your concern, and I wish everyone cared as much as you do. I think you should trust the boss's judgment—he believes I can do the job. I also hope you will give me a chance to prove myself. I want this lab to do well just as much as you do—so we share this, but I need your help, Mike. You're competent, and you have a lot of experience. Suppose you tell me when you see any signs of problems, and we can talk about them. I know it's hard for a lot of men to work with a woman. (She does not say, work *for* me, or *for* a woman, but *with* a woman.)
> MIKE: Well, I don't know, we'll see."
> SANDRA: Will you give us both a chance to work together?
> MIKE: I guess so.

Her efforts paid off. She became accepted because of her competence as a chemist, and even more because of her sensitivity in dealing with difficult issues.

Scenario 3

You are being promoted into another department. Although you know the organization, you may have only a vague notion of who your new people are or what they do or what is expected of you. You're an old hand and a newcomer at the same time. This is a very treacherous situation, because your tendency will be to do things as they were done in your former place, which may not fit the needs of the new place. Information, as well as misinformation, about you may have preceded your entry. You, too, may have gathered impressions from hearsay or previous contact with the people there. Both sets of ideas may be wrong because whatever stories you or others have heard were relayed through someone else. Entering a new position is like getting married. Everything depends on how the people involved work out the specific differences among themselves; the issue is the relationship between you and your workers. Just as you change for the better or worse, depending on whom you're with, so do workers behave differently depending on who their boss is, on who the other workers are, and on the nature of the job.

Moving from one department to another is an opportunity to learn the norms (the unwritten rules) from scratch. Don't assume you already know all about your new area. Observe who does what, how, when, with what consequences, and for whom. Find out what kind of boss was there before you and how he or she did things, and whether or not it was satisfactory. If the previous boss was very much liked and is now missed, you'll have a harder time because you'll be expected to fit someone else's style, which can never be done. The way to deal with this situation is to be up-front and say that you have heard how wonderful the former boss was and that you hope to do as well, but that everyone's style is different. On the other hand, if the former boss was ineffective or disliked, your subordinates may have unrealistic expectations that you can save them. Unless you help them to adjust their expectations to ones that are reasonable, you and they could face serious disappointment or even failure.

Whatever your situation, find out for yourself everything you need to know by talking directly to each person in your department. Never rely on hearsay or secondhand information. Use your newness to your advantage.

Just as your workers will want to see the same patterns repeated (there is security in the familiar), you will have a tendency to manage as your former boss did; you will do the things that worked in your other department. Observe, take stock, and learn about your new place and new position. You should be willing to do some things *their* way and not only *your* way, or work out a compromise.

You may be expected to know specific things you do not know, yet you do know many things that would normally take years to find out. In being transferred and promoted, you have the best and the worst of all possible worlds.

Henry moved only two floors down, but what a difference in the work climate! For example, in his old department, the coffee break was scheduled and observed from 10:00 A.M. to 10:15 A.M.; in the new department, it was somewhere between 10:00 A.M. and 11:00 A.M. (more or less 10 to 20 minutes), and no one seemed to care either way. Henry knew that if he were to institute a rigid 15-minute break, he would make people angry, so he decided to see if people would take advantage of a flexible break and whether it would reduce productivity. He thought if the time taken off were to stretch to 30 minutes too often, he would say that 15 minutes was all that was allowed, but that it could be taken anytime between 10:00 A.M. and 10:30 A.M., thus offering some flexibility within a more rigid time span. Henry was prepared to go along with the norms as long as they were not unproductive. He also had a plan ready in case he needed an alternative. As it happened, he was tested only once by an employee who did take a long break of 35 minutes. Henry's preparation paid off. He spoke to the worker, reminding him not to take advantage of the flexibility. The offense was not repeated. Henry had set the limits not only for that one subordinate but for all the others who were waiting to see how he would react. (It is always a good idea to check with your boss to be sure he or she will back your decisions.)

Scenario 4

You have been newly hired as a supervisor. You have a college degree, an expertise in a specific field, and a track record, but you know next to nothing about the company that hired you and even less about the people you will be supervising. You go in on the strength of your expertise and your boss's confidence in you. Obviously your boss saw your potential. The expectation is that you'll render good service—not right away, immediately, tomorrow, but IN DUE TIME. Don't expect perfection from yourself or anyone else, let the work proceed as it has been, observe, and make notes on what you see or hear. Make a list of your workers, and note what they do. Study their job descriptions. Do they actually do what their job descriptions say they do? Do they do more, less, or something entirely different? Are they productive, and do they seem content? List the patterns you observe. Who comes in early or leaves late? How much socialization is there? How hard do individuals work? What is the mood in the office? Is the work boring or challenging? Study file records on turnover rates, absenteeism, sick leaves, and complaints. In other words, do as an anthropologist does in an alien culture: study the ways of the natives. Little by little, you will begin to make sense of their culture. Establish a relationship with your employees: talk, ask questions, get a feeling for their weaknesses and their strengths. Don't make quick judgments or promises. Wait for a while before you take action. What may seem disruptive at first may not be in the long run. New managers are always eager to show their ability and therefore tend to start making changes too early. Tell your workers you need time to observe and think about what you see, and only then do you plan to make decisions about what will continue as is and what will be changed. If you feel there is pressure from your supervisor for you to perform immediately, ask him or her for the time you need to be informed.

The anthropological attitude when you enter a new job or a new position is always a helpful stance to take at the beginning, because it lets you be more objective. It's harder to be as analytical if you're promoted from the ranks because it's also *your* culture, and it's almost impossible to detach yourself enough from it to pretend you're an outsider looking in.

Steve had been an assistant buyer for some years and knew the clothing business well, but there he was, hired to manage a department in a large appliance discount store. There were either hectic periods when the salespeople were bustling about trying to serve impatient customers or quiet periods when there seemed to be little for them to do. He noticed that while there was work to be done during slack times, the salespeople stood around chatting and then, as soon as customers came in, sprang into action. He thought of changing this and assigning tasks, but he decided to wait and see. He was right. Salespeople were active when they needed to be and took the needed rest from the pressure when they could, managing to keep up with the paperwork in between, without having it rigidly scheduled. Had Steve insisted on setting specific times for the work to be done, he would have run into resistance. The atmosphere was friendly, people helped one another, and the salespeople needed to relax in between very busy times. Steve decided to keep observing and to do nothing unless he noticed that work was not being performed adequately.

How You Look Makes a Difference

Before you begin your day in your new role, think about the image you want to project. Clothes express three messages: they tell something about your company, about your position in the company, and about the way you feel about yourself. An advertising agency and a bank may want to convey very different images to the public. A clerk and an executive need to convey different images. For example, in your plant or shop, do the supervisors wear overalls as the workers do? In your hospital or lab, where everyone wears white coats, is the supervisor's the same as the technicians' or different? In your office, do most female workers wear slacks or dresses while most female managers wear suits? Do most male managers wear ties? If you're a woman with no women supervisors whose clothing you can use as an example, look at the men. Are they wearing jackets? This will give you a clue as to how formally you will be expected to dress.

Pay attention to what you wear; it often dictates how you act. We all alter our behavior according to our dress. I put my feet up or sit cross-legged in jeans, but I sit up straight in a suit. I also stand straighter when I have a jacket on, and my handshake is firmer. Your clothing need not be expensive, but it must be becoming and fit well. If you are a woman, avoid too-tight skirts or low-cut blouses. Don't buy skirts with side slits because often more shows than is intended. Blouses can be feminine, but they never should be see-through. Buy skirts that let you get into a car comfortably without their riding to midthigh.

Do the men and women in your place of work wear easy-to-care-for polyester, or do they dress in materials that look like cotton, silk, linen, or wool? Adapt your clothes to whatever seems to be the norm.

Are the colors of your clothes muted? Do people dress conservatively? Who wears ties, and what kind? What about belt buckles? Shirt colors? Check to see what is commonplace. In other words, follow the examples that are there for you to observe.

If you're at a loss as to what to buy, you will find that most department stores now have personal shoppers who will advise you at no extra cost. Shoes should be simple pumps in neutral colors with comfortable heels. Many women I know have bought briefcases that can hold a small purse containing their personal items and whatever papers they need. If you get one, you will find that a side pocket is useful for papers too big to fit inside. You do not need to carry all your makeup everywhere you go. Have everything you will need to use in your office drawer as well as in your home, and carry only touch-up items.

Cologne for men or perfume for women is acceptable as long as the fragrances leave with you when you go.

Women often ask me about makeup and nail polish. You can use them, but be conservative—you don't want to look "made-up," nor do you want attention to be focused on very long, very bright red nails. You should wear your clothes and your makeup, they should not wear you. Eyeglasses studded with stones are not for work; neither is gaudy, noisy jewlery. If you have very long hair, gather it in a neat fashion. Remember, understated is considered more elegant. You can begin to be more creative in the way you dress only after you have been there awhile and have earned some credibility.

How to Begin

As a worker, you were responsible only for what you did, but as a supervisor, your job is to be responsible for what everyone else does. In other words, you are accountable for other people's performance. If they don't do well, you get the blame. If all goes well, you get the credit; if performance is above expectations, you may even get praise. What is performance, and how do you know when people are performing well? As a supervisor, you are responsible for a product or service—whether your subordinates make airplane parts or fill out and file insurance forms or answer phone calls. Whether your workers use their hands to build or type, their heads to study and to think, their voices to answer phones, or their faces to smile when greeting visitors, they are all doing something that can be done well or done poorly.

What must you know and what must you do to be a good supervisor? On the first rung, most supervisors are teachers. You will probably have to know how to operate equipment in your area and what is expected from each employee. You also need to know the standards you will use to measure a job well done, whom you can depend on and who depends on you, the resources available to you, and what will be expected of you. When you know these things, you can decide the means by which you plan to achieve your goals.

As a supervisor you will be in charge of three basic tasks: (1) what needs to be done; (2) who will do it; and (3) how it will be done. It will be your responsibility to make these decisions, fitting the worker to the job, helping those who need it, creating an atmosphere where people can be productive and enjoy their work and each other. It will be your chance to influence a large part of the lives of your workers so that they go home at the end of the day feeling good about themselves and the work they do.

A supervisor has power. What you do and say has impact. If you're not satisfied with one of your workers, your expression of that dissatisfaction may mean loss of self-esteem or loss of a job. If you are pleased, your attitude may mean a boost in confidence or even a pay raise. You are now in a position of influence, and you have a responsibility to be fair, honest, clear, direct, and supportive. Enjoy your promotion and learn to be the best boss your workers ever had.

Understanding the Big Picture

The big picture for you is the whole organization. What is the purpose of this organization? What are its short-term goals? What are its long-range goals? Where is it going? Can you discern a value system, such as "Let's have the best-trained people in the field" or "Let's get this done the fastest and cheapest way" or "Let's beat the competition or be the first" or "People's problems outside of work are not our business" or "We're a company who cares"? Even though each organization is basically concerned with overall productivity, the means used to get to that goal represent the company's value system.

I will discuss the big picture first because the tendency for a new supervisor is to remain identified with the workers. It is now important for you to start identifying with management. You are now part of the management team, and even though you may feel your support comes more from your workers than from your equals or your superiors, do not fall into the trap of settling in where you are most comfortable, but work at getting to know your new peers.

It is important to understand *what* the organizational goals are and what means are used to obtain them in order to find out *who* in the organization seems to be fulfilling these expectations best—those are the people with power. For example, if your company wants to be in the forefront with new products, innovations will be valued; therefore, the people who are willing to take risks and test new ideas will do better than the conservatives who do it the way it's always been done. If your company is run by older, more careful people who know a good thing when they have it and prefer to stick with it, a person with bright ideas on how to improve matters will not be welcome.

Expectations will also be affected by whether the organization is in a period of growth and expansion, in a period of stability, or in a period of trying to survive by cutting back.

Power flows to the people who meet the most critical organizational needs. Let's take some examples: Procter & Gamble may focus most on marketing; Intel (a computer company) would want to push ahead through research and development; and Chrysler, which used to emphasize production, now heavily depends on its finance people. If resources are scarce, purchasing agents are more important to the company. If a school is in financial trouble, funding has to be developed and students have to be recruited.

Right after World War II, when getting the economy back on its feet was the first priority, the people in *production* were most influential. Then *marketing* gained importance as increasing demand became the goal. When funds were short, *financial* experts developed influence. Today the people in power have to be good at *negotiation*; they need interpersonal skills to deal with conflict. According to a recent report, three job functions that are moving into preeminence in top management are *corporate planning, human resources,* and *marketing*.[2]

Because there are always tensions in any system, you will need political understanding to survive. The balance of power is always changing, so you must keep reading the signs to know what is going on.

At the beginning, try to fit the mold—it is visible if you look for it. Only much later, when you have gained credibility and are well established can you dare to be a maverick and try to change conditions.

What Is at Stake

Early on, do a stake-holder's analysis for yourself. A stake-holder's analysis means determining who has what at stake. Each unit, department, and section has a vested interest in the continuation of what it is doing. Each division tends to believe not only that it is more important than the others but also that it does not have enough recognition. So each wants more resources and more influence.

As a new supervisor, you will need to know: (1) What is important (and for whom)? (2) Who knows it (or who has it; resources)? (3) Who needs it (is vulnerable)? and (4) How can you provide it?

When you have begun to figure all this out, you are in a position of power because you have information and will know how to play the system. But how do you find out?

Most organizations have an unofficial company historian—an old-timer who is happy to talk about the good old days. Listen carefully because history both repeats itself and swings in opposite directions. Like a pendulum, it moves away, only to return. Find out what you can about how the organization was started and by whom. Is there a tradition? Are people promoted from within or hired from the outside? Is seniority important, or does merit count more? Is complying with affirmative action a big issue? Have there been policies that have been discarded?

Why should you pay attention to all this? Because you will need to know who has power today and who is most likely to have power tomorrow. Your own future depends on how well you can obtain and use the available resources and how well you fill the organizational and departmental needs.

There are other ways to find out who has the power. Observe who calls meetings, who sets the agenda, whose agenda gets worked on and gets implemented, whose work gets done first, who interrupts whom, who has lunch with whom. Start looking for nonverbal behavioral cues, such as who seems uncomfortable with whom, who sidles up to whom, who gets upset and by what, who and what seem valued and rewarded, who and what goes unrecognized.

There is a world out there for you to learn about as you perform your supervisory responsibilities. Don't miss any opportunity to observe, take note, and remember. I have two mottos I live by: "You never know" and "Just in case."

You Never Know and Just in Case

"You never know"
and "just in case"
are the two phrases
I live by

So I notice
what seems insignificant
and remember
unimportant events

I do some things
not for the doing
but for the having done

I collect experiences
and live through events
which are not all
especially pleasant

But I do not mind
and keep doing it still
because just in case,
you never know . . .
something may come in handy

What we have just been looking at is the informal organization. There is also a formal one, and you need to know how it works. Most organizations are divided into departments. This division may be by function, such as production, marketing, finance, or personnel—each with a manager who reports to an overall manager. It also may be by product or service, such as food, laundry, equipment maintenance, cleaning, or products A, B, and C.

Another division may also be by location, such as regions, cities, or the south wing on the third floor. Most divisions are mixed—you may be supervising a department that manufactures a particular product under a plant manager who reports to a regional manager, who reports to the production manager, who reports to the company executive.

Try to find an organizational chart, as shown opposite, and write yourself in.

As you look at this chart, it will become clear who your colleagues are, who the other supervisors are, from whom you will get your information, and to whom you will give it. Plant C manager is your boss and a critical person for you to get to know, but you might also want to get to know others if, for example, what you produce must rely on specifications drawn elsewhere or if your product goes to another department for completion. You will need good rapport with the people who feed you information as well as the people down the line from you.

You're a cog on a wheel, and you must be familiar with the other cogs to make sense of where the wheel is going. What you will need to do is to establish relationships with the people who are significant to your operation. Talk to them in their offices. Ask them to go out for a beer or a cup of coffee. Seeking information in order to perform better is a legitimate and valued quest.

You will also want to pay attention to what types of people seem to be in decision-making positions. Are there any women, blacks, or ethnic minorities in administrative positions? What is the highest rank a minority has reached? If you are a minority person, this survey will tell you a lot about what advancement opportunities there are, who your support system might be, and how you may be viewed if you're assertive or ambitious.

Understanding the Little Picture

The little picture you must look at is composed of your workers. It should be detailed, and you should keep filling in the missing pieces with small brush strokes as you learn them. Who is a grouch? Who can be trusted? Who works fast? Who is sloppy? Who has family problems?

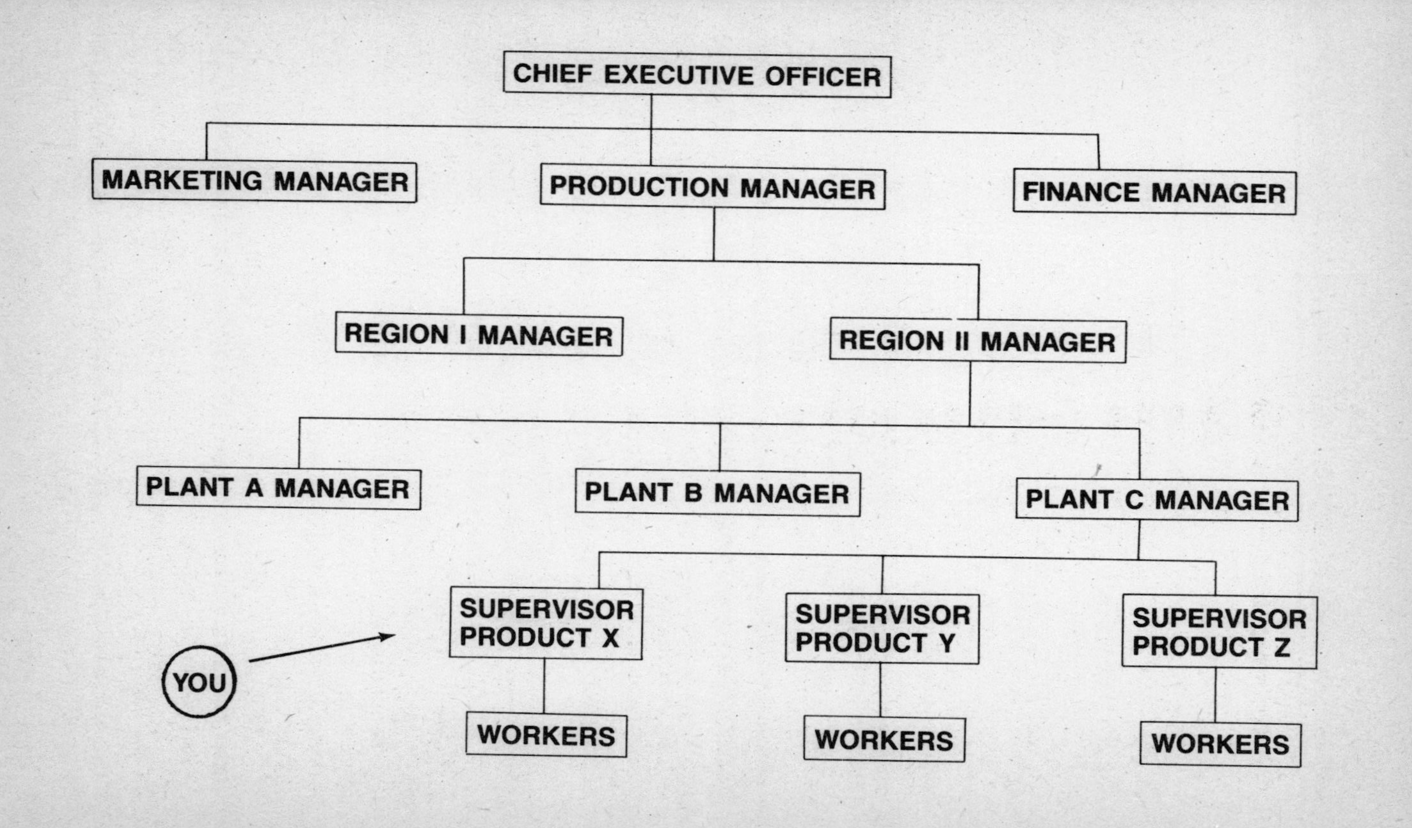
CHIEF EXECUTIVE OFFICER
MARKETING MANAGER
PRODUCTION MANAGER
FINANCE MANAGER
REGION I MANAGER
REGION II MANAGER
PLANT A MANAGER
PLANT B MANAGER
PLANT C MANAGER
SUPERVISOR PRODUCT X
SUPERVISOR PRODUCT Y
SUPERVISOR PRODUCT Z
YOU
WORKERS
WORKERS
WORKERS

Where You Fit

Be actively assertive and seek out other people at your level or above, even though you may not feel particularly welcome. This is your new peer group, and you cannot work in isolation. Ask to join them; don't wait to be invited. If they're a tight-knit group, you will have trouble getting in. As a new person, you may even be suspect. Can you be trusted? Will you report what you overhear? Will you be loyal and protective? There is always a period in which a new supervisor is in limbo. You have lost your old peer group and have not as yet been accepted by a new one. This is a lonely time, perhaps scary, and you may wonder, "Who needs this?" Don't let yourself be overwhelmed. Stick around, become familiar to your peers, do them some favors, study what a good group member must do, and eventually you'll be accepted.

It is easiest to ask questions at the beginning. If you wait too long, people will wonder why you've suddenly become interested. As a newly hired or promoted person, you're expected to want to get on board as fast as possible. As you learn the details of what you need to do on a daily basis, keep your eyes and ears open to the total picture to pick up any information you ought to know about.

You can share what you learn with your workers so that they will feel part of the organization and will understand how their work fits into the scheme of things.

People are more motivated to work if they see how what they do individually or as a small group results in something tangible. Even tightening screws or filling out forms all day seems more worthwhile if you know why you are doing it. Surprisingly, under certain circumstances some workers prefer routine, monotonous, simple jobs but still want to feel that they are a part of a larger organization.

What you will need to know next are the specific expectations the organization has for your department. Your immediate supervisor is the one to tap for this information.

It is surprising how often managers do not tell their supervisors exactly what the output expectations are. You should be fully aware of how much work is to be accomplished, what the standards of quality are, and the amount of time allotted for that piece of work. Insist on enough time to discuss this fully with your boss so that you are satisfied with the answers.

You cannot meet objectives set by others if you don't know what they are. If your workers perform well, they make you look good; if you perform well, your manager gets the credit. A supervisor is always caught between management demands and workers' needs. You will always be pulled between these two forces. One of your main responsibilities is to represent your workers to management and to explain management requests to your workers. A supervisor often acts as a buffer between the demands from upper management and the capabilities of the workers.

The Supervisor

I'm in charge of him
but she's in charge of me
She is in charge of him
but only through me.

I tell her his needs
I tell him her wants
He needs to work less
She wants him to work more.

And I'm in the middle.

Exercise

This is the first of a series of exercises that you will find at the end of each chapter. The purpose of these exercises is to increase your awareness of the issues discussed and to help you become more effective as a boss. Do you have a colleague, a friend, a family member you can share your answers with? If not, take a few minutes to jot down some impressions. Even though most people don't like answering questions, these are for your own benefit, so I urge you to answer them.

Think about your workers and answer the following questions:

1. If you are different (race, gender, ethnic background, age, and so on) from any of them, will that person be affected by your being "different" from him or her? If yes, how

can you help this worker become more comfortable with you? Try talking with that person more often.

2. Are you experiencing any discomfort being the boss of any particular individual? If yes, can you figure out why?
3. If you were one of your workers, how would you perceive yourself as a boss? Try to describe yourself as seen through the eyes of someone else. Do you like the image? If not, is there anything you are able to change?
4. Do you suspect that some of your workers have never worked for someone like you because you're a woman, a minority person, older, younger, and so on? If the answer is yes, take an opportunity to become better known to that person.

2

GETTING TO KNOW YOUR WORKERS AND YOUR BOSS

Your first few days are behind you. You are still mostly observing and learning, although in many organizations, you will also be expected to be actively supervising. Who you are and whom you supervise will influence both how you manage others and how others perceive your management style.

Men Supervising Men

If you're a man supervising other men, you can expect the usual issues that exist in any hierarchical situation. The men may envy you, may compete for your position, or may be jealous of each other and compete for your favors. Some may try to get away with as little work as possible; others will want your approval and work very hard for it. In other words, you will have the normal people problems. Most books on supervision are written for men supervising other men. Let us take a look at some specific issues when that is not the case.

Men Supervising Women

If you are a man supervising women, you are in the most traditional man/woman relationship. Because of their early training, most boys grow into men who are more focused on tasks and achievements, and girls grow into women who are more focused on relationships and on nurturing others.

This pattern of relationship between men and women is reflected in attitudes at work. Many women are taught that achieving a good relationship is what society calls being successful. Women learn early how to compete effectively for men; their concern about clothes, hair, makeup, weight, charm, and sex appeal, all reflect the attempt to please. It is not surprising, then, that at the workplace, some women will compete for the attention of the boss or the strongest male who can offer some protection or give some special privileges.

Competing behavior takes many forms, from very subtle kinds of seductions to quite brazen ones. Some women play at being a "helpless little girl," using childlike gestures and voices. This makes some men feel needed and powerful—they like playing "Big Daddy." Some women play at being a "femme fatale," acting as the sexpot, the vamp, one who makes implicit and sometimes explicit sexual promises. This attracts some men, and they feel flattered that women find them desirable. Some women play at being the "good mother." They sew on a loose button, bring in coffee, and are solicitous and hovering. Some men are comforted by such nurturing and feel cared for and loved. Some women play at being a "tough tease." They are sarcastic, hold back no punches, deliver barbs, poke fun, and generally exchange pointed remarks with men who may be challenged and attracted by this kind of matching of wits. It's a competitive game of who outsmarts whom and who has the last word. If the man wins, he feels like a champion; if he loses, he might become angry or come back for more. However, some men are very threatened by this kind of woman and will do everything to avoid any encounters with her.

The little girl, the femme fatale, the good mother, and the tough tease are all after the same thing. They want to get their boss interested in them in some special way, to be liked more than the others, to win extra favors, and to be on more intimate terms with their boss than the other women are. I have heard some managers say that they have been bothered by women in subordinate positions who try to use their sex to get a promotion, a pay raise, a training opportunity—or anything else they want.

We have all witnessed women behaving this way and have cringed, wondering if any man could be foolish enough to fall for it. As long as there are men who do, there will be women who will attempt it. And women are not alone. Men, too, try to ingratiate themselves by acting as yes-men to top executives. It is important for a male boss not to encourage his female subordinates in behavior that is out of place in a work relationship. If he seems to like it, it will only reinforce that behavior. A good boss rewards good work, not good looks; he praises his worker's performance, not her cuteness; he pays attention to her ideas, not to her body; he recognizes her value as a worker regardless of her sex, not because of it. As a boss, it is his responsibility to set the standards and make the women who work for him aware that they are in a working, not a courting, relationship.

Many men believe that women work just as a hobby or for luxuries and thus lack the ambition, aggressiveness, and dedication necessary to really succeed in business. They believe that women have higher rates of sickness and absenteeism and that they cannot understand technology. These are myths that undermine work relationships and keep men and women from understanding and appreciating one another. Today most women work to earn a living; many are single heads of households. They are equally dedicated to their jobs, and if one compares men and women in similar jobs, their rates of absenteeism and turnover are the same.

It is critical for a male boss to remember that it is because he is the boss and not because he is a man that women might make a play for him. For some men who think that many of the women who work for them are attracted to them, it may be bad news; but it is power that is the magnet, not the strong profile or broad shoulders.

Kathy is obviously attracted to her boss, Henry. She flushes when she talks to him, and then laughs a bit too loudly; she is always thinking up excuses to see him in his office, brings him cookies, and generally is making a big play for him. At first, Henry was flattered, but then he started feeling embarrassed and worried about what the other workers would think. It had to stop, but how? He decided to call Kathy in and talk to her honestly, as follows:

HENRY: Kathy, I can't help but notice that you go out of your way to be nice to me. It's great, but it's also embarrassing.
KATHY (flushing): I don't know what you mean.
HENRY: You come into my office more often than anyone else;

you bring me cookies. Yesterday it was flowers for my desk. I think people might begin to gossip.

KATHY: So, who cares.

HENRY: I do. I want to maintain a professional atmosphere here and it's important for you and me to be professional. You don't present the image of a serious worker.

KATHY *(defensively):* I can do whatever I please.

HENRY: Kathy, there are certain standards we must maintain. It is best for you not to bring me gifts, even though I appreciate the thought. I know this conversation is difficult for you—it is for me. (Kathy starts crying.)

HENRY: It's okay to cry, Kathy. I understand how upsetting this must be to you. I would like to help you become a more professional woman. You're a good worker, and I don't want to lose you.

KATHY *(still crying):* I knew all along you didn't like me.

HENRY: I like you just as I like my other employees. I care for all of you and want you to do well.

KATHY: I don't ever want to see you again.

HENRY: Kathy, your feelings are hurt, but that's a matter of pride. I won't tell anyone of our conversation. I would like to see you in my office again in a few days. (Kathy leaves without saying anything.)

Henry was direct, firm, but nonpunitive. He remained the helpful boss, but he made his expectations known. His message was clear—their relationship was to be professional.

Women Supervising Men

The toughest thing of all for women who want to be professional—who just want to do their work and who see themselves as colleagues—is contending with men who play "Big Daddy," "Little Boy," "Roving Romeo," or "Put Down." A man in a position of authority can reprimand a subordinate for unbecoming behavior. A worker cannot reprimand her boss for the same behavior without worrying that her job may be on the line. This power differential is the crucial difference between who can say what to whom and with what consequences.

If you're a female, male workers may find accepting you as boss a culture shock. A female boss with a mostly male work force has problems that can be difficult to handle, especially if she is the first woman for whom these men have ever worked.

From childhood, schoolmates, coaches, or fathers often shame the little boy who has allowed a girl to overtake him in competition. Somehow, losing to a girl is far worse than losing to another boy. When little boys grow to manhood and suddenly get a woman as a boss, that childhood conditioning can still influence attitudes. Something does not feel right; they question whether they are inferior men if they allow themselves to be led by a woman.

These feelings are especially true in traditionally male enclaves, such as police work or fire fighting, where work is hard, even dangerous, and so a person must be tough to take it. If a woman can take it, too, then maybe it's not so tough, and maybe they're not the men they thought they were.

The stereotype that women are the weaker sex is true in terms of body strength. What is not true is that *all* women are weaker than *all* men. Some women are taller, stronger, tougher, or faster than some men. For some men, having a female boss is like being surpassed by a woman. Having a woman dictate, evaluate, reward, or punish is uncomfortable. It reminds men of their subordinate relationship to their mothers. Men who choose difficult physical work may have made that choice so as to be in the society of men.

The male culture has its own rites, norms, and inside jokes for male eyes and ears only. Every primitive tribe has some sort of special house only for men, a particular rite only for boys, work that only men can do, or ceremonies only men can perform.

In the United States, we are no different. Witness the clubs, societies, and associations that exclude women and in which members are sworn to secrecy. Witness the antagonism these male societies exhibit when women try to join.

Many women who do not understand the special kind of male bonding that occurs in all-male groups are irritated that they are excluded. The cohesiveness of the group is based on the fact that some can be members and some cannot. If everyone can be "in," then there are no boundaries, and no one then is "out." To feel "in," you have to have some who are kept "out."

To Be "One of Them," You Must:

Dislike the cafeteria food
Complain about the boss
Discount your subordinates
Joke about the women
Disparage the men
Make passes you don't mean

You pay the price of membership
by acting according
to others' expectations
If you conform
you're one of them

And so you become
more like the boys
than the boys themselves

Perhaps that's not
how you want to be
Perhaps you're not
the only one
to feel this way
If you're afraid
to check it out
how are we ever going
to change the world?

There is no question that something is lost when doors are opened to the opposite sex. I know how special it feels to be in a group of all women. We laugh, tell stories, share experiences, and talk about the men in our lives in ways we could never do if men were present. The same goes for men. They joke, brag, and talk about women in ways that women would not understand or enjoy. Women inhibit men; if, however, the men decide to not be inhibited, the women present are offended and think the men are rude.

The comments men make are not considered crude within their culture. What they say may sound awful to female ears. It is not meant to offend, but it does just that when women hear it. Yet it is important to include both sexes even in informal gatherings to foster comfort with each other and good relationships. Many important decisions are made or work-related information is passed on at these men-only meetings, thus effectively excluding women from opportunities to learn, share, participate.

Just a Little Fun...

The men talk about the women
sexist remarks
about scoring
and measurements

The women gossip about the men
laughing behind their backs
but within hearing distance
ridiculing them

Inside jokes
shared secrets
no harm meant
no pain intended

Yet it hurts
in hidden ways
Those at whose expense
we're having
just a little fun

What should you do? A woman supervisor must be aware of these dynamics. She will see to it that the male employees have opportunities to be by themselves during breaks or lunch, but she also needs to spend time with them, get to know them, and see to it that other women in her department do too. It is important to let them know that she does not enjoy sexual jokes or demeaning comments about women and doesn't want to hear them when she's around. I have found that the women who join in the crude joke-telling are often resented as being "unladylike." Each organization will have its own norms

What is important here is for women to understand the resistance they will be most likely to encounter. It is not directed at their person but at their femaleness. By facing the issues as they come up, they can eventually earn credibility. The period between initial entry and acceptance will be fraught with difficulties. The female supervisor may be mercilessly teased. She may undergo a hazing process to test if she can be one of the boys. She may be isolated, not be given important information, sabotaged, or insulted. She may find on her desk bizarre objects, nude photos, or cartoons. She may be tested to see if she is tough, can take a joke, has standards, is flexible, and knows her boundaries. If she can laugh with the men who are subordinate to her and not tolerate poor performance at the same time, she probably will make it.

The following reasons are why some men say they don't like working for women bosses:[3]

1. **Women don't appear confident.** People prefer bosses who seem to know what they are doing.
2. **Women don't have clout.** People prefer working for bosses who have the support of upper management. Can a woman boss bring resources, prestige, and clout to her department?
3. **Women don't know how to play the game.** Women are seen as not delegating responsibility or working in teams.
4. **Women come on too strong.** Women are seen as overcompensating by acting too tough, using strong language, trying to be one of the boys.
5. **Men don't know how to treat a woman boss.** Many men feel awkward with women executives in social situations. They tend to be overcomplimentary because they think they have to be nice to a woman.
6. **Men believe that working for a woman will make them look bad.** Over one-half of the men surveyed said they felt inferior when their superiors were female.
7. **Men believe that some women are promoted because of affirmative action and therefore are not qualified.**

What is important about this list is not whether these statements are true or not, but that they represent the feelings of many men. If women bosses understand the prejudices, they will be better able to deal with them.

Nora has been around for a long time. She knows that men like to talk about women as they talk about games: who scored and how many. The prize goes to the one who gets the most unattainable woman (the big catch), or to the one who gets the most women (the successful hunt). It has nothing to do with how they feel about particular women they have relationships with. Nora, herself, does not mind such talk, but knew that some of the women at work were offended by the way some men talk at times in their presence. Nora decided to be straightforward with her male subordinates about comments they made that could be offensive to other women employees. She asked them to meet with her and started the discussion by asking how they felt about having a woman supervisor. She said that she understood that for many men it could create a problem, thus allowing that negative feelings are normal. Then she talked about how some women might not appreciate the joking nature of sexual comments; that often what men say "in fun" can hurt, demean, or embarrass; that whenever the men are by themselves, they can do as they please, but with women around, they should curb their comments or take the chance of being seen as being sexually harassing. In other words, Nora set the standards of behavior.

Even though blue-collar workers may be more open in expressing their prejudices, white-collar workers share the same feelings but express them differently. Blue-collar workers tend to be more physical, use stronger language, and express anger by shouting and fighting. White-collar workers are more verbal, have fewer opportunities to vent their frustrations, and may be more underhanded in their expressions of disapproval.

Shouting on a construction site is very different from shouting in an office. Kicking a piece of equipment in a plant is different from kicking a piece of furniture in an office. Obscenities on an assembly line sound different than they do around a conference table.

I am neither passing judgment nor am I trying to reinforce class differences; I am making these comments for women who will be supervising men in various settings. It is a reality they will have to deal with, and they need to be prepared for it.

Popular assumptions are often based on stereotypes. Many men accept the false notion that women are psychologically unsuited to supervisory jobs, that their temperaments are bound to create difficulties. Here are some facts you can use to refute these prejudices.

"There is considerable evidence to support the fact that women managers are not significantly different from their male counterparts and that they may even possess superior attributes and skills in some areas related to managerial effectiveness. The differences that do exist would serve to *increase* probability of women functioning well as managers. The largest difference that has been found is that women place a higher value on interpersonal relationships, especially those with peers, than men do.''[4] Although some male supervisors to whom I have talked say that some of the women they work for bend over backwards not to appear as ''nurturing females'' and thus act tough, this is probably not a natural tendency and, I would guess, might disappear as women gain in credibility and, therefore, confidence.

''Another report finds that by a 2-to-1 margin, female managers report greater satisfaction from their careers than from their home life. Sixty percent of the women choose careers as more satisfying compared with 37 percent of the men. The survey also notes that women are more willing than men to work long hours, to accept a job promotion even if they have doubts about their ability to handle it, and to give up activities at home if work activities conflict.''[5]

Women Supervising Women

Most women have been brought up to expect to see men in authority positions. How many of our mothers have threatened punishment with ''Wait until your father comes home—you'll be sorry . . .''

Women have been used to obeying, respecting, and fearing people in authority, and in our lifetimes the authorities have most frequently been men. Even today our children get the same messages we did when we were growing up. If you watch the commercials on television, you may see a helpless woman distraught in front of a dirty sink, dirty floor, or dirty laundry; a male voice then booms out and announces to her that her troubles are over if she will only use Product X. In other words, men know best even about products most men never use. It is the voice of authority that counts; and obviously advertisers must know that women will believe a male voice's message more readily than one delivered by a female voice.

Things have not changed much today. Although most elementary schoolteachers are women, the principal is often a man; more doctors are men and more women are nurses; and 99 percent of all top administrators and decision-makers are men.

If your female staff previously had a male boss and you are their new female supervisor, you will have to pay attention to some very specific dynamics:

1. There will be some discounting of your authority—what do you (as a female) know about being in charge? Many women still hold stereotypes about women being able to take orders but not being able to give them and, in fact, may even believe that women should not be in leadership positions because it makes them unfeminine. In our culture, in the eyes of many people, masculinity is enhanced by success and femininity is diminished by it.
2. There may be jealousy—what made you better qualified than they? What your promotion means to other women is that they cannot rely on the face-saving device of saying, "They don't promote women here," but need to accept the fact that it may be their own limitations that hold them back. This is not a pleasant realization. If your being boss makes them feel inadequate, their anger may be turned against you as the generator of the bad feelings. This is an unconscious process; most people are not in touch with what goes on inside of them and are only aware of their anger. This will have nothing to do with you as a person but with you in the role of a woman supervisor.
3. There may be testing—"If you're so good, let's see if you can take it." You'll experience some forms of sabotage; workers may test you to see if you report them when they make mistakes.
4. There may be gossip—talk about your personal life or allegations made about your sex life with people in the office. It may be fun for some to gossip about one's superiors, and speculations can quickly begin to sound like facts.
5. There may be attempts made to become your friend—being close to the seat of power is a strategy used by people who want special privileges and favors. In this case, *you* are the person who has influence over your workers' lives.
6. There may be assumptions based on sexual stereotypes—because you're a woman, you will be more understanding and therefore more lenient, less demanding. If you let it be known that you expect the same output and quality of work as your predecessor did, you may be regarded as having no

sympathy. If you try to be more sympathetic to the problems of your workers than your predecessor was, you may be dismissed as having no standards.

Should you be discouraged? No. You may not encounter any of these reactions, but you should be prepared to deal with such attitudes because they often do exist. You may find that many women will be delighted to have you as their new boss. It will make them feel good that one of them has made it, and they will identify with you and make your job easier by being helpful, cooperative, and concerned that you do well.

I wanted to tell you about reactions women bosses frequently encounter so that you'll know you're not the only one if they happen to you. You don't need to feel that there's something wrong with you or with your style of management. Place the cause of the problem correctly on the shoulders of your testers.

Wherever I have lectured throughout the country, I have heard from disappointed women who complain that their female boss is a "bitch" or a queen bee, when they had expected that working for a woman would be easier. What is interesting about this is that I do not hear the same disappointment if the male boss is a "bastard." If *he* is not helpful, it doesn't hurt as much as when *she* is not helpful. Why? The expectation makes the difference; if you expect a female boss to be a sister or to be like your mother, and she's not, you feel that she doesn't behave the way she *ought* to and you're angry at her for not meeting *your* expectations. On the other hand, if your male boss, from whom you make no particular demands of brotherhood, is not helpful, you may wish he were, but you don't feel violated. The different expectations from male and female bosses are really sexist; you're expecting more from one than from the other. There is no evidence that women bosses are any different from men bosses, either in their management style or in the results they obtain. Therefore, it really seems that the difference is only in the perceptions of employees. Sometimes, of course, we find women bosses who are indeed harder on their female subordinates.

Why might that be so? One reason might be that they are going overboard to be fair so that they will not be seen as prejudiced. Another could be that they are afraid they will be taken advantage of, and a third reason might be that they are fighting their own inclinations to favor women, wanting to be liked. In my own research, I have found that people who have struggled the most in their careers make others struggle too so as not to diminish their own fight up the ladder. Since it is women who struggle more than men because of discrimination, the few women who finally "make it" sometimes protect their hard-won territory by not permitting it to be easy for other women. And, finally, those who have succeeded in being accepted by "the old boys" sometimes don't want to risk that position by being seen as "one of the girls" all over again.[6]

Although knowing the reasons may not be very helpful in any particular case, it is important for subordinates to understand why their bosses act the way they do, and it is equally important for the bosses to recognize that they may want so much to be "one of the boys" that they will become "the best boy" there and neglect the well-being of their employees. Bosses should try to fight that tendency and remain available and helpful to their workers. Although I have been talking about men and women, the same interaction occurs among blacks. I hear complaints from lower-level blacks that some of their brothers and sisters who have "made it" have become unreachable. The reason for this is the same: survival in the system.

If you encounter a problem, one of the questions to ask yourself is: "If I were Mary or Nancy, how would I feel about me?" By placing yourself in other people's shoes, you can better understand what motivates them. If you observe that one or more of your workers seem to have difficulty accepting you, identify what behavior gives you that sense. Does Mary avoid you or fail to answer fully when you talk to her? Does Nancy show she is upset by slamming doors; does she take long breaks, talk excessively with coworkers, or perform her tasks poorly? Call each of them into your office individually and ask how she feels about her work. Share the concerns you have, being sure to describe the behavior you have noted. This should not be judgmental, but done in a caring way. For example, "Mary, you seem to be avoiding me. Is there something going on in your mind? I would like to be helpful to you." If you get a reply such as, "I don't need any help!" you may want to say something like, "I think if we cooperate, we can make each other's job easier. If I can count on you, you can count on me."

I should note here that men and women both say they prefer to work for male bosses unless they have had experience working for female bosses; once they have, they say it makes no difference. Having the experience of working with and for both sexes shows people that it is the person, not the sex, that matters.[7] Whatever sex you are, the first thing you must do as a supervisor is get to know your workers. This is accomplished by observing them and by talking to them. Even though workers may be on their guard at the beginning, a new supervisor can convey the message that he or she cares enough to take the time to find out how the workers feel about their jobs, about the company; what their hopes are, their worries, their strengths, and their frailties. There are ways to humanize the workplace; taking the time to talk is the way to begin.

Getting to Know Your Boss

Your immediate superior is the most important person in your work life. Your boss can make your job easy or impossible, and make the atmosphere pleasant or unbearable. Your function is to see to it that your workers perform according to expectations (your boss's expectations) and to make your boss look good. Just as your workers can make you look effective or ineffective, you can make your boss look like a good manager or a bad one.

Most managers have very little time to sit down and talk. They move from one thing to another, always under pressure. You need to insist on discussion time with your manager at the beginning and on a continuing basis to check on progress.

Make a list of your questions for that first discussion, as follows:

1. Clarify *exactly* who reports to whom.
2. Do the people involved have this information?
3. Is there anything you ought to know about recent or current difficulties that your department has in
   a. meeting productivity goals?
   b. climate at the workplace?
   c. workers' individual problems?
4. What does your boss feel unhappy about or proudest of?
5. What is your boss most concerned about?
6. What would your boss like to see you accomplish:

   a. ideally?
   b. realistically?
7. How can you be most helpful to your boss?
8. Together with your boss, get some tentative objectives for yourself.
9. Put a next meeting date on both your agendas to talk about how things are going for you.
   a. This can be in a week.
   b. This can be a few minutes at the beginning or the end of each day.
   c. It can be set up as a regular time that both of you can count on.
   d. It can be "catch as catch can," but be aware that you'll be responsible for doing the catching.
10. Understanding your boss means accepting him or her as a human being with fears, hopes, and frailties; someone who needs encouragement as much as you do, perhaps even more so if support is not given from above.[8]

Some bosses have poor communication skills, are overworked, grouchy, or just won't like you. Despite these barriers, you must tell your boss that in order to perform well, you need to have some initial information—be sure to get what you need. You can then stay out of the way if you have to.

Some bosses like to have tight control over their supervisors; others want their supervisors to figure things out by themselves and leave them alone.

Figure out your boss's style as well as your own. What makes you most comfortable? There is no right or wrong way; it is a matter of matching styles of working together. This is important because it is natural to assume that the kind of boss you would want for yourself is the one your workers would want for themselves, too. People have different needs and hang-ups about issues of authority, and what may work for you, may not work for others.

If you're a man with a male boss, remember that his initial ease with you will depend on how similar to him you seem to be. Do you share hobbies, have the same church affiliation, like the same sports, have similar educational experiences? Some bosses prefer their subordinates to be very much like themselves; others may prefer subordinates who are very different in order to fill in the gaps. For instance, if a superior realizes that his greatest weakness is paying attention to detail, he may want someone to work for him who is very detail conscious. Most people in authority positions are lonely. Your boss may be feeling very isolated and would welcome feedback on how he is doing and would appreciate your recognition of his work.

If you're a man with a female boss, get in touch with any prejudices you may have against women in positions of authority. If you have a prejudice, it will show up in your relationship with her. Talking about it may help.

If you're a woman with a female boss, do you expect special treatment or do you expect the worst? Your expectations may not be based on present reality but on either past experiences or hearsay. Give your boss a chance, but always expect and insist on a professional relationship. If she becomes a mentor, so much the better; but don't be angry with her if she doesn't.

If you're a woman with a male boss in a traditionally nonfemale work setting, you may be the first woman your boss has had on his management team. We all react to new life situations by using what we have learned in similar previous events. The best predictors of future behaviors are the patterns of past behaviors. Your boss may be at a loss as to how to deal with you. It is up to you to show him how. Be professional and never flirtatious. Maintain high standards for your own performance; try to figure out things by yourself when you can; never play "poor helpless me," but assertively ask to be told or shown as a matter of course. Do not share personal matters with him. If you are interested in upward mobility, say so. Some men assume that women are not ambitious. If his wife does not work, he may have preconceived notions about women, such as: women should stay home; they only work for pocket money; they'll quit because their families come first; they are overemotional; they are not really interested in a career or in added responsibility; they cannot travel or relocate.

You may represent a threat to your boss's sense of values, as well as a threat to his wife, who may worry about her husband's working with a woman. Some men have a tendency to discount women because they have been raised to expect women to hold subordinate or nurturing positions as mothers, daughters, wives, servants, or nurses. Very few men are used to dealing with women in positions of authority. Their teachers were women, but the principal was a man; nurses are usually women, but the hospital administrator is a man; secretaries are women, but the chief executive officer is a man.

If you are a black woman, a Hispanic, or an Asian, you will have even more difficulty in establishing your credibility. Blacks, in our culture, have held the lowest-paying jobs; Asians and Hispanics (like more recent immigrants) have also done the more menial work. It is not easy for a man to make the transition from seeing women of color in only low-level jobs to accepting them as colleagues and even worse—superiors. The women, in turn, may find being assertive with a man, especially a white man, after having experienced so much discrimination and so many past put-downs, is next to impossible, or else some may overreact and become overly assertive.

In such areas as Africa, South America, the Middle East, or Asia, males have dominated and subjugated women for centuries. It is hard enough for a white woman to put on her three-piece suit and say, "I'm your equal," and be listened to. It is incredibly difficult for a woman of color to break through the barriers of custom. As a supervisor, you are in a position to help your workers overcome their ingrained fears of rejection and your own boss's unthinking emotional responses to women or minorities.

What can you do? Make yourself known to the people in power by becoming a familiar figure—visible, predictable, trustworthy. This kind of familiarity breeds promotions.

Familiarity Breeds Promotions

Familiarity also breeds understanding, comfort, and acceptance, regardless of formerly held prejudices. If I asked you who your friends are, you would probably answer, "People with whom I share interests, value systems, with whom I am comfortable." Your friends are probably a lot like you in many respects. Unconsciously, you choose clones of yourself; there is a bit of you in this friend, another bit in that one. People hire, promote, and enjoy working with people whose behaviors are predictable because they are most like themselves. The clonal effect in organizations is unconscious and pervasive.[9] I became aware of it when I was teaching at the University of New Hampshire. At that time, we were interviewing candidates for assistant professor. My most dynamic and aggressive colleagues looked at the candidates and said, "They all seem depressed." My quietest and most reflective colleague looked at the same candidates and said, "They're all so hyperactive." The candidate I liked best was a short, freckled woman with curly red hair. (I'm a short, freckled woman with curly reddish hair.) It was then that I realized that we all attempt to surround ourselves with clones in order to find a level of comfort. Subsequent research has confirmed this.

If you are different from your boss in age, sex, color, religion, education, or ethnic background, you will need to work at becoming familiar to him or her. Workers who are similar to their bosses don't have this need and aren't concerned with it.

Most people have prejudices against the unfamiliar. Most of us have grown up believing the stereotypes about certain groups of people. The old are senile; the young are irresponsible; women are overemotional; white men are arrogant; black men are aggressive; black women are promiscuous; Asians smile too much; Hispanics are lazy; Jews are greedy; Catholics are rigid; Irish are hot-tempered; Germans are authoritarian; Arabs are terrorists; the English are uptight. Add your own list about Italians, French, Scandinavians, the handicapped, the obese. PUTTING PEOPLE IN CATEGORIES IS STEREOTYPING; ATTRIBUTING NEGATIVE QUALITIES TO THEM IS PREJUDICE. Prejudice is common to all people, but it is discrimination—the acting on the prejudice as if prejudice were fact—that results in unfair and illegal decisions.

It is only by becoming known to your superiors that you can undo the stereotypes associated with the category to which you belong. I'm not saying, "Become the opposite of what you are." I'm saying that regardless of your sex, age, or social background, and perhaps even because of it, you can be a good supervisor.

It is important for us to stop apologizing for our differences and to start celebrating them. Most work groups are homogeneous. Everyone is similar, but even though it's more comfortable, homogeneity may be neither creative nor challenging. The "different" person can provide the heterogeneity that sparks creative approaches to problems. Innovative solutions come from different perspectives, different frames of reference.

How do you become known, become familiar? Move closer to the seat of power, both in space and time. Sharing space means you are visible, you are around, you work close to, next to, are involved with the more powerful persons. Sharing time means you are with those people, not only during working hours, but at breaks, at lunch, after hours, so that they get to know you better, so that what becomes foremost is not your difference but, in fact, your potential contributions in terms of hard work, good ideas, and interest in your job and in the organization.

People are hired and promoted because of two criteria. One is competence to do the job, the other is "fit." Fit is the perceived compatibility between you and the rest of the people. Once you become familiar, it will be easier to get support, and people need to feel supported in order to succeed.

Familiarity Breeds Promotions

It's not only what you know
but who
it's not only who
but what they are willing to do
for you

Why should they do it?
because they know you
because you're around
because you're good
publicly, not quietly

When you are close
to the seat of power
it rubs off
like lint
so take a few specks of it
put it on your sleeve
for all to see
that you're one of "them"

Familiarity will always
breed promotions

Research has shown that male managers are hired more often if there are male subordinates, and women if there are female subordinates.[10] Fit is more easily obtained when subordinates are similar to oneself. This, of course, is always to the detriment of the "different" person. What goes for hiring goes for promotions—a promotion involves a "firing" from the old position and a "hiring" into the new one.

Exercise

Here are some characteristics of a good boss. (Indicate your answers as *always, often, seldom,* or *never.*) Be honest with yourself so that you can work on your weak points. Don't expect to be perfect, but expect that willingness to acknowledge trouble spots is the first step to improvement.

1. You praise good work that merits it.
2. You help with work that needs improving.
3. You provide the information and guidance needed so that your subordinates can work effectively.
4. You communicate to your subordinates the reasons for important decisions.
5. You encourage criticism and feedback from your subordinates regarding your policies and your management style.
6. You consult with your subordinates before making decisions regarding their work.
7. You organize and plan well.
8. You give additional training, encourage professional growth, and provide opportunities.
9. You are willing to take risks by delegating authority to subordinates.
10. You make your expectations clear.
11. You evaluate fairly and regularly.
12. You have patience.
13. You are self-confident and decisive.
14. You promote team spirit.
15. You are able to deal with conflict.
16. You are flexible.
17. You are sensitive to people's feelings.
18. You have a sense of humor.
19. You keep confidences.
20. You trust people.

21. You can make the difficult decisions to take corrective action in disciplining.

Here are some don'ts:

1. You have no favorites.
2. You do not reprimand a subordinate in front of others unless there is a specific reason, such as making an example.
3. You are never rude, unpleasant, or sarcastic.
4. You are not secretive, vague, or evasive.
5. You do not abuse your power by intimidating subordinates.
6. You do not act in a condescending or patronizing manner.
7. You do not check on employees unexpectedly.

PART II

BUILDING RELATIONSHIPS

3

COMMUNICATION: YOUR LIFELINE

Building relationships is probably the one *most* important aspect of a supervisor's job. You cannot achieve anything without your workers' cooperation, and you will be left floundering if you don't know your superiors' expectations.

This chapter should increase your interpersonal skills and make you aware of barriers to communication. It focuses on the ways we "speak" to each other and on the cultural differences among us that often lead to misinterpretation and, thus, poor communication.

Your main function as supervisor is getting information and passing it on. Perhaps the single most important skill you need is the ability to deal with people successfully. You may be an expert in your field; you may have been promoted because you're so good at what you were doing as a worker. But this does not mean that you can teach what you know to others or that you know how to manage people.

I am often called in as a consultant to high-technology organizations because they promote their best engineers and scientists to managerial positions, and many of these people have no skill and often no interest in "managing." Frequently these new managers do not know how to tackle people problems, and they make blunders that affect climate and productivity. How they communicate will determine their success.

Written communication—letters, memos, minutes, notes, or telephone messages—can be difficult to interpret because we cannot hear the tone of voice or see the gestures of the person who is communicating. Yet putting thoughts in writing gives the writers a chance to think out what they want to say and to choose the best, clearest way to say it.

It is important for all managers to be able to communicate clearly through the written word. If you are not good at writing, take a business writing course. It will serve you well throughout your career. Even a general notice that is posted and does not require a personal response should be written concisely and grammatically. It is also wise to put things in writing in situations where misunderstanding or misinterpretation can occur. There are many instances when you will need to keep a record on file.

Most communication, however, is verbal—speeches, orders, directions, and conversations. Although a message communicated in this form is usually more personal because the sender is actually present to deliver the message, misunderstandings can arise.

When you are not quite clear about what you want to say, you can tell your listener that you need his or her help in clarifying exactly what you mean. Together you can reach an understanding. Even if you're very sure of what you want to say and you feel you express yourself well, you still may not be communicating clearly.

The Communication Loop

If you are sender A giving a message to receiver B, you will probably alter your message based on your perceptions of B's ability to understand your message. If you think B is as smart as you are, you will give the message as it is in your head; but if you think B is a bit slow or is very sensitive, you may simplify your message to make it easy to understand or soften it so as not to offend. Your feelings about B will affect either the content or the style of delivery of your message—your message is being filtered through your perceptions of B. In the meantime, B also has feelings about *you*. You may be B's boss, subordinate, friend, foe, relative, or acquaintance, and depending on how B perceives you, he or she will have different feelings about the message. We all have said to someone at some time, "*You* go and tell them; they'll listen to *you*." Sometimes a message is better received when the messenger is changed.

Not only do A and B have feelings about each other that can influence how the message is sent and heard, but both have feelings about the message itself. If it is good news, A will love to tell B (who will be glad to hear it). If it is bad news, A may hedge, be too tentative or too abrupt, and B might not hear it correctly or completely. The chart below shows the communication loop:[11]

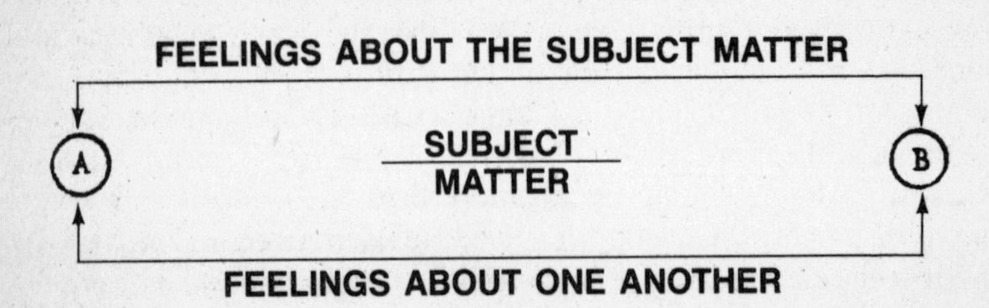

For example, Jennifer has done a sloppy piece of work. Nora, her boss, likes her, thinks well of her, and is surprised by the inadequate performance. She might tell Jennifer, "This is really poor and not up to your standards. I'm surprised. You're usually so thorough. It will have to be redone." Jennifer, who trusts her supervisor, may answer, "I know, I got preoccupied with other things and rushed. I'll redo it." Nora knows that it will be redone satisfactorily.

Now suppose Nora does not like Jennifer. Her message would be the same in content, but her tone might be more curt. If she omits, "You're usually so thorough," it will sound very punitive. Jennifer, on the other hand, if she mistrusts her supervisor, might be afraid that her job was on the line. She could become defensive and say, "Well, I have too much to do," or, "You didn't explain exactly," or even admit to the sloppiness but with surliness such as, "Okay, okay, I'll redo it . . ."

In the first case, the relationship was strengthened by the ability of Nora or Jennifer to be honest with each other; in the second case, the relationship was jeopardized by the lack of trust and the inherent dislike.

What can a supervisor do to avoid falling into the trap of the second type of communication?

Before you read on, take a few minutes and try to answer that question yourself. Imagine that you are Nora talking to Jennifer. Examine how Jennifer might feel; then switch roles.

The feelings the boss has toward a subordinate must be examined before he or she gives a directive or conveys dissatisfaction.

The message and the tone of voice will be colored by the subject matter and by the feelings toward the subordinate. The strategy is to get in touch with how you *feel* about your subordinates so that if you don't like them, mistrust them, like them very much, or whatever, your message about one particular current behavior does not express past grievances. Some people tend to trust almost everyone unless that trust has been broken. Other people are generally mistrustful and you have to gain their confidence over time. What type of person are you?

Tone of voice can be trusted more than the words because your tone of voice is usually subconscious and reveals the real way you feel about the content and the other person.

Tonal communication operates through the speaker's voice (high/low, fast/slow) and the feelings expressed through voice inflection. This can greatly add to the clarity of communication or it can be a barrier to understanding. Tone of voice that tends to support the message the sender wishes to communicate is helpful. Otherwise, it can confuse the listener and the message. For example, if someone says she is happy to stay and work late but says it in a low, tightly controlled voice, the message may be that she is upset about working late and is not happy at all. The receiver then would not know whether to believe the content of the message or the tone of it.

This is also true of nonverbal communication which is revealed by the cues a person gives when interacting with another person. Body language, posture, and hand motions are all forms of nonverbal communication. Sometimes a touch can mean more than many words. Again, these cues can support or distort the message depending on how they are intended by the sender and how they are interpreted by the receiver.

Although many forms of communication are universal, people from all cultures and classes recognize the friendliness in a smile and the rejection in a growl. There are ways we have been taught to communicate by our parents; that communication may be misunderstood when the background or origin of the sender is different from that of the receiver.

In order to be able to understand others and get one's own messages across better, let us consider the four dimensions of nonverbal communication: space, time, appearance, and gestures.

Space: How Close Can You Get?

The first dimension of nonverbal communication is *space*. Space has different meanings for people in different countries. It is interesting to note that the farther north on the globe that you travel, the more space people put between themselves and others. The farther south you go, the more comfortable people are at being close to one another. An Englishman will need distance when talking with you; an Arab will want to bathe you with his breath; and a Japanese will cover her mouth while laughing so that her breath does not touch you.

What this means is that workers who are from the Middle East might expect you to stand close to them when you talk or they may feel rejected. If you stand too close to New Englanders, they may feel that their space is being invaded and be very uncomfortable.

Staring can also be felt as an invasion of space. When you're in crowded quarters such as an elevator or a bus, you cannot gaze at a person who is standing or sitting a few inches away without seeming to be offensive. As you draw closer to strangers on a street, you tend to direct your eyes away from them. Looking too long at a member of the opposite sex is seen as being either rude or as making a pass. If you touch someone accidentally in crowded quarters, you usually say, "Excuse me."

In many European countries, men can walk down a street with their arms around each other, women can hold hands, and no one suspects homosexuality. In some countries, men can kiss each other as an expression of friendship. In the United States, many parents of boys confuse displays of affection and expressions of emotions with sexual preference. They urge their sons not to show warmth or tears, for these are seen as feminine behaviors, not appropriate for "real" men. These boys grow up to value control. The only people they are allowed to touch with any kind of affection are women and children. They can only show affection for a man by punching his arm or slapping him on the back.

Recent male immigrants from European countries may feel free to hug one another until they learn that in America a more distant handshake is more acceptable.

It is important for supervisors to know the backgrounds of their workers and, whenever possible, give the more recent arrivals the comfort of being with someone of similar origin for a part of the day. It is also important to let others with whom the new person will be working know about the cultural differences: distance, affection, what is acceptable and nonacceptable. Place a newly arrived Italian worker with a group of Germans, and you may have an unhappy person. However, this does not mean you have to segregate your workers according to background. They must also have a chance to be with people different from themselves so that they can learn the new ways.

Accommodating differences stemming from different cultural backgrounds is important, but one must also pay attention to individual differences. Don't move in too quickly. Let the other person establish his or her comfort level. Be aware that space exists as an important factor in all human communication. The way you use space conveys a message.

If you speak from behind a desk, you send a different message from when you sit next to a person, as shown on the chart below:

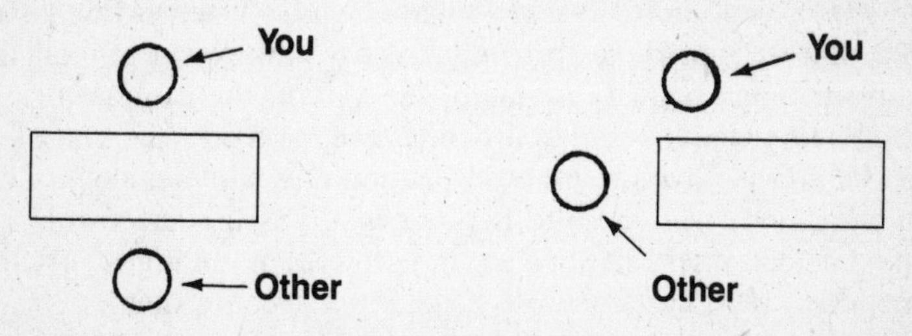

Where you move your chair in relation to another says how much formality you want or how much informality. In a restaurant, I always feel easier sitting next to good friends than opposite them. You can test this formality issue by the following exercise. Next time you're in a restaurant, place some objects of yours (your cigarette case, your glasses) on your dining partner's table setting. More often than not, your partner will either move them back toward you or squirm in his or her seat. You have invaded private space. Be aware of your own comfort level in terms of space with the various people in your organization. Are you more distant with some than with others? What messages do you give by the way your office is set up? Become conscious of the way you use space.

Some people take up more space than others. The taking up of more space is also a measure of one's self-confidence and one's status. Only bosses put their feet on the table, thus extending their bodily space, or put their hands behind their heads, again extending their space. They can do this in front of a subordinate. The subordinate would rarely feel free to do the same in front of a boss. If a boss were on the phone, the subordinate would most likely wait at a polite distance until the call was over. If a subordinate is on the phone, the boss might hover over him or her to express impatience.

Time: Does It Mean the Same to Everyone?

The second dimension of nonverbal communication is *time*. The example just given also shows that a subordinate knows that he or she must wait for a boss to be finished yet cannot make that same boss wait in the same way or for the same length of time. Whether a visitor stops at the door of an executive, then walks in halfway, stops again, waiting to be asked to sit down, or whether this visitor walks right in and right up to the desk of the executive—all this says something about the status of the visitor, the national origin, the education, the level of self-confidence, or a combination of all four. Timing is also important in determining who sits down first, who talks first, who gets up first, or who has the last word.

In some countries, seasons are important, but not hours. You get things done by a certain season, not by a specific time.

American business people in some Mid Eastern or South American countries have had a lot of difficulty inculcating the notion of being on time. That necessity is not shared by the people who live there. "What difference does it make whether you arrive at 8 or 9 as long as you get there?" The well-known "mañana syndrome" means "tomorrow will be soon enough; why rush now?"

However, promptness is a Western cultural phenomenon made necessary by industry. Nonindustrialized nations don't feel these same pressures. If a supervisor has a work force of people for whom time does not have great importance, it may be necessary to ask your boss if you can install flexible working hours so that if someone comes late, he or she stays later. Most people don't mind working a full day; they just have trouble arriving at a specified time. Yet some industries and service organizations require promptness. In this case, it must be explained that it is a requirement of the job.

I would like to caution you, however, that not all South American people have problems with time, and that some North Americans do; that not all Arabs use space the same way; and that there are individual differences among all of us. This generalization is just to help you become aware that some problems do not arise from your good or bad supervisory style but can be the result of ingrained cultural patterns that may not be easily changed or violated.

Some people are quick; others are slow. I get impatient with very slow talkers and must be careful not to finish their sentences for them or assume I know what they're going to say. Become aware of what you like and dislike in others so that you don't judge their performance unfairly because of your own idiosyncracies and preferences.

Appearance: The First Test

The third dimension of nonverbal communication is *appearance*. The way one looks usually communicates who one is and how one feels about oneself. This also includes posture, walk, clothes, hair, and makeup.

First impressions last a long time. You will be remembered by how you were first seen. Posture and walk are so much a part of a total appearance that I include them here. Do you walk confidently or tentatively? Do you stand up straight or slouch? Clothes that don't fit, messy hair, slips that show, untrimmed nails, smeared lipstick, spotted ties, and shirttails that hang out are all messages that you send to others. If you are doing manual work, spots on clothes or dirty nails may be accepted while you're involved in your job, but nowhere else. Sloppiness is an expression of personality, and some people may draw conclusions about sloppy ways of thinking, sloppy management, and general unreliability from that kind of appearance. "If they can't manage to pull themselves together," people will say, "how can they manage anyone else?" However, others may like the informality.

We judge by appearance more than we realize. We all carry categories in our heads of what is acceptable and what is not, and we match people to our categories. It would be useful for all of us to find out how we think others *should* look so that we would be less prejudiced by appearances. Here again, there are different cultural norms. Norms of cleanliness are not shared by everyone in the same way. When I was a little girl growing up in France, I had a bath once a week, and when I came to the United States, I was amazed to discover that people took daily showers.

Appearance is also related to fads. Remember the outcries at the young men who wore long hair during the days of the Beatles? Young people often follow extreme fashions, and you as a supervisor may have to set some standards as to what can and cannot be worn to work, but be aware of what is "in."

When I was young, I wore a pompadour, and my brother had a butch haircut. As teenagers, my son wore an afro, and my daughter pressed her hair with an iron. I wore saddle shoes and bobby socks; today people wear high heels with pants, which would have been in dreadful taste twenty years ago.

When my students at San Diego State University come to class in a bathing suit top and short shorts, I still do a bit of a double take. Are these the managers of tomorrow? It is sometimes difficult not to be an old fuddy-duddy! A friend of mine related this story about appearance. After several weeks of student teaching, her sixty-year-old supervisor took her aside. "Carol, you are an excellent teacher, and I most enjoy you as my supervisee, but your short skirts, beads, and frizzed hair do not match your professional style. I know it's the fashion, and I know you, in particular, feel strongly about being 'who you are,' but I must suggest a compromise. I am conservative and set in my ways, but I am willing to put aside my prejudices about your dress, and grade you according to your ability as a student teacher. I ask you to consider that how you dress conveys a very significant message to your students and your peers. Is it more important to cling to your statement about yourself or to reinforce your authority and presence by how you look?" Carol compromised. This twenty-two-year-old "hippie" and the sixty-year-old supervisor learned from each other. He was able to set aside his prejudices and see a job well done; she was able to compromise and learn from experience, thereby increasing her effectiveness.

Gestures: What Do They Tell You?

The fourth dimension of nonverbal communication is reflected by *gestures*. What is important to remember about gestures is that not any one gesture is significant by itself, but the pattern that gestures form has meaning. If you smilingly say, "I'm very upset" or stamp your foot when you say, "I'm not angry," the message is garbled because the gestures do not fit.

There are some generalities one can make about the meaning of certain gestures, but again, be aware that alone these gestures may not mean much. The following is a list of the more generally recognized meanings of gestures:[12,13]

1. Covering the mouth while speaking (unsure or lying)
2. Wiggling a foot (bored)
3. Putting objects in one's mouth, such as pencils (need of more information, anxiety)
4. No eye contact (concealing something)
5. Feet pointing toward door (ready to leave)
6. Rubbing nose (rejecting what is being said)
7. Rubbing eye or ear (doubt)
8. Touching ear (ready to interrupt)
9. Hand to throat (need reassurance)
10. Clenched hands (anxious)
11. Clenched fist (determined, angry)
12. Pointing a finger (reprimand)
13. Sitting on the edge of a chair (ready for action)
14. Moving forward on a chair (agreement)
15. Arms crossed tightly across upper chest (unwilling)
16. Unbuttoning of coat, uncrossing of arms and legs (opening up)
17. Leg swung over a chair (unconcerned)
18. Sitting backward on a chair (dominance)
19. Hands behind one's back (feeling superior)
20. Locked ankles (holding back)
21. Rubbing palms (expectation)
22. Thumbs in belt or pants (everything under control)
23. Unconscious throat clearing (apprehension)
24. Conscious throat clearing (admonishment)
25. Hands together pointed toward ceiling (confidence, pride)
26. One hand above the other on one's lap (sure of oneself)
27. Sitting with one leg under oneself (comfort, unconcern)
28. Women send sexual signals by preening themselves—touching their hair, playing with a necklace, caressing their legs, crossing and uncrossing them

29. Men preen themselves by straightening their ties, pulling up their socks, pulling at their pants, checking their fingernails
30. A person may be lying when he or she blinks a lot, covers the mouth, wets lips, clears throat, swallows repeatedly, sweats, or shrugs shoulders

These gestures may be different for different cultures. For example, an Asian or Hispanic young woman may have been brought up not to look a superior in the eye, particularly a man, while talking to him. A white woman may have been brought up to maintain eye contact while talking, which can be just as disconcerting to some people as no eye contact at all. Again, examine your own prejudices and preferences, so as not to let them get in the way.

Nonverbal Messages

What is important to remember is that nonverbal messages are picked up, interpreted, responded to, and stored without much conscious awareness. We say things like "I had a feeling that . . . ," "I can't put my finger on . . . ," "She's not my type . . . ," "He makes me uneasy . . . ," "There's something about her . . . ," or "He reminds me of . . ." without really knowing what we're referring to. We are picking up information from nonverbal behaviors that form patterns we recognize and trust as a basis for judgments. It is important to start paying attention to what cues we pick up so that rather than reacting unconsciously, we will make conscious decisions as to how we choose to respond.

A colleague of mine recently told me the following story. She walked into a conference room and felt that something was wrong. Trouble was brewing, but she did not know how she was picking it up. She trusted her instincts and said, "Something's going on here; what is it?" This opened up the discussion, and the people present were able to say what was troubling them. What did she notice? Her boss's jaw was set a little tighter than usual; one colleague was shifting about in her chair; another greeted her with a voice pitched higher than normal, and still another avoided eye contact with her. Not one of these alone would have been significant, but together they indicated that something was amiss. She trusted her recognition of the signs, she read the nonverbal communication, and she took action to clear the air.

What nonverbal messages are you sending? Be aware of the way you come across to others. Review the way you walk into a room, the way you sit, what you do with your hands, feet, eyes, the distance you keep from others. Do you touch people as you greet them? Do you start the conversation? Do you show disapproval by your facial expressions? Do you smile only when things are pleasant, or do you smile all the time, even when expressing disapproval?

Many women have been brought up to hide their feelings of anger and displeasure, and many men have been taught to hide their feelings of pain and vulnerability. To be angry is not regarded as feminine; to show hurt is not masculine.

Yet our nonverbal messages often manage to get through, and our true feelings become known to others even though they pretend not to notice. It is time to show our emotions, to become more expressive, to allow women to be angry and allow men to be sensitive. It is time for us all to be *aware* of our nonverbal behaviors and to accept them as true expressions of ourselves.

Listening Skills

We have discussed what you observe with your eyes. Now we must turn to what you hear with your ears. Just as observation is a skill that can be perfected, listening is a skill that can be learned and practiced. Many people think of listening as passive. They expect to be bored, and they lose energy if *they* aren't doing the talking. Good listening is active; it involves the listener as much as the talker. The reason most people don't *really* listen is that if they did, they would be "open" to new information, open to how someone else sees the world, and based on this new knowledge or new perception, they might have to change their own ideas or preconceived notions. Most people don't like to change their usual ways of thinking. It feels safer to fall back on the familiar than to experiment with new frames of reference. However, we won't grow and we won't become good managers of people if we don't make a concerted effort to understand them.

Seven barriers to effective listening are as follows:

1. **Physical discomfort.** Being hot, cold, tired, or having a headache affects one's ability to listen and pay attention to the speaker.
2. **Interruptions.** Telephones, typewriters, fans, and other parts

of the physical environment can detract from the flow of communication.

3. **Mental preoccupations.** Having other meetings, deadlines, and reports due can be distracting.
4. **Preconceived answers.** Having pat answers to people's problems or trying quickly to categorize their problems can interfere with really listening to other people.
5. **Boredom.** Expecting to be bored with certain individuals means already beginning to tune them out before they have had a chance.
6. **Talking about oneself.** Being preoccupied with oneself disrupts communication.
7. **Personalizing.** Assuming that people are talking about you, even though they are not, can inhibit listening.
8. **Feelings about the other.** Liking someone or disliking someone can distort one's listening.
9. **Selective listening.** Taking in only part of what a speaker is saying because one's personal opinions or beliefs contradict the message being communicated is akin to not accepting what was said as being true for that person.

Active listening means temporarily suspending one's own values and trying to understand how things are for the speaker—putting yourself in that person's place. The first component of active listening is to *listen for the total meaning* of what someone is saying; this is sometimes expressed as listening for "the music behind the words." It is not enough to hear only the content of what someone is saying; the speaker's feelings and the emotions that color what he or she is saying should also be heard.

The second component is to *respond to the feelings* one hears; it isn't enough merely to hear the feelings being expressed. One must also respond so that the speaker knows that he or she is being heard. Sometimes the content of the message is less important than the feelings the speaker is trying to convey, as when someone says, "I'd like to melt this typewriter down into scrap!" Responding to the content of that statement would be ridiculous; it is the feeling that is being conveyed that is important. "You must be terribly upset or feel overworked" would be an appropriate answer.

The third component of active listening is to *note all the cues* the speaker is using to communicate his or her message; these can be nonverbal as well as verbal. Body language, tone of voice, and facial expressions are all part of the message. Active listening is a special skill and one that people can develop. We all have latent abilities in this area, but you must first be willing to be open to others' opinions and take the risk of being changed by that openness. A good way to check whether or not you are listening well is if you can paraphrase what the speaker has said, both the meaning expressed and the meaning that underlies the words. You can test yourself by saying, "Do you mean . . ." and then repeat the statement made by the other person.[14]

Active listening is important in all manner of communication, whether the communication is upward, downward, or horizontal. Upward communication occurs when you talk to your boss or other superiors, send them memos or reports, or do a presentation for the upper echelon. Downward communication happens when you talk to the people who report to you or to others in other positions subordinate to yours, when you post a notice or write an evaluation. Horizontal communication takes place when you deal with people at your own level: vendors, clients, visitors, or other supervisors.

Pay attention to how much you do these kinds of communication and whether you listen as actively when you listen to a subordinate as when you listen to your boss. It is usual for people in subordinate positions to put in a lot of effort in trying to find out what people in higher positions want, need, and expect. They "psych them out" so that they can meet those needs and expectations. People in high positions often do not see the payoff in finding out what subordinates may want, hope, or expect. Their own needs are being met, and that's enough. Be the kind of supervisor who cares both about what your superiors think and also about what your workers think. In addition, be a good colleague to people at the same level. Listen just as openly, eagerly, and actively to your boss, your peers, and your subordinates.

For example, Henry, your boss, tells you how much he enjoyed his last holiday, giving you details of where he went and what he did. You listen with great attentiveness, trying to pick out clues about Henry's likes and dislikes. You are pleased that your boss treats you like an equal. You respond with interest, making the moment last. A bit later, Mike, your subordinate, wants to tell you about his holiday. You may not really care whether he went to the beach or the mountains, but you listen politely while thinking that he's wasting his time and yours. While listening to Henry, you encourage him to tell you more by saying, "And then what did you do?'' or ''That's fascinating!'' While Mike is talking, your responses are polite, but you hope to end the conversation by saying, ''Oh, yeah,'' or ''Mmm,'' or ''Glad you had a good time,'' or ''What about those defective parts you mentioned earlier?''

These two conversations will have a very different impact on the two people you talked with. You would not like to be treated by Henry the way you treated Mike. Good communication is the key to managing people. It takes good interpersonal skills both to take in information and to give information. The good manager is one who sees each person, regardless of rank, as worthwhile, with something that is worth listening to.

Communications Upward

If I compliment my boss
He'll think I'm buttering him up
Trying to ingratiate myself
The words are: "apple polishing"

If I criticize my boss
He'll wonder: Who the hell I think I am
telling him what to do?
The words are: "the arrogant kid"

If I say nothing to my boss
He'll discount me as indifferent,
As a person without opinions.
The word is: "invisible"

Verbal Skills

When we talk about verbal skills—how you say what, to whom, and when—we are talking about feedback. You listened actively, you picked up the cues, you noticed the body language, you heard the message, you noted the feelings behind the message; and now you are ready to respond. You must ask yourself what it is that you now know. There is a truth that you have learned—how can that ''truth'' be translated so that it can be understood?

Let us take the following example: Jack is a good worker but seems to avoid you. When he does talk to you, he is abrupt, on the verge of being unpleasant. As long as he does his work, you may decide to say to him, ''You're a good worker, Jack. I know you prefer to be left alone, and I'm glad to do that as long as the job gets done.'' This establishes a contract between the two of you and gives you both the permission to keep a distance from each other, which says that you understand and respect his way of doing things. It could also be that *you* think Jack wants to maintain distance, while Jack may be shy or ''keeping his place.'' In that case, you could ask him if he is uneasy around you, if he wishes to talk about it, or what would make him more comfortable.

If, however, Jack does not perform well, you will have to call him into your office knowing that he will probably have trouble listening to what you have to say. ''I know you prefer to be on your own, and I can respect that, but your work is not good enough. I want to talk to you about improving it. Are you willing to do that?'' If your conversation is going well, you may want to say, ''I'm glad we can talk to each other today.'' If not, say, ''I feel you have trouble listening to me.'' Deal with the problem you have in communicating with Jack.

Women are generally better at interpersonal skills than are men. While little boys were playing ball, little girls were talking to one another, talking about each other, trying to figure out why people behave the way they do, trying to sort out feelings. Girls had time to practice these skills and grew up knowing how to communicate. It is harder for boys who were expected to talk about things and events instead of sharing intimate thoughts and feelings. Men who often have trouble recognizing their own feelings have even more difficulty reading the feelings of others; and because they don't see the available clues, they don't understand and tend to diminish the value of interpersonal communication. ''I tell them what to do, and they had better do it. They've got to know who's boss around here'' is a very male type of statement. On the other hand, ''I couldn't sleep last night because of what you said,'' or ''I really care a great deal about what you think of me'' are more female types of statements. It is difficult to imagine many men saying these.

It is important for us to realize that because women are more comfortable with feelings and expect them to be shared, and because men are uncomfortable with them and expect a minimal amount of sharing of anything personal, each sex often violates the other's norms of what is good communication.

It is also important for us to be aware that many of the suggestions given here may work well with one group of people and less well with another. The critical component is the realization that people are shaped by six major categories.[15]

1. **Heredity.** The individual's genetic makeup will influence that person's capacities and limitations.
2. **Gender.** What people learn about sex roles early in life will influence their behavior and their expectations of others.
3. **Race and ethnicity.** People of color have had a very different experience from that of whites growing up in the United States. The constant threat of discrimination makes people wary.
4. **Family.** A close family of four members in which both parents are professionals may produce children with different concepts of independence from a family of seven children without a father. Religious attitudes are also developed within the family.
5. **Class.** The socioeconomic background includes educational opportunities. People who live in the barrio with English as a second language will hear a supervisor's criticism differently than will a person who went to an American university.
6. **Geography.** Where people were born and raised makes a difference. A person from the South will view the world differently from someone born in the Northeast. The Southerner may tend to speak slowly and politely; the Northerner may speak more quickly and abruptly.

As you read this, try to relate yourself to these six categories and try to understand how you are shaped by them. If you can understand the forces that made you who you are today, you will be able to have more tolerance toward those people who are different from you.

Cultural Differences

While all of us have grown up knowing people from other families, from some other state, or from different educational backgrounds, many of us have not been in day-to-day contact with people from different ethnic groups. As more and more minorities are entering the workplace and for the most part in the lower-level positions, it is up to the first-line manager to be able to supervise these people effectively. The reason that gender differences need also be understood is that even though men and women have had experience with one another in social settings, many people have not worked with with the opposite sex and thus do not know how to behave professionally.

White people should be sensitive to the fact that they view the world from a white frame of reference without being aware that it is a specifically white perspective, and even more specifically a white male perspective. The result is that we describe as "normal," "healthy," and "effective" those people who function most like white males. Women who don't conform to the male model are often seen as being "too emotional." Nor does it occur to most men to think of men as being "not expressive enough" and thus different from the majority of the population, which is almost 53 percent female.

We define the acceptability of people of color by how closely they resemble us and fit into our culture. Blacks, Hispanics, Asians, American Indians—all have characteristics they share as racial groups, as ethnic minorities, and as individuals.

For example, Puerto Ricans, Mexicans, and Cubans share a language but are of different ethnic origins. Asians include Japanese, Chinese, Vietnamese, to name a few, and have some similarities but many differences. Because these groups of people share more similarities with each other than they do with whites, some people tend to lump them together and say, "all blacks..." or "those Asians..." or "every Hispanic..." Since it is impossible to make a cultural profile for every culture and every ethnic group we may come in contact with, let us take a hard look at the major values and beliefs of the white culture.

White Culture[16]

We believe in rugged individualism; the individual is the primary unit.

We believe in the Protestant work ethic. Hard work brings success.

We are competitive; we strive to be number one. Winning is everything.

We focus on the future versus the present (becoming versus being). We save for a rainy day and value continuous improvement.

We are action-oriented. We must always *do* something about

situations. Our need is to master, control, harness, exploit both nature and the environment. We would rather schedule our lives than be spontaneous.

We emphasize the scientific method. We want to be objective and rational. We believe in cause and effect, and dualism: either/or, mind/body, good/bad, right/wrong, the polarities. Numbers are meaningful to us.

We make decisions by majority rule. Our organizations are based on the pyramid hierarchy chain of command.

We believe in one God (Christian), and in our white system as superior to other cultural systems. Our ideology is to bring other groups up to "our standards."

We value self-disclosure, direct eye contact, limited physical contact or touching. We handshake and control emotions. We each need our own space; we are territorial. We like owning space.

We adhere to time schedules. Time is viewed as a commodity and is considered precious; time is money. Hours, minutes, and seconds count.

Our holidays are tied to the Christian religion (Christmas, New Year's, St. Valentine's Day, Easter) and to white leaders and historical dates (Presidents' Day, Columbus Day, Fourth of July, Thanksgiving Day).

We believe in romantic love, marriage, and children. We assume that the man is the breadwinner, head of house, and strong. We also assume that woman is the homemaker, subordinate to the man, and nurturing. The family is the primary social unit, and our organizations are structured on these roles.

Music and art are based on European culture. There is competitiveness around attractiveness for women—Miss America (blond, blue eyes). Men compete around athletic prowess (tall, dark, and handsome).

Status is achieved by what one owns, money, credentials, titles, positions, roles.

Although the younger generation may not recognize itself in all of these, it still applies to the generation in power, the people in their 50s and 60s. As you look at this list, it makes it easier to take a step back and ponder whether our culture is necessarily the best or the only valid one. Must all others adapt to our way of doing things?

Let us examine some different approaches to life and to work. Some nonwhites believe that the group is more important than the individual and that it is better to live in harmony with the environment than attempt to change it. Feelings and intuition are valued more than rational or intellectual thought. Silence may be more valued than talk. Keeping eyes cast down is a statement of respect.

For example, many Asian-Americans believe that feelings are not to be shown, that silence is important, that elders and authority figures are to be respected, that advice is to be sought. They also feel that an individual who does poorly risks disgracing his or her family; therefore, it is extremely important to do well. Hispanics are often family-oriented, believe in group-centered cooperation, and have a different time perspective. Many blacks tend to have a sense of "peoplehood," are action-oriented, have immediate short-range goals, and place a great deal of importance on nonverbal behavior. Most American Indians tend to be creative, experiential, intuitive, nonverbal. They are most often cooperative, not competitive, and use a wealth of folktales or supernatural beliefs to explain life.[17]

As a supervisor, if you think that a person who does not make eye contact is devious, if you believe that a person is weak-minded if he or she doesn't speak out, if you feel that a person is withdrawn because he or she is quiet, or if you think that being logical is the only way to understanding, then you will probably have difficulties not only working effectively with a nonwhite population, but you may also have difficulties working with anyone.

Communication Flow: You Are the Key Link

As a supervisor, you are the person in the middle of the communication flow, between your workers and your own boss. For each product or service your department is responsible for, you must find out what your superiors expect from you in quantity, quality, and time of delivery. Then you need to give this information to your workers. You are responsible for their output, and you are accountable if anything goes wrong. You must tell your superiors what progress you are making and discuss with them any problems you encounter that you cannot solve yourself. The communication flow looks like this:

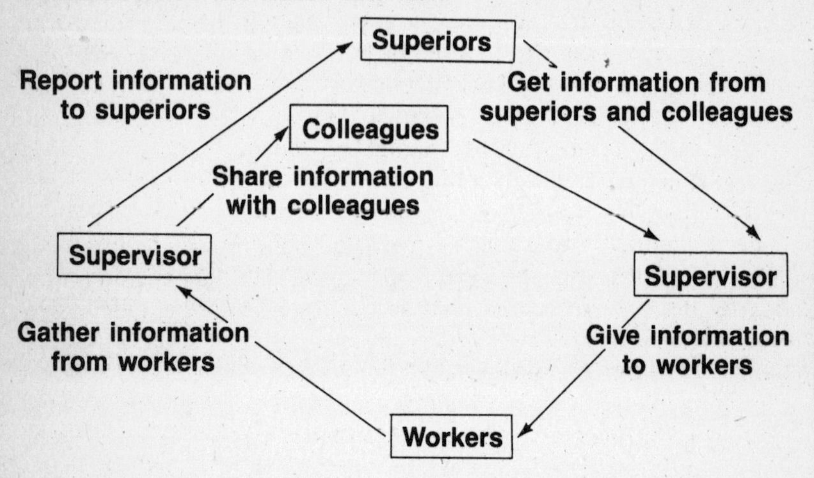

Your job depends on maintaining a continuous flow in the give-and-take of information. This will be influenced by two factors: the level of trust between you and others, and your skill with the whole communication process. This chapter suggests ways that can help you to understand yourself better, to be more tolerant of others, and more settled in your new middle-person position.

Exercise

Apply the communication loop to yourself.

1. What information do you get from your boss?
   a. Is it sufficient and clear?
   b. Is it timely?
   c. Is it difficult to come by?
2. What information do you get from your colleagues (other supervisors)?
   a. Are you included in the informal network?
   b. From whom do you usually receive information informally?
   c. Do you check your sources?

3. What information do you give your workers?
   a. Do they feel free to ask for information from you?
   b. Are they satisfied?
4. What information do you get from your workers?
   a. Is it from observation?
   b. Is it from their telling you?
   c. Are you open and available for feedback?
5. What information do you report to your boss?
   a. Is your boss interested, open, and available?
   b. Do you feel he or she understands your difficulties?
   c. Do you report only on major issues or do you have the possibility of ongoing discussions?
6. What information do you share with your colleagues (other supervisors)?
   a. Do you offer support to them that may help with their jobs?
   b. What kinds of information do you feel are appropriate to share?

After you have completed this exercise, go back and look at your answers to see if you are satisfied with them. If not, you will know where you need to increase your communication flow, and can make plans to do it.

4

MANAGING CONFLICTS

Conflict is inevitable. It is not possible for everyone always to agree on everything and for problems never to occur. As a supervisor, you are responsible for dealing with conflict at your place of work when it affects your workers, yourself, or productivity. There are four main types of conflict you may encounter: (1) conflict within yourself, (2) conflict between you and your workers, (3) conflict between you and your boss, and (4) conflict among your workers.

Conflict within Yourself

You encounter conflicts between your personal life and your professional life or between your own values and the organization's goals. As a supervisor with new responsibilities, you may also find that it is harder to manage your home life as well as you had before. If you have had a hard day at work, you may have to decompress when you get home. It is very difficult for most people to just "switch off" when they leave work; instead, frustrations, disappointments, and hurts carry over into the private life. During job changes, there is more spillover, especially if you feel that the fit between you and the new position is not very good.

Spillover means that your family gets the brunt of your being upset; you get impatient or annoyed with a spouse or a child when you are really upset about a work-related problem. Spillover decreases as you begin to feel more competent at work, as you begin to enjoy it, and as you feel proud of what and how you do it.[18]

How much energy do you invest in your job? Do you take work home evenings or on weekends? Do you go to work earlier or stay later than anyone else? If you do, it is at a cost to your private life. If you're a woman, there may be pressures to be in charge of the home and children; if you're a man, there are more expectations today to share in household duties and family responsibilities. As a beginning supervisor, you may need to increase your work time with a consequent reduction in private time. If this is temporary and family members know it, it can probably be managed without conflict, but if work commitment at the expense of private time continues, you may get into the mañana trap: "Tomorrow I will invest in my private life." When "tomorrow" finally comes, the family is not there anymore; they have either grown up and left or just have gotten tired of waiting. It is very difficult to become a "born-again private-lifer."[19]

The other personal conflict that may occur is when your values conflict with organizational goals. For example, the company you work for makes an inferior product or disposes illegally of hazardous materials or treats workers unfairly. Not everyone can have the luxury of walking away from a job. Times may be hard, and you may have many family responsibilities. What should you do? You may have to work despite the continued conflict between your integrity and the need to survive until a time when you can quit or confront the problem with your superiors. You may just need to stay in the unhappy situation, although you have little commitment or loyalty to the organization. Sometimes you can derive satisfaction from working in isolation or in having one's own department function well; still, the knowledge that one's value system is being violated will remain as an unresolved issue and one that is difficult for you to live with.

Conflict between You and Your Wokers

This conflict most often occurs when you and one of your workers have different standards and different expectations.

You want one worker to finish more quickly; she thinks you're unrealistic—you become frustrated, and she becomes upset. Another worker expects better working conditions than you can provide—he's angry, and you don't know what to do. One of your workers is rude to you; another is inappropriately flirtatious. How do you handle unpleasant situations with people who depend on you for their livelihood, and on whom you depend for their productivity, since that is *your* livelihood? (1) First, you must define the conflict; (2) next, you must identify what led to it; (3) then, you must take a look at the obstacles that need to be overcome; (4) after that, you must examine the resources or options at your disposal for dealing effectively with the conflict; and, (5) finally, you must predict the consequences of resolving or not resolving the conflict.

To illustrate these five points, let us take the following case:

1. You're supervising Phyllis, who is too slow and does not seem to be able to meet minimum standards of efficiency. You have talked to her, observed her work, suggested ways to improve—all to no avail. She gets upset whenever you start talking to her about her work. To define the conflict, you would have to say that Phyllis and you have different standards of what is acceptable work.
2. The triggering event was your calling her attention to it.
3. The obstacle appears to be Phyllis's unwillingness to talk with you about it, but it may also be her inability to do better.
4. Your options could be that someone else train Phyllis or that you change Phyllis's job or that you reduce your expectations.
5. The results of not dealing with this conflict will be your continued frustration. The results of confronting her with it might be an improvement in Phyllis's work and better communication with her—or Phyllis's quitting or being fired. The question to be answered is: Are you willing to take a chance on Phyllis's quitting? If not, you may have to live with the conflict.

Let us take another case, as follows:

1. Marc complains of the noise in his unit, and when you are unable to do anything about it, he's rude and insults you. The definition of the conflict is the difference in concepts of what constitutes acceptable behavior.
2. What led to it is his belief that you, as his boss, could have taken care of the noise but were unwilling to do so.

3. The obstacles you face are Marc's continued disbelief and the existent noise.
4. The resources are your skills at talking with Marc and getting him involved in helping solve the problem, for example, by suggesting he wear earplugs.
5. The consequences are that Marc will either change his behavior or he will continue to insult you until you are forced to transfer him or fire him. Let us listen in as Marc and his supervisor have the following talk:

SUPERVISOR: Marc, I was very upset when you shouted insults at me. If you have something to say, I wish you'd wait till you calm down and then ask to talk to me. Now, what's the problem?
MARC: You know what the problem is—you don't care about any of us. The noise is giving me headaches, and what do you do? Nothing.
SUPERVISOR: I have talked to my boss, who consulted with the engineers. Apparently nothing can be done; however, it's terrible for you to have headaches. Would changing your position help or would wearing earplugs make a difference? What do you think? Do you have a better idea? I would be happy to do what I can.
MARC: (Grumbling) Maybe if I worked closer to the window...
SUPERVISOR: Try it for one week, and if it's not better, let's talk again—calmly.

In this case, the supervisor has given Marc alternatives and made it clear that insults are not acceptable.

There is another possible consequence of having dealt with the conflict: although it seems positive for both parties now involved, how will the person feel who has been working near the window when Marc will work there, too? The supervisor should also talk to that person to ensure that no new conflict will develop between the two workers.

Conflicts occur because people do not have the same information (Marc thinks you can take care of the problem), or have different perceptions of the problem (Phyllis believes she's good enough), or have divergent goals or values. For example, in conflicts of interest, one person wants the same resources as another person.

Conflict Between You and Your Boss

In this conflict, let's reverse the tables. You think that your boss has unrealistic expectations (just as Phyllis thought you had) or is dragging his feet getting you needed resources (just as Marc thought you did). Your boss is angry with you; you are frustrated with him or her—what should you do? There are ways to reduce potential conflict. Analyze your boss's style by answering these questions:

1. Does your boss prefer written memos, drop-in visits, or formal appointments?
2. Does your boss like to discuss things at some length or prefer to be brief and to the point?
3. Does your boss value attention to detail or creativity and initiative?
4. Does your boss have prejudices against a category of people you represent or bend over backward to support certain people?
5. Does your boss accept feedback even if it's negative, or want to hear only pleasant things?
6. Does your boss like to solve problems or have only solutions presented?
7. Does your boss freely want to share information or hold on to whatever is known?

It is important that your working styles, as well as your personality styles, be compatible with those of your boss. For example, if your boss tends to explode, a *compatible* style would be to remain calm; if your boss wants things done immediately, an *incompatible* style would be to procrastinate.

Getting to know your boss is a first step. The second step is to get to know yourself and see how you can fit your boss's expectations of what a subordinate should be like.

Managing the relationship is as much your responsibility as it is your boss's. Also, be aware of your boss's pressures at work and the expectations his or her superiors have that must be met.[20]

There may be a time when your boss will be angry with you. If the anger is legitimate, acknowledge it and explain how you plan to do things differently as opposed to defending what you did wrong. If the anger is misplaced, say so, and explain that you understand the frustration but that it should not be directed at you, that, however, you would be glad to help think through some alternatives.

Being a boss, like being a parent, is both a skill and an art. The skills can be learned, but the art is a predisposition to being a teacher, a coach, a role model, a leader, and an empathetic authority figure. Some bosses are better than others, most have some good points; all have some bad ones. If you can't improve your relationship with your boss, you may have to change bosses, unless your work is such that you can keep avoiding contact.

Conflict Among Your Workers

You are responsible for a productive work climate. This means that conditions at work must be such that your workers will be able to work efficiently so that you can meet your productivity goals, and that people are satisfied so that you won't have excessive turnover or grumpy employees.

You can accomplish this by being the kind of boss your workers can talk to, by knowing what's going on, and by mediating between them if there is trouble. The kind of boss someone can talk to is a boss who will always listen carefullly, take even seemingly small complaints seriously, be available, and show care and concern. Knowing what's going on means making it a point to solicit information by asking how things are going, seeing if anyone needs help, and picking up small clues for impending problems (a worker who slams doors, drops tools, shouts, or comes in late). It is best to address the problem before it worsens, especially if it involves other workers. No one wants to have unpleasant people around, and one problem worker can make the environment unpleasant for everyone. Suppose you have two workers who continually bicker. Is it a friendly, joking kind of banter—a way to tease each other, a way to relate, or is it nasty and hurtful? If it is the latter, you may need to become a mediator.

Some people are afraid of conflict and think it should be avoided at all costs; others love a good argument and enjoy doing battle. Which one are you?

Not all conflict is bad; sometimes different viewpoints need to be aired. If people feel free to have divergent opinions and to disagree, and if they do not see debates as threatening but as healthy, then you and your organization will benefit from such diversity. After all, if we all agreed on everything, we would have no challenge, no creativity, no learning from each other. For example, if two of your workers disagree as to the best way to handle a problem and become quite heated about it, you can show that you appreciate how much they care and either work out a compromise or see the stronger merits of one particular position.

If you see conflict between individuals, listen to each person's complaints privately without taking sides. When people are angry, they make wild statements, such as "I'll never show you any specifications again," which, of course, can't be implemented. Avoid head-on confrontations. For an employee to be able to talk to you about feelings can reduce tension. After things cool down, you can determine what each is willing to do to keep meeting the company's objectives.

Do not expect the adversaries to kiss and make up, but do tell them you expect them to act like adults with politeness and restraint no matter how they feel. You have the right to make the rules. These are some guidelines you can give: no name-calling, no sabotaging of one another's operations, no refusal to cooperate, and no use of violence for any reason.

One of the problems in these situations is that the other workers may take sides and you may find half your unit warring against the other. Unless it is absolutely clear who is at fault, do not take sides yourself; rather, insist on the job being done. Getting people to confront each other will only work if it is done in the privacy of your office or outside the workplace and if you feel you can be truly impartial, and that your negotiating skills are sufficient to get each to see the other person's point of view.

One of the things I have found helpful is to get each person to pretend to be the other and have them talk as if they had the other's job or position.

Often people fight over what seems to be trivial, childish matters. But don't minimize the importance of the fight. At issue may be territory, self-esteem, or status—none of which is trivial. Although squabbles will always exist, you should set the tone for how they are to be handled.

Sexual Issues Between You and Your Boss

What do you do if your boss makes sexual comments, innuendoes, or asks you out for dinner when you know it won't be for business purposes?

If, after an initial rejection, he (in the majority of cases it is a "he") continues, ask to speak to him privately and say, "I'm sure you mean well when you compliment me, ask me for dinner, and put your arm around me, but I prefer for you *not* to do this. I do *not* date people I work for. Evidently you don't believe me because you keep after me. What can I do so that you will really believe me when I say I don't want it? It is important to me to do the best job I can, and I don't want anything to interfere with that."

It will be up to your boss to come up with an answer. If you're not satisfied with it, you can still say, "Is there something in my behavior that makes you think I'm interested?"

Again, he'll have to come up with an answer. This approach makes the boss take the responsibility for his behavior. *Don't make him the problem, make him part of the solution.*

If he continues, you can threaten to tell his boss and threaten to sue him and the company for sexual harassment. This process, however, is very unpleasant and costly; and even if you win, your reputation as a troublemaker may make future employment difficult. Women who are willing to do so have great courage.

What constitutes sexual harassment is any sexual behavior that is unwanted, unwelcome, jeopardizes your effectiveness as a worker, and makes you afraid to put a stop to it because it may affect your job and your future. You should know your company's policy on sexual harassment. If the problem continues, go to your supervisor's boss and eventually to the personnel department and the Equal Employment Opportunity Commission (EEOC) officer.

Different Tunes

She sings:
"Someday my prince
will come"
and she dreams
of tenderness
and a long life together

He sings:
"There is nothing like a dame"
and dreams
of quickies
here today, gone tomorrow

Sexual Issues Between You and Your Employees

These problems occur most frequently in situations where men supervise women. A supervisor must *never* initiate a sexual relationship with a subordinate! Why? Because some employees will believe that if they refuse, the supervisor might feel rejected, become angry, give them the worst shifts, take away privileges, or withhold further training. The supervisor might give them poor performance appraisals and even fire them. If a supervisor uses a position of power to try to take sexual advantage of a worker or even to make sexual remarks in jest, such behavior is viewed as sexual harassment, and the supervisor can be taken to court.

Don't touch your workers and don't tell them about your sexual exploits, fantasies, or problems. This kind of behavior can make them uncomfortable and will almost always be misinterpreted. Don't ask personal questions unless it is clear that you are doing it either because you wish to know your workers better or you think there might be a problem you could help with.

Don't talk about personal matters unless the atmosphere of the workplace is one where people share family concerns. If one of your workers is seductive, you must not take him or her up on it. If you do, you are taking advantage of your position as supervisor.

Sexual Issues Among Your Subordinates

Observe whether or not there is sexual joking among your workers. Some women will resent it but may be uneasy about stopping it. Some women may seem to enjoy it, but many do not and just pretend to in order not to be seen as prudes and excluded from the group. Also, there are men who are uncomfortable about sexual comments but who won't say anything. It is the supervisor's responsibility to stop that kind of behavior. Also be aware that there are a significant number of reports concerning homosexual harassment.

Most companies know that the best defense a company can use

in preventing sexual harassment is to have a written policy that spells out the fact that management will not tolerate a supervisor's use of his position to secure sexual cooperation of his subordinates, nor will it tolerate sexual misconduct on the part of their workers.

Courts have broadened the types of interaction they see as sexual harassment. If a female employee becomes the object of sexually derogatory, oral or written remarks, jokes or gestures, and the situation is brought to the attention of the employee's supervisor, failure to act on the matter would be judged as management condoning the conduct.

If a worker encounters such harassment, and if she informs her superior of such harassment, the superior is held just as responsible as the harasser for the harasser's conduct if he or she doesn't do anything about it. The only exception to this is when the employee takes legal action immediately without informing the employer or allows the employer no time to find out about the incident.

In any case, most incidents should be handled at the supervisory level. Because a lot of legal involvement can be avoided if supervisors handle sexual harassment cases effectively, the following are some steps that a supervisor should take when a subordinate confronts them with allegations of sexual harassment:

1. Find out your organization's policy on sexual harassment. Every personnel manual should have a policy or a "speak-out" program concerning sexual harassment if the company wants to avoid legal involvement. If the company does not have a policy, sexual harassment would fall under Title VII of the 1964 Civil Rights Act.
2. Determine your role in implementing the policy. If the organization does not have formal training programs for supervisors on handling sexual harassment, familiarize yourself with the Equal Employment Opportunity Commission guidelines, contact your personnel's affirmative action officer for advice, and ask the person being harassed these eight key questions*:
   (1) Who harassed you?
   (2) What did he/she do?

*Note that these questions are the same questions that the harassee should be able to answer for the complaint to appear credible.

(3) What did he/she say?
(4) When did the incident occur?
(5) Were there any witnesses?
(6) Has this happened before?
(7) Has this happened to others?
(8) What would you like me to do?

3. Inform your staff of the company's sexual harassment policy. Be sure that all present as well as new employees are made aware of any sexual harassment policies. It is not enough to post the policy and distribute it. Sit down with your people and discuss the problems. You can rent a videotape on sexual issues or present a workshop.[21]
4. Act immediately and appropriately when an incident occurs. As soon as you see or hear of an incident of sexual harassment, do not wait for it to go away—take action in a professional manner. It is important that you do not let the sexual aspects of sexual harassment frighten, confuse, or anger you into not acting appropriately. Also, it is important to remember that all discussions should be conducted in private.
5. Investigate all incidents objectively and empathetically. As a supervisor, you should investigate in a calm, journalistic manner. Explain to the victim that it is best to document incidents if further action needs to be taken.
6. Determine a course of action with involved parties. Ask the victim what she wants you to do. The employee may be asking for advice on how to handle the situation herself, or she may want to file a complaint and want to ask you to investigate the situation. In some cases, you should report the sexual harassment to the personnel department immediately so that they may investigate.
7. Follow up on all courses of action. If, after talking with the victim and the personnel department, the situation does not get better, begin investigating the workplace. If sexual harassment is found, initiate disciplinary action.

If supervisors follow these procedures, the harassment problems may end here without legal complications. Be sure that the policy statement includes a definition of unacceptable employee behavior, an explicit statement of employer disapproval of misconduct or sexual harassment, a discussion of detrimental effects of sexual harassment, and an indication of corrective or disciplinary actions that will be taken when sexual harassment occurs.

For example, the policy statement could contain the following:

> Sexual harassment of the employees of this organization will not be tolerated.
>
> This means that the following behaviors are grounds for disciplinary action:
>
> 1. Abusing the dignity of an employee through insulting or degrading sexual remarks or conduct
> 2. Threats, demands, or suggestions that an employee's work status is contingent upon the employee's toleration of, or acquiescence to, sexual advances
> 3. Retaliation against employees for complaining about the behavior described above
>
> If you encounter such abuses from supervisors, fellow employees, or clients, you should contact your supervisor, the personnel office, the equal opportunity coordinator, and/or your union steward.
>
> We want all employees to know that they can work in security and dignity, and are not required to endure insulting, degrading, or exploitive treatment.[23]

Not only may subordinates' jobs be on the line if they refuse sexual advances from a superior, but there have been instances upheld by grievance committees and courts of law where subordinates have been found to have sexually harassed superiors, thus creating a hostile and intimidating work environment. Harassment can also exist between coworkers, creating an atmosphere that is not conducive to working effectively. Sexual harassment is seen as a power ploy because it demeans people it is forced on, making them feel powerless and helpless and, conversely, making the harassers feel more powerful because they're having fun at the expense of someone else.

I have found that it is the people who are the least sure of themselves who need to downgrade others. They are the ones who abuse children and harass women. The coworkers who do nothing are not innocent observers but accomplices, for it is up to everyone to stop demeaning actions wherever they take place.

Boys Will Be Boys

A leer
A comment about her legs
A dirty joke
A brush against her
A swear word
with an apology
for the lady present

A conversation that stops
when she comes in
The whispering when she's there
The laughter when she passes by
The relief when she quits.

Women just can't take it
They have no sense of humor
and overreact to a little "innocent fun"

Office Affairs

Other sexual issues besides harassment may influence productivity and work climate. What do you do if two of your workers are having an affair? Nothing, if it doesn't seem to affect their work or anyone else's. However, office affairs can be disruptive. The couple may not always behave appropriately—they may take longer lunch hours or find excuses to work on the same projects. Other people may be irritated by their behavior and even feel threatened if one of the partners has a higher position and can confer privileges on the other. In this kind of situation, whatever rewards the other person gets will be regarded as unfair. If, as the supervisor, you see that such a situation has negative consequences, you must talk to the pair and consider transferring one of them. The transferred person should not necessarily be the woman (although this often is the action taken) just because the woman usually is the one in the lower position or the one who is more easily replaceable.[24]

Homosexuality is not an issue a supervisor must deal with unless, again, it affects the work climate through inappropriate behavior. This does not mean that if some employees don't like homosexuals, you can use that dislike as an excuse to fire such individuals. Be aware that you, too, have your own prejudices about sexual behaviors. You may be very upset if one of your married workers is playing around, or you may have been brought up to dislike gays, or you may think that flirting is disruptive. You cannot impose your value system on others, but you can maintain an atmosphere conducive to good work, cooperative relationships, and trust. You can make yourself available so that your workers can come and talk openly with you without fear of retribution.

Harassment of minorities may not be sexual, but it can have a very serious effect on them. Racial jokes, innuendoes, and exclusion from the group are all very painful, and minority workers often will not complain to you but will suffer in silence. Their productivity will diminish, and the work climate will deteriorate. Be observant and put your foot down when you see such harassment taking place. Your influence can change an entire group's work climate. You will be respected for your values. This is a time to be tough. As a supervisor, you must see to it that your work force operates well together.

One of the main causes of conflict is resistance. There are two basic assumptions that need to be understood in order to deal creatively with resistance. First, most people will always resist that which is not in their best interest and second, resistance needs to be respected as an expression of need. Even if you believe that it is ridiculous or unwarranted to resist in a specific situation, the resistor may feel righteous, and it is up to you to understand the reason for the resistance in order to overcome, compromise, or give in. First, allow the resistance to surface as a legitimate expression, listening carefully to the reasons given. Acknowledge that the resistor has a right to the feelings expressed. Explore whether the resistance is about a specific situation or about a general attitude toward change, new suggestions; or ask for specific objections and for alternative ideas. If there is room to negotiate, do so. If not, explain your positions and request cooperation even though you sympathize with the objections. People can be very strong and creative when they resist something they perceive as being potentially harmful. You may need to reassure them by honoring their concerns, but at the same time, you must be adamant about the desired outcome.[25]

Your Conflict-Management Style

It is important to identify your own preferred style for managing conflict because that is what you will fall back on most often. Do you tend to withdraw, do you confront problems head-on, do you find compromise solutions, or do you attempt to smooth things over? Whichever is your tendency, it is sometimes necessary to do what is least comfortable. Every conflict situation may necessitate a different approach. Sometimes it's not worth a fight, so you withdraw; other times it is important to put your foot down, so you confront. Getting people to agree may be critical, so you compromise.

Examine the situation, the needs of the people involved, the possible consequences, and then act. Conflict management will be one of the more difficult tasks among your supervisory responsibilities.

A supervisor will often have to act as an arbitrator. The following step-by-step conflict management model will help you in mediating between workers who fight or complain about each other:

1. Both parties should declare their interest in resolving the conflict; if not, you should make the necessary decision.
2. Both parties should be asked to define the conflict as each sees it and to state the reason for it (misinformation, values conflict, territory, self-esteem, and so on).
3. Both parties must be prepared to look for something they can agree on, such as a goal of enhanced productivity or a better work climate.
4. Both parties should state what they wish the other would do.
5. Both parties should state what they are able and unable to compromise on.
6. Both parties should explore mutually acceptable, if not completely satisfactory, solutions that will settle the conflict.
7. Both parties should set up monitoring devices to ensure that the conflict will not recur.

Exercise

Find out your company's policy regarding sexual harassment. Observe whether there are any indications of such harassment among your workers. Invite the women of your unit to come to your office as a group and ask them if there are any issues they would like to discuss. Do the same with the men and with the minority groups. Offer to see your employees individually if they feel they can't talk publicly. Promise confidentiality, and keep your promise. Is there help available from the personnel department? Are there training packages or consultants who are experts in this field? Find out, for these tools can make it easier for you to deal with these issues.

PART III

GETTING SETTLED

5

MANAGING TIME

You feel overwhelmed! There is more to do than you can possibly get done during the workday. If you have so much to do that you don't even have time to think about time management, then *you know* you need to do something differently.

Time management includes how you use your own time and for what purpose, as well as how you schedule the time of others. Decisions about your own time require goal setting and planning; decisions about your workers' time require planning and scheduling.

Personal, Professional, and Organizational Goals

You need to take a couple of quiet hours with a "DO NOT DISTURB" sign on your door. If you do not have an office, find a quiet spot (unless quiet time is so impossible to arrange at work that you have to do this at home). Make three lists: professional goals, organizational goals, and personal goals. Make a separate time plan for each: three years, one year, and tomorrow.

Professional goals are those you want to have achieved three years from now. For example, you may want to be in your boss's shoes, or you may want a better job in a different company, or you're just waiting to go into business for yourself, or perhaps you want to stay put and expand your responsibilities.

Organizational goals are the objectives you set for the workers you are supervising. For example, you hope that Joseph will be retired by then, that Susan will have moved on, and that your unit will expand its operation.

Your personal goals may include spending more time with your growing children, learning about computers, or getting in better physical shape.

Set priorities for all these goals: professional goals A, B, and C; organizational goals A, B, and C; and personal goals A, B, and C.

Your Tomorrow Starts Today

If, for your professional goal, you want to be in your boss's shoes in three years, then a year from now you should arrange that he or she delegate some responsibilities to you, and tomorrow you should make a list of what these might be. If a move is what you want, then a year from now you should talk to people from other companies, and tomorrow you should start finding out about possible contacts.

Next, take your organizational goals. In what way can you be preparing Joseph for early retirement? What training does Susan need to take the next step? From whom are you getting support for expansion?

Priorities for your personal goals should also be set. Enroll in a computer training program or in an exercise class, or plan an activity with your family.

The three-year projection is your hope, the one-year projection is your plan. Tomorrow is the action; today is the preparation for it.

Schedule Your Time

You now need to make a chart. It should include all your activities at work, as well as your activities outside of work. If your days are fairly uniform, make a daily chart. If your duties are different each day, make a weekly chart.

My chart is for an average day, and it gives me information: I should work less and have more time for myself.

A glance at your chart will tell you how much or how little you are doing for yourself, and how much or how little satisfaction you are deriving from it. If most of your time is spent on energy-draining activities, you will deplete yourself and cease being effective. Ask yourself: (1) Does the activity really need to be done? (2) Can it be done some other way? (3) Can it be done by someone else? (4) What would happen if it were done differently,

Daily Chart [mine] Based on a 5-day Week
(Divided into Half-hour Segments)

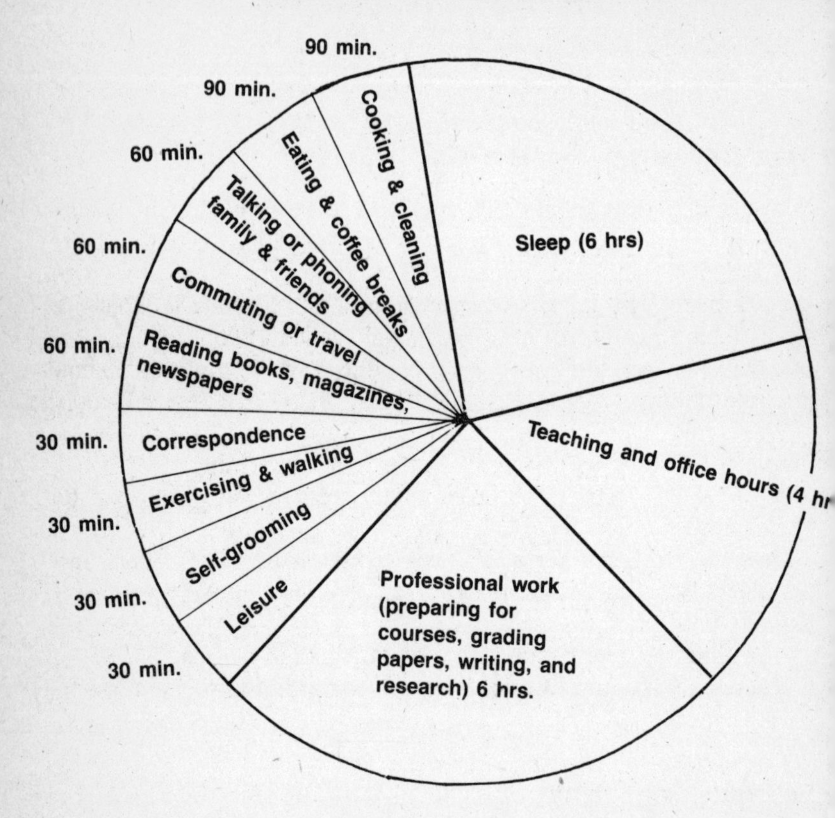

not done by me, or not done at all? (5) Is there a better time for you to do the unpleasant tasks, such as getting them done early so they're out of the way, or giving yourself a reward for doing them?

In your chart, mark your spaces to approximate the time each activity takes. For example, if you sleep eight hours, it should take up one-third of your chart.

I hope the quality of your life is better than the following:

Quality of Life

I jump out of bed
throw on some clothes
gulp down my coffee

put a note on the fridge
wave to my husband
run out of the house
hop into my car
dash into my office
glance at my mail
scan the paper
scribble a note
get rid of a visitor
cancel a luncheon
order a sandwich
eat at my desk
my ear to the phone
make a rapid decision
hurry to a meeting
refuse an invitation
read a summary
draw a quick conclusion
speed out of the office
go to a fast-food place
pick up a pizza
throw something in the oven
grab a bite
ask him about his day
not really listen
flip through a journal
skim through a report
turn on the TV
watch a 10-minute newscast
blow him a kiss
hit the sack

Your Time at Work

Start each morning with a "To Do" list for that day.[26] Underline in red what needs to be done first, in green what should be done next, and in blue what can wait until tomorrow. As you do them, cross them out. Today's blue may be tomorrow's red or maybe stay blue for so long that it eventually gets crossed out anyway. You can devise your own system, but you should have a system or you won't know what gets done and what doesn't. Keep the crossed-out lists in a file, They may come in handy when you are given a performance evaluation by your boss.

Notice if you do a lot of firefighting. This means responding to crises rather than going through your planned activities. If you are, then you need to schedule time for trying to prevent the crises from occurring. This may include studying the patterns. When, where, who? Do the problems always involve the same people? What are the causes? You may want to hold a meeting with the people responsible and help them brainstorm ways to avoid crises.

A manager's job is fraught with interruptions; it is fragmented; the interactions with others tend to be brief and the activities varied. In other words, what you don't have is nice, long, predictable, uninterrupted time. Women are often better than men at juggling many things at the same time and have a quicker start-up time after being interrupted. Perhaps this is true because women have watched their mothers—or are themselves—coping with multiple chores.

To accept the fragmentation as part of a supervisor's job is important because one must learn to work around it and be able to accomplish things in bits and pieces. If you wait to have a large amount of time set aside to start a project, you may have to wait forever.

The following are time robbers:

1. Procrastination or avoiding a task
2. Telephone interruptions (Have phone calls screened, if possible, and return all calls during a block of time when you have the least energy for doing other jobs.)
3. Misplaced items
4. Drop-in visitors
5. Waiting for people (Always have something you can be working on.)
6. Failure to delegate
7. Unnecessary meetings (Consider what your role is to be at the meeting, and decide whether there is need for you to be there.)
8. Unnecessary correspondence (I will often make a note on the same letter that was sent to me if a short answer is required and mail it right back, thus avoiding the usual "Dear so and so" and other formalities.)

The following are time savers:

1. Refuse to make decisions under stress unless absolutely necessary.
2. Consult other people.
3. Do not expect to anticipate everything.
4. Don't be afraid of making "a" wrong decision versus "the" wrong decision.
5. Realize that not everything worth doing is worth doing well.
6. Go on to something else, once a decision is made.
7. Manage each day according to a predetermined plan.
8. Set out your goals for each day in order of priority.
9. Make a "To Do" list every day.
10. Use dictating equipment whenever feasible, if you have access to a secretary.
11. Upgrade and downgrade priorities constantly.
12. Ask yourself, "What is the *best* way to use my time *right now*? Then do it.
13. Divide large projects into sections so that you won't need a large block of time in which to do them.
14. Tell your superior what you plan to drop or delegate to others when you are given too much to do, and ask for advice.

Who Does What Best?

What are you responsible for? Is it a product, a service? Whatever it is, certain activities are needed to fulfill your department's required output. It can be the paperwork to produce a certain type of service; it can be the making of a product. List all the steps needed to produce the desired outcome. After you have identified *what* needs to be done, you will need to figure out *who* will do it.

You cannot make a schedule until you know two things: what needs to be done and what skills your work force needs to do it. You should look for the best fit between the person and the job. For this, you will need to make a chart of your own activities and have your workers do the same for themselves.

Ask your workers to prepare a chart similar to the one shown on page 106. Have them make three columns for their activities: those they do on a daily basis, those they do on a routine but nondaily basis, and those they do nonroutinely (just once in a while). This is what your own chart may look like:

Activity	Daily	Routine Nondaily	Nonroutine
Read mail	X		
Return phone calls	X		
Take inventory		Monthly	
Write reports		Every two weeks	
Make performance evaluations		Twice a year	
Interview applicants			X
Lunch with customers			X
Make a "To Do" list	X		
Schedule workers		Weekly	
Report to boss			X
Order office supplies		Once a month	
Hold staff meetings		Once a month	

As you look at your own activities chart, you may decide that you would prefer to have regularly scheduled meetings with your boss instead of on a catch-as-catch-can basis, or that you only need to write reports monthly. Looking at the charts your workers have prepared will give you a basis for discussion with them: what they're good at, what you want them to improve, what they can change. It will also give you information about how you use your work pool. Do the women and minorities perform more of the daily tasks, and do the white men do more nonroutine and unusual tasks? This may be the case, but you won't be aware of this type of subtle discrimination until you have read these charts.

Make your own chart based on what your workers do and on your perceptions of their strengths and weaknesses, using the chart on page 108 as a guide. The X-marks on the chart are the original scheduling, and the zeros are added after you have looked at the chart and reevaluated.

As you look at this chart, you can see the problems right away. Often someone is needed to take over for Jane. This cuts into the work to be done. She will have to be more reliable, or there should be one person who automatically replaces her, or you might rotate replacements. If Mike is fast but inaccurate, it might be a better idea for Susan to answer mail unless Susan could be made responsible for checking accuracy when Mike types. Jack should not be filing anymore and ought to teach the system to someone else, possibly Susan. Kathy might be a candidate for a computer training program, and the next person who is hired ought to sit down with Jack and be told about the department's norms since he is the company historian. Someone else should also learn to take dictation; check to see if Mike is interested, and at the same time, see to it that he gets help to improve his accuracy.

None of these decisions should be made by you alone. Whenever possible (if a decision affects the work of a person), the person or the work group involved should be consulted. If no choice can be offered, then an explanation is due about the reasons for the change, with a chance for the person involved to have a say.

You can also make changes after your reevaluation because you believe that Mike would be offended if his typing is checked by a coworker, that Kathy needs to be challenged, that Jack needs to slow down and get some recognition for his long time with the company, and that Jane may have to be let go if her absences continue (unless a good talk with her can get to the bottom of the trouble). You might also notice that some of the ordering of office supplies that you now do could be done by someone else. Only after you know the jobs that need to be done, after you identify your workers' strengths, weaknesses, and preferences can you make your schedule intelligently. You will also need to remember that it is common practice in most agencies to give first choice in shift, location, or type of work to senior people. Check with your boss about your organization's policy regarding seniority.

	Answer Phone Receptionist	Answer Routine Mail	Type	File	Take Dictation	Strengths	Weaknesses
Jane	X		X			Good on phone	Often absent
Mike		X	X		0	Fast, cheerful	Inaccurate
Jack	0		X	X		Knows everything about company	Near re-retirement, often tired
Susan		0	X	0		Accurate, quiet	Slow
Kathy			X		X	Young, bright, ambitious	Quickly bored

How do you approach your workers with the suggested changes? Most people tend to resist change. Since it's easier to keep doing the same thing, you can predict initial rejection of your ideas with all kinds of arguments as to why they won't work, or can't work, or have failed when tried before, or have never been done. Your best strategy is to sit with people individually, explain your reasons, listen to their arguments, and try to arrive at a mutually satisfying decision. If you can't get agreement, you will have three choices: back down, put your foot down, or compromise.

Here is a conversation between a worker and you:

> YOU: Mike, I'm reorganizing the office for better efficiency and want to talk to you about some of my ideas.
>
> MIKE: All right.
>
> YOU: You are among our fastest typists and can really get the work out. I appreciate that, but you pay a price—accuracy. I can understand that it's hard for you to be both fast and precise, but it takes time for me to correct your work. You don't seem to be able to find your own mistakes. How would you feel if Susan made the corrections instead of me?

MIKE: But Susan isn't my boss.

YOU: No, and I understand your feelings. She will not be your boss, but she is very good at proofreading. Will you give it a try, and we'll talk again in a couple of weeks. You can let me know how it's going.

MIKE: Okay.

If you can predict smooth sailing, you should meet with the whole group, but if you expect resistance, do not meet with them all together because they will only reinforce one another.

A word of caution. Not everyone wants to be consulted. As strange as it may seem, some people are so used to following directions that they feel threatened when they have to make any kind of a decision and may lose respect for the person in authority. Their sharing of decision-making is interpreted as "My boss doesn't know and needs to ask others."

I once had an Iranian student who became very upset with me when I did not know the answer to a question and admitted it. He told me after class that it was a shame for a professor to admit not knowing something. The Socratic method of teaching by asking students questions does not work with certain people.

I had a similar experience with a Filipino student who apologized to me after class for his fellow classmate, who he felt had been rude for disagreeing with the teacher, when in fact I encourage students to challenge me. What this shows is that you cannot assume that all workers, regardless of their backgrounds, will respond favorably to your attempts to involve them in their own scheduling, and that even if they disagree with you, you won't always know it. Awareness of differences and respect for them are the first steps toward understanding. Explaining North American habits, norms, and expectations is also very helpful, for ours is a culture foreign to many people.

The same caution applies to different age groups. Young people may not be knowledgeable enough about their own abilities and either underrate them or have unrealistic expectations of what they can do. They could be counterdependent: whatever you say, they disagree and think they know better. They graduated yesterday and want to be company presidents tomorrow; they think you're too old-fashioned. Older persons may have difficulties with a younger supervisor, believing they know more and should not be told what to do.

There is no single way to manage everyone. To manage most effectively, learn about the individuals who work for you and try to see them as individuals; know what needs to be done and then be concerned with what each person can do, is willing to do, and expects to do.

What motivates *you* may leave me indifferent; my greatest aspirations may leave you cold. Adopt your supervisory style to the needs of others, while recognizing your own tendencies and patterns.

Delegation: The Newest Part of Your Job

Be aware that there is more comfort and security in performing the work you're used to doing than in doing what is unfamiliar. Learning to manage is a new and unfamiliar skill; allow yourself not to be perfect at it just yet.

The tendency for many supervisors is not to let go of their previous jobs but just to add on supervisory responsibilities. You cannot add on without taking off something—or you'll get exhausted and nothing will get done well enough. Some supervisors just do less of whatever they were doing before; others stop the former activity completely. Telephone company supervisors answer only their staffs' special questions and do not sit at the switchboard. They may each be responsible for 15 to 25 operators. In the telephone company, this is a routine arrangement; supervisors do not decide on their own to take a switchboard position unless there is a special crunch. In places such as a factory, supervisors may be tempted to keep their hands on the tools or the machines; sometimes it is expected; however, it is important to make certain that if "to supervise" is a full-time job, "hands on" is only for training and demonstration purposes.

To delegate is to entrust an activity to another person. It is not assigning unpleasant tasks to others; it is giving someone else the authority to make decisions and the opportunity to act in your place. If unpleasant tasks need to be divided, however, then you should admit that a task may not be pleasant but that it still needs to be done. Don't pretend it is a great opportunity when it isn't.

Why is it so difficult for some people to delegate? There are several reasons:

1. **If you assign a job that you do well yourself, it may not be done to your standards, or as quickly, or exactly the way you would have done it.** So the perfectionist in you says it won't be done as well. The question to ask is: Will it be good enough for the purpose? If not, can that person be taught to do the job well enough?
2. **If other people do your job, the insecure person in you may fear that they will do it better and that you'll be replaced.** If you delegate a task of a routine nature, you can take the time to do more creative things, such as thinking of ways to increase productivity. If you can be replaced by someone you have groomed to do your job, you can move on to the next step, too. You should delegate to teach others and to free yourself for bigger and better things.
3. **If you give up your responsibilities, you'll have nothing to do.** People with a very small territory are afraid to give any piece of it away for fear they will have nothing left. You give up some territory only to increase your ability to do more managerial tasks and to assume pieces of your boss's territory.
4. **You don't have time to teach someone how to take over.** The less time you have to train someone, the more you need to do it. It's a matter of priorities, and perhaps you unconsciously want to hold on, for one of the first three reasons.
5. **There is no one to delegate to.** This is the reason most commonly given by supervisors for not delegating. This does not necessarily mean that no such person is available, but rather that the people available are not regarded as competent or are too busy or unwilling to accept the delegated work. All of these reasons can be overcome if you're willing to put some time and effort into it, if you're *really* convinced you want to delegate. Your own resistance may

> be the first thing to deal with. What do you fear? If you have reason to be afraid that you may be out of a job if one of your subordinates should make a mistake, the atmosphere in your place of work is such that there are no growth possibilities. You may want to discuss this with your own boss and get some support for the risk you're taking in delegating. If there is no available person to delegate to and you are overworked, you may want to consider hiring someone.

The three major components of delegation are *what, who,* and *how. What*: Define what needs to be done and see to it that it gets done. *Who*: Define who can do what and train them to do it. *How*: Use interpersonal-relations skills to create a productive work climate.

Before you delegate a task, you should (1) analyze your own workload; (2) analyze the resources in your department; (3) brainstorm your options; (4) select those options that logically and intuitively make good sense; (5) begin doing them; and after the task is completed, (6) track the results.

In the *what* component of delegation, you should make a list of all your activities—tasks, duties, actions, and responsibilities—and divide them into four categories:

1. Work that can be done only by you as manager; work that is never delegated such as performance reviews
2. Work that can be delegated immediately to someone who is trained to take on the responsibility
3. Work that can be delegated as soon as you can take the time to train someone to do it
4. Work that should be delegated, but no one is available who can do it

In the *who* component of delegation, if you see yourself as the only competent person around to do the work you believe others should be doing, you may need to examine your own attitude. The best predictor of the future is the past. Is it your usual pattern to do everything yourself, whatever the reason? Although it may be true that you do the job better or faster than anyone else, the question to ask is whether it will be done well enough or fast enough by someone else to accomplish the results needed by the organization. "It's easier to do it myself," is only true in the short run. People who say that often become firefighters, that is, they go from one crisis to another, always doing everything themselves, not taking the time to plan and delegate.

If you have competent people to whom you can delegate, but who may be unwilling to take on an extra burden, you should explain that you are offering more responsibility and more autonomy as an example of your trust in them. Then your subordinates may be motivated to take on the added duties. Be sure that they understand that it is not a question of their doing your job for you but is instead an opportunity for growth. The issue here will be your ability to accept other people's way of doing a job that may be different from your own. Even though you may be convinced that your method is the best (most efficient, fastest, cleanest), their results are all that need to be evaluated. A confident supervisor will be able to recognize a job well done and congratulate subordinates if they meet or exceed expectations.

If you have to train someone to take over a particular job, you should realize that training takes time and patience. Both of you must feel that it is worth the effort even though mistakes will be made. How tolerant can you be of an error? How tolerant can your organization be? If *no* mistakes are made, no one is learning or growing. It is unrealistic to expect that things will be done correctly from the start or that they will be done as efficiently, quickly, or neatly by a beginner as by a veteran.

How do you know who is ready to be trained? Observe your workers. Who seems to be interested in the work and likes the job? Who does good work, is helpful to others, and seems to be liked by others? Who can initiate and work independently? There are other clues. Who seems bored? Who may need more to do or more challenge in what they're doing? Who seems dissatisfied? Find out by asking and by being ready to listen to suggestions as to what they think they could take on. Women and minorities may be less obviously upwardly mobile because they have been taught to keep a low profile. There are cultures that deem it rude to try to advance by asking for opportunities. You need to ask what your subordinates' ambitions are and help them with career plans.

In the *how* component of delegation, you should show enthusiasm at the opportunity to teach others new skills. After all, it is as good for you as it is for them. However, the issue here is patience with the slowness of others to understand. If there are language problems, be aware that not only do they not understand you, but it is also equally your problem that you may not be able to explain in their languages. The burden of difficult communication is a shared one. You may have to have another worker act as translator. Many people are intelligent and are ready to learn more but are handicapped by their lack of English. Don't let that stand in the way of teaching them new skills and giving them more responsibility.

It is important that the people to whom you delegate see the task as an opportunity for growth and not as an extra burden you want to get rid of. This may not be clear to people, especially those from other cultures, and you may need to take the time to explain in positive ways your reasons for choosing them above others and what such a move could do for them.

It is possible that a worker may wonder, "Why am I being given this job when my supervisor is being paid to do it?" Being selected to be trained should be seen as a reward for good work, and the supervisor can make this clear by saying so and complimenting the trainee for past performance. People should know that what they do is valued by their supervisors. You might say, "I like the way you helped settle the dispute that Joe and Harry had yesterday; you have good people skill," or, "I appreciate your extra help with the work; your efforts are not going unnoticed," or, "You're doing good quality work; are you interested in more responsibility?" Workers need to understand how accepting delegated responsibility will benefit them.

Delegation must be both interpersonal and individual. As such, it depends to a large extent on the relationship between you and each member of your staff; however, as listed below, there are some general guidelines to follow:

1. **Delegate on the basis of results expected.** Some people need to be taught procedures and must have every step explained; other people should be told only what you expect, and they will find out how to do it. For example, if you ask a worker to check on the prices of a product from the competition, this may be enough information for some. For others, you may have to tell them to call five supermarkets

and speak to the suppliers. Be sure you don't overexplain to those who don't need it, and that you give enough information to those who do.

2. **Set standards by which you can measure performance.** People need to know what you consider a successfully completed project.
3. **Establish ongoing controls as needed.** Some workers' progress will need to be checked on a regular basis. Decide ahead of time when you will get together so that your worker understands it is not an issue of trust but part of the plan. Other workers will resent being checked on and can be relied upon to complete the job on their own. Be sure to give people a chance to prove themselves.

When you delegate a task, you have the following methods to choose from:

1. Your worker investigates and reports back; then you make the decision and take appropriate action.
2. Your worker investigates and recommends action; then you evaluate the recommendation, make the decision, and take action.
3. Your worker investigates and devises an intended action; then you evaluate the decision made by your worker and approve or disapprove.
4. Your worker investigates and takes action and advises of the action taken; then you display faith in your worker's ability but explain that you want to be kept advised as to what's going on.

When you delegate a task, you should (1) explain the results expected; (2) set performance standards; (3) give all the relevant information; (4) delegate only to qualified people; (5) establish control in terms of quality and time.

Remember that we tend to trust most those who are most like ourselves. Check if the person you trust most is very similar to you in work style, values, or background. But be careful not to clone yourself unconsciously. It is unfair to the others who may be equally, or perhaps even more, competent than the person you are most comfortable with.

Listed below are some things that can go wrong when you delegate a task:

1. **The subordinates make mistakes.** Because you are accountable to your organization for the errors in your department, this will not only make you look as if you have poor judgment, but it may also lose your company money. A good boss will, of course, understand that you took a necessary risk and will not chastise you for the error.
2. **The subordinates do better than you, which is good for the organization, but bad for you.** You can point out to your boss that the excellence achieved by your subordinates is due to your effective training methods.
3. **The subordinates do not want the added responsibility and complain about the extra work.** This should have been dealt with before you delegated the task; however, if it was not done or your subordinates did not understand what the job entailed, you have two choices: take away the tasks and give them to someone else or insist that the workers do the job as part of the workload, explaining the reasons for your decision.
4. **Other workers are jealous and complain.** It is important to announce the exact new responsibilities of your subordinates to everyone and to praise them if the job is well done.

Listed below are some positive aspects that may occur when you delegate a task:

1. The supervisor now has time to concentrate on other work.
2. The subordinates' growth and development are stimulated by the freedom to act and experience success as well as failure.
3. The supervisor is now a teacher and a coach.
4. The necessary two-way discussion of objectives and results increases interpersonal communication.
5. The subordinates have the opportunity to show what they can do, giving them self-esteem.
6. A continuing relationship develops of trust and confidence.

Here is a possible dialogue between a supervisor and a worker that might take place if the supervisor is considering delegating some duties to a subordinate.

HENRY: Susan, I have been watching you, and I really like the way you go about your work. You're a quick learner, you are very efficient; you don't make the same mistakes twice, and you get along well with people. Have you thought about advancement?
SUSAN No, I can't say I have.
HENRY: Would you be interested in learning some new skills—being in charge of a project?
SUSAN: I'm not sure I could do it. What is it?
HENRY: Up to now, I have been making the decisions as to whose work gets typed by whom. I have been doing it on a first-come-first-served basis. There have been complaints that I don't pay enough attention to priorities. Would you like to try to develop a system that would include dealing with emergencies?
SUSAN: Hmm, let me think about it. Would I get a pay increase?
HENRY: No, not yet. But if you do a good job, there will be more opportunities for you to show what you can do, and I wouldn't be surprised if you got a promotion and a raise, although I can't promise anything.
SUSAN: Okay, I'll give it a try. In fact, I already have a couple of ideas.
HENRY: Good, why don't you give me a plan. When do you think you can have something worked out?
SUSAN: Oh, in two or three days.
HENRY: That's fine. I'm looking forward to discussing this with you. We will also have to tell the others. There might be some resentment because you're a woman and also because you're very young. Perhaps you can think about that, too.
SUSAN: Yes, I expect that Mary will give me a hard time.
HENRY: Yes, and it may be very subtle; let's talk about it if it occurs.
SUSAN: That's good to know. Thanks.
HENRY: Good luck.

We see here an example of a supervisor who checks first whether the worker is willing and feels ready. He delegates a project, offers to discuss the plan, makes sure others will know about it, and promises support in case of difficulties. We have a feeling from this dialogue that things will work out well.

Eventually, the supervisor may, in fact, be grooming an understudy, a person from the staff who can take over many of the responsibilities of the supervisor. It is important that your boss does *not* see you as irreplaceable at your present job, or you can never be moved up without loss to the company.

In order to prepare yourself to move on, you must train and develop a right-hand person who can take charge during short absences, one who could assist you when there are special projects or rush jobs. That person should have good technical skills, be able to instruct others, show initiative, work with very little need of direction, and get along with people. Be careful not to overload this person with all the jobs you dislike, but delegate the kinds of responsibilities that will permit challenge and growth.

Exercise

If you have not done the exercises in the body of this chapter, take the time to do so now. These exercises included making three lists of goals: professional, personal, and organization (p. 100); an activities chart (p. 102); a daily To Do list (p. 103); a chart scheduling your workers (p. 108)—and finally, the exercise dealing with delegation (p. 113).

6

MANAGING STRESS

Because you must be feeling quite a bit of stress coping with a new role, dealing with subordinates, reporting to a new boss, evaluating your organization, I believe that some understanding of stress and its management will be helpful to you at this stage.

Stress is the process of adapting to the demands of the environment. If the demands of the environment are greater than one's resources to meet them, then stress is increased. If there are too few demands, there is no challenge, no excitement; then the result is apathy. If there is too much demand or the wrong kind of demand, then one reacts with physiological changes such as sleeplessness, an increased heart rate, an acidic stomach, or headaches. Different people have different ways of translating stress into bodily reactions.

Too much stress makes you feel that you can't cope; that things are piling up; that things aren't working out; and you begin to feel anxious, upset, or afraid. Not enough stress makes you feel that you have too much time on your hands; that you are bored; that nothing is happening; and you begin to feel listless and depressed, believing that life has no meaning.

Stress is not necessarily negative. For example, when I make a speech in front of a large audience, I feel under stress. My heart beats rapidly, I breathe faster, and I feel nervousness in the pit of my stomach; yet I also enjoy the feeling of excitement and look forward to the act of speaking because this initial stress has given me energy. Anxiety when taking a test produces adrenaline, which could benefit the test-taker; however, an overproduction of adrenalin might produce the opposite effect—an inability to concentrate.

One of the major factors causing stress in managers is the unrelenting pace of their activities. These activities are characterized by brevity, variety, and discontinuity.[27] What does this mean?

A study of 56 foremen in the United States found that they averaged 583 activities per eight-hour shifts, an average of one in every 48 seconds;[28] thus they were constantly doing something. Other studies confirm this. For example, 160 managers in Great Britain found that they worked for half an hour or more without interruptions only about once every two days.[29] All the studies show that supervisors jump from issue to issue, responding to the needs of the moment. Half of all managerial activities last less than nine minutes.

If there is no time to think quietly, no time to pursue one idea or project without interruptions, no time to take a breather, is it any wonder that many supervisors are under stress?

What can you do to avoid this condition?

Knowing that the tendency will be to work at a relentlessly fast pace all day long, plan to take breaks for yourself. Every hour and a half, take five to ten quiet minutes and do nothing but sit and think. Relax, breathe deeply, stretch, drink a cup of tea or coffee (without caffeine, for that adds to stress). Don't allow yourself to just keep pushing—you will become less effective if you don't stop to refuel. If you know that you should expect your new activities to be brief, varied, and without continuity, it will be easier to deal with those facts.

One source of considerable stress is the result of expectations that haven't been met, either one's own or someone else's. In a work situation, unmet expectations are probably the boss's, but sometimes your own unrealistic standards may be even worse. We also come to work under stress because of family matters. We arrive upset because we are worried about a sick child, worried about a spouse's job, or angry about a fight with a friend.

Stress also comes from anticipating problems that may never occur. For example, I often feel stress before flying because I'm afraid the plane might crash, or I feel stress before an interview because I'm afraid I will fail. An important key in dealing with stress that comes from expectations that are not met, is to identify the expectations and see in what way you might fall short of achieving them. Once you have done this you can then negotiate with yourself to set a level of output toward which you are willing to strive. You can also ask yourself how reasonable the demands of others are. If you believe they are not, perhaps you can negotiate to have them changed. I do this for myself. I have learned that I expect to accomplish much more work than I ever seem to be able to do, so that at the end of the day, I'm upset with myself for having done less than I had planned. My current effort is to decide ahead of time to expect to produce less work than I previously would have thought myself capable of, thus becoming less frustrated with myself for not doing it all.

Early Signs of Burnout

What is burnout? It is depression and/or exhaustion because of overwork or being under too much stress. You may be suffering from burnout if you are tired *all* the time; if you take no pleasure in what you are doing; if everything feels like "too much"; if there is nothing you look forward to; if you have difficulty with concentration or with finishing a task; if you keep misplacing things, forgetting appointments, not really hearing what others say, not remembering what you have just been talking about; if you notice that you keep rereading the same paragraph; and if tasks take you longer than they used to. A few days' holiday will do wonders; but you should realize that you will be coming back to the same situation, and *that* is what needs to be changed. Again, you must determine what you can delegate, how you can manage your time better, and what you can do for relaxation. You will need to replenish yourself—you will need to refuel so that your engine can function effectively once more. Talking to a friend, seeking professional help, restructuring your job or even changing it, may be necessary so that you do not burn out.

How Some People Cope

People deal with stress in five possible ways:

1. **Wallowing.** These people seem to enjoy their condition and complain to everyone about it. They feel victimized by others and by the system, but they never seem to want to do anything about it.

2. **Depression.** These people withdraw, grow sad, feel hopeless and helpless. They blame themselves and say "It's my fault," and they feel guilty whether or not the unmet expectations are their own or those of others.
3. **Denial.** These people try to talk themselves into being cheerful despite obvious stress, pretending all is well and keeping a stiff upper lip. By not admitting they feel bad, they often convert their emotional problems into physical symptoms.
4. **Anger.** These people blame others and the world for their difficulties. They accept no responsibility and feel used. They say, "It's not my problem. It's yours."
5. **Problem-Solving.** These people try to understand what the expectations are, whether or not the expectations are reasonable, and whether or not resources are available to meet such expectations. They confront unrealistic expectations head-on. In order to be a good problem-solver, you must know yourself, your capacities, your abilities, and your stamina—you must know what you can expect from yourself. In order to be a good boss, you must be a good problem-solver.

Stress is greatest in the beginning of your responsibilities as boss, when you are not yet sure to whom you can delegate jobs or how best to manage time and you have the burden of trying to prove yourself. That is the time to reduce all outside sources of tension. Don't undertake too many social or community activities or take extra evening courses. Delay joining clubs that are demanding of your time. Postpone becoming an officer in an organization or an active committee member. Commit yourself only to those activities that promote understanding of your job, camaraderie with others at work, and emotional support outside of work. This is a time to eat well, to get enough rest, to exercise (which, by the way, seems to be the last priority of many working people and should be first), to take opportunities to have fun, and to think of other things besides work.

Who Is Under Most Stress

You can usually assume that most minority workers and most women experience a great deal of stress. Many of these workers feel that they are not being given equal opportunities, that their work is going unrecognized, that they are not being accepted in the informal networks dominated by white men—that their mistakes are noticed more, that they are in dead-end jobs and that they must perform better and work harder to get ahead.[30]

Categories

If one woman goofs
everyone says
we shouldn't have hired a woman

If ten men goof
no one says
we shouldn't have hired a man!

Many of these workers also say that they are made to feel they were hired because of equal employment opportunity goals and not because of their ability. It is important for you as their supervisor to understand that these feelings are strong and painful and that you may never hear about them directly. People often assume that if you are of a culture different from theirs, you will not understand them—that if you are a man, you will not understand women; that if you are a Caucasian, you will not understand an Asian. It is interesting to note that both men and woman rate female bosses as being more effective supervisors because they are more open and communicate more easily with their subordinates, an important stress-reducing element.

As a supervisor, you will need to become sensitive to the assumptions made about you, for these can be barriers to good communication. The only way I know of to keep the doors of communication open and thus reduce your workers' work-related stress, is to be an understanding boss. Ask questions, express concern, and get in touch with your own unconscious prejudices about people different from yourself.

Let us take an example. Black men especially are the victims of stereotypes and distortions. They are often depicted as "street-corner men": criminals, deserters, hustlers, ineffective, and irresponsible. These images of black men result from poor research, which tends to focus on pathology rather than on strength, on low-income groups in the black community, and on captive subjects, such as prisoners and mental patients. This all adds to the prejudiced image whites may have about blacks. More than any other groups, black men die from personal injuries on the job. Because of the racist structure of the labor market, black men work in some of the dirtiest, most dangerous job situations in this society. Blacks face a 37 percent greater chance of suffering an occupational injury and a 20 percent greater chance of dying from a job-related injury than do whites. It is thus not surprising that black men are more prone to stress.[31]

Perpetual Guilt

Most organizations are structured today as if the traditional family pattern, where the man works and the woman is at home taking care of everything, were still the norm. With today's changing family work patterns, the wife often takes care of the family *and* works, and the husband has more responsibilities at home than he used to. Thus they both experience more stress. Many working women I know are always feeling exhausted and guilty.

Perpetual Guilt

If I'm in the office
I wish I were home
With the children

If I'm home
With the children
I know I should be
In the office

I always should be
Wherever
I'm not!

Managing a career and a family is stressful because we do not have the structures available to deal with them both effectively. If we had more and better day-care centers, if we had flexible working hours and understanding bosses, life would be more manageable. Many women have asked me how they can become less ambivalent about working *and* having children. I answer that the reality of today's world makes ambivalence appropriate. Not to be ambivalent would be to deny the problem. We will not change the world by becoming less ambivalent; we will change it only by getting the men and the top administrators who make policy decisions to become more ambivalent themselves because there is something to be ambivalent about. I do not believe that children are the sole responsibility of the mother; they are the equal responsibility of the father. If your workers talk to you about their families, you can be the kind of supervisor who shows concern about your workers' families. A worker who is not under stress because of family problems will be a better worker.

Here we run into cultural differences. Some men may consider it demeaning to be involved with child care, while others may feel it is their responsibility and their right to have some time off to take care of their children. Indeed, there are many men who feel stress because they are not able to meet their expectations of being a good father: too many missed Little League games, too few dinners at home. You as the supervisor need to be aware of your own inclinations so you do not impose them as a preferred value system on your workers.

It is also important to realize that there are cultural differences in how one exhibits stress. Most Asians, for example, prefer not to share any inner turmoil and try to hide any kind of upset, no matter how severe. Many Hispanics, on the other hand, who have been used to sharing feelings, frequently express anger by shouting or pain by crying. We must also be aware that within each culture, there are also individual differences. Some Italians are very reserved and some Asians are very outspoken. Putting people in categories can lead to prejudice through stereotyping. We must use such categories *only* as a way to begin to understand cultural differences. Such general observations help us accept others' ways of doing things, of thinking, feeling, and reacting. However, we must also remember that an individual may not fit the cultural expectations.

Men, Women, and Stress

Do men and women manage differently? No—unless they are under stress. Men when stressed are more likely to become dictatorial; women under stress are more likely to become conciliatory.

Men and women have the same emotions but express them differently. The way men and women behave under stress varies.

Women tend to cry and share their upset with others, whereas men tend to withdraw and not share their feelings. Men express anger with more ease. Because the manly thing to do is to seem to be invulnerable and not show signs of weakness, a man will have little tolerance toward a woman's tears and even less so toward another man's tears.

A study based on 300 responses from women in top executive positions shows that 52 percent of the women surveyed were single, compared with only 4 percent of the men. In addition, 61 percent of the women were childless, but only 3 percent of the men were. Seventeen percent of the women were divorced compared with 2.4 percent of the men, and more than one-half of these executive women said that their careers played a part in their separation.[32]

What do these numbers reveal? Handling both a career and a family is difficult for women who are upwardly mobile but not as big a problem for men. It is important for female supervisors to know these statistics so that when they are faced with difficulty managing their personal and professional lives, they will at least know that they are not alone and that it is a common syndrome. Although there is no real cure, some improvement is possible through better time management and more delegation, and by using effective methods to deal with the inevitable stress.

Besides the issue of juggling both a career and a family, women encounter stress due to behaviors directed specifically at them.[33]

There are ten categories of behavior that men in organizations commonly impose on women who work for them.[34] These behaviors are usually motivated by traditional (stereotypical) assumptions about women; this is how many men were taught to act toward women and perhaps even what the women in their personal lives expect from them.

However, it is generally reported by all levels of women in work environments that these behaviors are *disabling* to women. That is, when male peers, subordinates, and managers behave in these ways toward them, women tend to lose effectiveness and motivation; they miss out on development opportunities; and their morale and their activity tend to decrease steadily. (Please note that most of these behaviors are also displayed by whites to blacks and other minorities, with equally disabling effects.)

If you are a man reading this list, any one of these behaviors may seem too petty to be concerned about. It must be kept in mind that, if you were a woman, you might experience innumerable versions of these "little" things—daily, weekly, continuously. The small things form a pattern, and the pattern is indeed disabling. As you read the list, try to feel what it would be like to be a *woman* and have these things happen to you daily:

1. **Overprotecting her.** (Probably the number one complaint.) Holding back on criticism; soft-pedaling negative feedback for fear of her rejection; giving assignments that are too easy; not encouraging her to take risks; censoring rough language so that you won't even use words that one commonly hears; not sending her on business trips because of imagined sexual complications.
2. **Excluding, avoiding, ignoring, or forgetting.** Not dropping by to visit; not inviting her to lunch with the group; not including her in otherwise all-male groups; not passing along useful technical or organizational information; not getting to know her; not giving her supervision, coaching, training, or projects equivalent to that of her male peers; not *really* listening to her; not including her in meetings where she could contribute or learn; not routing information to her; not crediting her contributions, ideas, work in discussions with others; not shaking hands with her.
3. **Inappropriate sexualization.** Calling her by endearing terms; commenting on her body or clothes; turning neutral topics into suggestive ones; discussing other women in sexual terms in her presence; flirting; touching her in sexually suggestive ways; initiating conversations about her "love life."
4. **Male-oriented language structures.** Referring to hypothetical managers, directors, professionals, and people as "he"; referring to the human race as "man"; referring to adult females as "girls" and "gals"; using genderizing words to describe nongender functions (chairman, right-hand man, man-hours, and so on).
5. **Drawing her into traditional female roles.** Selecting her from a group of male peers to prepare food, run errands, take notes, copy materials; seeking her comfort and sympathy for your "personal story" without reciprocating; assum-

ing that she is a nonmanagerial or lower-status employee; explaining business matters with domestic or child-care examples.

6. **Staying one up.** Providing solutions rather than helping her think things through; telling her not to worry or that you'll take over for her; doing something for her rather than helping her learn how to do it herself; holding on to information, skills, or contacts that you have and she doesn't; trivializing her concerns; bestowing fatherly or brotherly pats on the head; lavishing praise on relatively ordinary accomplishments; responding to her suggestions with counter-suggestions instead of considering hers.
7. **Discounting and discrediting.** Assuming that she has inferior skills, capabilities, or understanding; regarding her as "not in the right field"; demanding more proof, data, or persuasion than would be demanded of a male peer; explaining or paraphrasing what she has just said for the benefit of others.
8. **Loyalty tests.** Joking or making derogatory comments about another woman (or women) and expecting her to appreciate the joke; telling her she's not like other women, she's special, she's unusual for a woman; that she thinks like a man; baiting her or teasing her in ways that she can't protest without appearing to be overreactive.
9. **Male solidarity.** Going along with another male's sexist remark or joke; joining in "locker room" comments about women, particularly when a woman is present; talking exclusively about topics that capture the interest of men in a group but not the women (or woman); promoting negative attitudes toward affirmative action in the company.
10. **Self-protection.** Trying so hard to avoid committing the errors listed above that you end up seeming formal, distant, and unreal; being afraid to make mistakes with the woman you could learn from; not letting her make mistakes and take reasonable risks for fear of consequences; not asking her for feedback on yourself; surrounding yourself with traditionalists and skeptics.

This list may seem overwhelming. (The experience of these behaviors certainly can have that impact on women.) Here is a suggestion for sorting it out: Go through the categories and write out for yourself the corresponding *enabling* behaviors that men can have to help women contribute their most effective effort to the organization. Then check yourself against both lists for a week, or periodically. Discuss it with some other women you work with.

Exercise

Start working on this six-step stress-reducing plan. Make a schedule for yourself starting now. Share your plan with at least one other person who will check on your progress.

Stress Reduction

A first step in reducing stress is the evaluation of expectations. You will need to sit down and make a list of all the self-expectations you are not meeting or those that others make you feel you're not meeting, and ask yourself if you can, in fact, meet those expectations. What are the expectations? Am I able to meet them?

The second step in dealing with stress is to prepare yourself physically, mentally, and emotionally to deal with whatever demands come your way. We all know that we ought to eat less sugar and salt, more fruits and vegetables and whole grains, less red meat, more poultry and fish. Food is the fuel that keeps us going, and we need good fuel. Poor nutrition will deplete us and make us less able to deal with stress.

Third, exercise is a good way to get rid of the excess adrenaline that accumlates from stress. When I'm really upset, I walk around the block, jump up and down in my office, or do stretching exercises to get rid of some of the tension accumulated in my muscles. Regular exercise has been shown to reduce heart attacks and high blood pressure.

Part of exercising is also learning how to relax; exercising is tensing muscles, while relaxing is the opposite.

Fourth, it is also important for us to know how to be quiet and how to be attentive to ourselves. Meditation is easily learned and is a boon to people who experience stress at work. To meditate, I set aside a quiet time and put a "Do Not Disturb" sign on my door. Then I close my eyes and say the word "Om" to myself over and over again for about 15 minutes. I am still meditating when other thoughts intrude, but I am not aware of them. I have stopped meditating when I'm aware that I've begun thinking other thoughts and continue to think them consciously. "Om" means "peace" in Sanskrit. The repetition of this word in a quiet environment is extremely soothing. When you're done, give yourself a couple of minutes to rest before becoming active again.[35]

The fifth step in reducing stress is to develop a support group. A support group means having a group of people you can talk to. Lonely people are the ones who experience the most stress and cope least well with life. We all need to have someone with a friendly ear to hear our complaints without judging us, and a strong hand we can hold on to while we cry. We need people with whom it's okay not to be okay.

Finally, let us not forget the importance of having fun. Taking part in activities that give us pleasure and being able to laugh are good antidotes to stress.

PART IV

BUILDING EFFECTIVENESS

7

INTERVIEWING TECHNIQUES

This section does not address itself to the hiring of new employees only. You may want to retrain an older worker, or try to motivate someone who has lost interest in the job.

Building effectiveness in others means becoming effective yourself. You first need to learn techniques that deal with interviewing, orienting new workers, and training them and motivating them to do their best. When you perform these skills well, you will have an effective work force.

Most new supervisors have their work force already in place and have no choice as to who their subordinates are; however, with time, you may need to hire additional people either because your operation is expanding or because you have to replace those who have left.

Remember how it felt to be interviewed? Remember how nervous you were, how hard you tried to make a good impression and how anxious you were afterward trying to figure out whether you were liked or not? No matter how nervous you are conducting your first interview, remember that the candidates are even more nervous and have more at stake—their jobs. You are probably worrying about what to ask or if the person will work out; wondering whether you will find anyone to fit the job; and wondering how to evaluate the applicants. I find that a rehearsal helps me to be more in control when the situation arises; therefore, practice interviewing with a friend or a spouse. Consider your first four or five interviews as practice interviews, and you'll be surprised at how quickly you will feel more at ease with it. If you make a mistake, especially if new employees have a probationary period, you can let that person go and start the process all over again.

Interviews have six steps: (1) preparing for the interview, (2) establishing a relationship with the interviewee, (3) eliciting information from the interviewee, (4) providing information to the interviewee, (5) closing the interview, and (6) evaluating the interview.

Preparing for the Interview

You cannot go into an interview cold; you must have done your homework. You should understand the requirements of the job for which you are interviewing applicants. It is important to have an updated job description. Make sure that you get this from your personnel department if they are responsible for maintaining it, or do it yourself if there is no one to do this for you.

In large companies the personnel department will do some preliminary screening, so you should work with the same job description they use. Check to see if it is accurate. Job descriptions are sometimes vague or even erroneous. In any event, you must know the characteristics of the job you are filling. See whether there are records of exit interviews with people who have held the job before. This will give you an indication of the problems encountered and suggestions for improvement. People often talk more freely when they are leaving an organization than they do while they are working there.

To help you select a person with the skills most vitally needed, do a job competency profile.[36] If you plan to hire a salesperson, for example, consider what the candidate must do to perform the job well. Let us say the duties are finding prospective clients, making calls, analyzing needs, making recommendations, following up, presenting a product or service, negotiating, and handling customer complaints. What skills are necessary for doing this well? Knowledge of the market, of the product or service, of the needs of clients; understanding the client's organization; interaction with decision-makers in the client's organization; the ability to close a deal and maintain customer satisfaction. List the qualities or competencies required. They are probably: initiative, assertiveness, analytic ability, problem-solving skills, ease in interacting with different kinds of people, persuasiveness, decisiveness, skill in negotiation, and the ability to listen well.

Find out about the applicants' specific skills by asking direct questions. For instance, they either know or don't know the market. You can ask them what they know about the product or services, whether or not they have ever closed a deal and how they did it. Have them tell you the problems they encountered and how they handled complaints. What you find out about their past experiences will help you to predict what they are likely to do in the future. The generic competencies are harder to evaluate; however, you can observe them in the interview process itself. You will see if candidates show initiative or are assertive or seem to be persuasive or negotiate well. If applicants can't communicate well with you, they may not be able to do so with clients. As a word of caution though, remember that the candidates are nervous during the interview process. Keep that in mind as you make your judgments.

Let us take another example. Suppose you want to hire an accountant. The task that needs to be performed might be to prepare month-end closings in entry journals, to review and verify accuracy of journal vouchers, to analyze and prepare accounts, to carry out monthly and quarterly reviews, to prepare tax reports and maintain tax records. The skills necessary for this would be accounting, budgeting, financial analysis techniques, knowledge of record-keeping and tax laws. Ask specific questions to determine if the candidates possess these skills and also ask to see some of the books they have kept. The general competencies they would need are logical, analytical, quantitative and problem-solving abilities; precision, attention to detail, skill in mastering new material, and synthesis of information. Whether they possess these attributes is harder to determine. You can get some idea by asking candidates how they would handle a specific situation. Their answers will help you judge how precise they are, how they deal with the new material you give them, how they solve problems, and whether or not they are logical.

The importance of doing a job-competency profile is that it will give you a set of questions to ask. If you have several candidates and you do not ask the same questions of each, you will be making unfair comparisons. Another important reason for doing a job-competency profile is that you may not need the *best* candidate, but the candidate who is most likely to do that particular job well. This is especially helpful in hiring women and minorities because a white male with a traditional work background may seem better because he may have had more opportunities or a longer work history; yet when attempting to fit the person to the job by using the competency profile, you may find that women and minorities are equally able to do the job. Thus, you will not be looking for the best person generally, you will be looking for the best fit between a person and a particular job.

In spite of the low regard older people face in North American society, mature women who have never worked or who have stopped work to raise a family are excellent choices for hiring, according to the Educational Testing Services in Princeton, New Jersey, for the following reasons:

1. Adult women have lower turnover rates than do younger employees.
2. On-the-job training costs are often reduced.
3. Over-40 workers usually attain higher performance ratings in a shorter time than do workers hired before age 30.
4. Older workers tend to have a more positive attitude toward work than do younger workers.
5. Women with experience in community and volunteer organizations have excellent managerial and interpersonal skills and have learned how to motivate people by using psychological rather than monetary rewards.
6. Volunteer experience shows such people are generally self-starters, dependable, and people-oriented.
7. Reentry women can help a company reach EEO goals.

If you are interviewing a reentry woman, be sure to cover *all* areas of experience and work, remembering that the best experience is not necessarily always the highest paid, or even paid at all.[37]

Occasionally, more candidates apply than you have time to interview. In that situation, you can do one of three things: (1) Send each candidate a detailed job description, thereby eliminating a few. (2) Have a group interview, where you explain the job in detail and then ask all of them to say something about themselves, their previous work, and why they're interested in that particular job. Allow some time for questions and discussion. This will eliminate a few people, and you can then have individual interviews with those who seem best suited to the job. (3) Evaluate the resumes against the job competency profile and rank candidates. Then interview a manageable number.

It is important to know the equal employment opportunity regulations of your company as well as the salary range, the benefits, and the length of the probationary period. You should also know special policies such as sick leave, bonuses, and perquisites.

There are some questions you cannot ask an interviewee. The reason they are forbidden by federal law is to avoid bias. For example, if you were to ask a man whether he is married or if he has children, the answer would probably not prejudice you for or against him; but if a woman were to say that she's a single mother with five children, you might make some erroneous assumptions about her availability. Following are the five types of questions you cannot ask in an interview:

1. You cannot ask if candidates are married, single, divorced, or living with anyone.
2. You cannot ask if candidates have children or if they plan to have children or who cares for their children.
3. You cannot ask candidates how old they are, how tall they are, or how much they weigh; nor can you make any comments about their sex or age unless it is a bona fide occupational qualification (BFOQ), such as specifying young women to model junior fashions.
4. You cannot ask candidates if they have been arrested or have served jail terms unless they need security clearance; nor can you ask what kind of military discharge they had, nor in what branch they served.
5. You cannot ask candidates whether they live in an apartment or a house or whether they own or rent.

One of the things that you may wish to say to the candidates is that you do not wish to ask illegal questions; however, if they have anything that they wish to discuss with you that would relate to the job, you would be very happy to listen to them. Remember that all interview questions must be job related. A note of caution: Be prepared to defend your selection process in court. Even informal comments may come up and cause trouble.

The Interview

So here you are. You have the job description; you know the needed skills to fill it; you know what you should try to find out; you know what you cannot ask; and you're ready for your first candidate. Be sure that the room you're in will make it possible for you to see the candidate well. It is preferable not to have a large desk between you and the person being interviewed because it adds distance and formality, unless you want that for a specific purpose. Arrange both chairs so that you can face each other. You may even wish to offer water, coffee, or tea. Try not to have interruptions, such as people walking into your office or telephone calls, although this is not always possible if you are a supervisor who must also be available to employees, suppliers, or clients so that you can deal with issues as they come up. If your boss wants to talk with you, it may not be advisable for you to say you are interviewing. Use your own judgment, but as much as possible, try to set aside time so that the interview will be uninterrupted.

Establishing a Relationship

Your candidate walks in, and you immediately form some first impressions. It is important to realize that some of us have prejudices. Many of us hold some stereotypes about women, older workers, blacks, Latin-Americans, Asians. You may have a bias about women who bleach their hair, men who are short, people with accents. It is important for you to become aware of your initial impressions so that your prejudices do not enter into your decision. If you are yourself a person of color or a woman, the candidates may not be expecting to be interviewed by someone different from themselves, and you will have to deal with their initial surprise, which may also have a negative effect. Remember that your candidates are anxious and want to make a good impression; you will be able to elicit the best information within a context of trust, warmth, and openness, none of which can easily be established in an interview situation. You may want to say something to the effect that interviews are very stressful situations for everyone. If your candidates seem *exceedingly* nervous, you may ask if they have been interviewed before or how often, and remark that it's all right to be nervous in this situation. This should reduce the anxiety level.

You can start with innocuous questions such as "How did you get here?" or "How did you hear about the job?" and then go into previous work experience, such as: how or what they liked about their jobs, what they disliked, what they liked or disliked about their bosses and their colleagues. You can ask them what their hopes are from this job and what they expect their future will be in your company. As you have this kind of general discussion, you should also look for body language to see if it matches what is being said. For example, look for sudden blushing or paling at specific topics or unusual fidgeting or signs of upset where certain subjects are mentioned.

Don't forget that your candidates are also looking at you to see if they are on the right track and whether or not you are approving or disapproving of what is being said. You should show interest at all times. If your interviewing technique is seen as being very threatening, the only information you will get is how your candidates respond to being threatened.

Eliciting Information

The more you get candidates to talk, the more information you will receive. How do you get someone to talk? You use open rather than closed questions. A closed question is one that can be answered with a yes or a no, or a date. For instance, instead of saying "Did you like your last job?" which a person can answer with a yes; you can say, "Tell me what you liked about your last job" or "Tell me what you didn't like about your last job." If you need to know about a specific skill, you don't ask whether they can do it, but how they acquired that skill, in what way that skill has been used in the past, and how they see it being applicable to the job they are applying for.

To help candidates to keep talking, you can make statements such as "Yes, go on" or "Could you tell me more about this?" or "Would you clarify what you mean?" If the candidates are not talking about relevant matters, you can interrupt by saying, "I need to interrupt you here because what I really want to know is. . ." Explain the interruption in order not to sound rejecting. You can go even further with this type of questioning. For example, instead of saying, "How do you get along with people you dislike?" you may want to rephrase it and say: "Tell me about a person you disliked with whom you needed to work, and how you managed it." Other interesting questions could be, "What are you most proud of in terms of your achievements to date?" "What is the most useful criticism you ever received? Tell me about it."

Ask why the candidates left their former jobs, what their career goals are, what their major strengths are, what their major weaknesses are as they might relate to the job, how their previous experience or education is applicable to this job. You can also ask what salary they expect, even though I urge candidates not to answer that question unless they know what salary is being paid for that type of position elsewhere. If the job requires teamwork or working alone, you may wish to ask how they feel about either situation and whether or not they have had experience with it.

During the period of eliciting information, you may very quickly determine whether the candidates are unsuitable. If you have made that decision, then you should end the interview without being rude, saying something to the effect that you have enough information and that you will let them know—unless you can tell them immediately that they will not be considered. You can do this only if you have a valid explanation. If candidates seem promising, then you should go on to the next phase of the interview.

Providing Information

If you're hearing the sound of your own voice too much, especially at the beginning of the interview, you are not eliciting information. Toward the end of the interview, it is important for you to tell the candidates about the job. This information should include what your expectations of performance are, how standards are measured, and how often they are to be evaluated. You should also talk about salary, benefits, and perquisites, especially if you know that the candidates are interested in the job and that you are interested in the candidates. You may also want to talk about the work environment, who the coworkers are, and what the promotion possibilities are. This is also the time when you should review the employees' qualifications and look at the job requirements to see where the fit is good or where there might be some gaps that could be filled by further training. Be sure to ask if the candidates have any questions. If you are interviewing several candidates, it would be helpful to tell them when they might expect to hear from you and that you have several more people to see.

Closing the Interview

One of the techniques I like to use is one I call the post-interview. If you have not elicited all the information you need, you may decide to change your approach. If you have been sitting in a certain position with, let's say, some papers and a note pad, you can push aside your note pad or the papers or the resume that is in front of you, and shift your chair by a couple of inches to either a closer or more distant position. This is to signify that something else is about to happen. You change your posture and say: ''Well, the interview is over. Tell me how you feel about it. How did it go for you? Were you able to say what you needed to? Did you get the information you needed?'' This often opens up the discussion to add items not usually covered during an interview, but that gives you a much better picture of the candidates. The candidates may relax more because the interview is over, and you can now talk about the process. One of the things I suggest to candidates is that if they are not sure how they came across, they also should use the post-interview technique by asking the interviewer, ''How did I do? How do you feel about my candidacy?'' This technique makes for a more informal dialogue.

Evaluating the Interview

Before you go on to the next interview or even before you leave your office, make some notes about what you have just experienced; jot down the candidates' physical description and a few salient points to help you remember them. You will be surprised at how easy it is to forget someone after you have seen a number of people. Make a preliminary judgment about the candidates, taking note of their strengths and weaknesses. This is an important process that can be accomplished effectively only if you do it immediately upon the departure of the candidates. If you wait, you will forget a great deal.

Interview Traps

A potential trap, and one that can have a definite effect on the interview itself, is the urgent need to fill a position. It is possible that unless a position is filled quickly, the department will suffer. If your applicant pool is limited, you may decide to hire a temporary person to alleviate the pressure to find a permanent replacement. Another trap is feeling sorry for the person who "really needs the job." You have no way of knowing who needs the job more, and need should not be a criterion. Still another trap is to talk excessively about yourself or try to impress the candidates with your power, prestige, or experience. Remember that the interview is fundamentally a forum for the candidates, not the interviewer. If you have heard other people's opinions about the candidates, be wary of their accuracy. People like or dislike others for a number of reasons, none of which may be applicable to the job requirements, so use your own judgment. Take into consideration what others say, but check it out for yourself.

When you do the hiring, you are in a position of power, and the person you hire will always remember that you were the one who provided that opportunity. There are managers who fire a large percentage of people in their department in order to rehire others they can count on as team members and who have no allegiance to previous managers. I do not advocate that approach, but if you are having problems with your employees that you have not been able to resolve, hiring your own people is one of the options available to you.

The Probationary Period

It is important to have a probationary period long enough to enable you to evaluate your new employee. In most organizations, the probationary period is set under state and federal regulations. It is imperative that you closely monitor the new worker in those early months of probation, making sure that your expectations of performance are the same whether your employee is young, old, male, female, white, or of a different culture, because you can be sued for firing an older person because of age discrimination, a woman because of sexism, or a minority person because of racism unless you document the difficulty and have given in writing ample warning of potential problems.

We have been talking about how you interview others. However, it is important to remember that if you are a woman or a minority, the person being interviewed will have some preconceived notions about you.

For many men, having a female or minority person doing the interviewing may be a new experience, and they may automatically assume that the interviewer is an assistant who is not authorized to make the final decision. If you, as a woman or minority person, are in fact the one who makes the decision or who at least makes the recommendation that will influence the decision of hiring the candidate, you should say so at the beginning of the interview. You should define your role: "I am the person who will make the decision" or "I am the person who will make the recommendation for the decision." If you suspect the interviewee might have a problem working for a minority supervisor or a female, it is best to discuss it openly.

The Benefit of the Doubt

White people are OK
unless they goof
and prove otherwise

Black people are not OK
until they prove themselves
as really OK

And then perhaps
maybe
sometimes
here and there
now and then
once in a while
some black people
may be OK

Might we consider
giving out equally
the benefit of our doubts?

There are certain things that are very difficult to find out during an interview, things such as people's integrity, initiative, persistence, or ability to follow through. Their recounting of their past working experiences will give you a better sense of these qualities.

After you have completed your first interview, go back over your notes and review this chapter to see in what way you used the information well and in what way you still need to improve.

Exercise

1. Remember when you were being interviewed for your job, and make a list of what you liked about that interview and what you did not like. Take that list and apply it to yourself as an interviewer and adopt the techniques you liked.
2. Look at the job description the personnel department has given you and see if it is correct. Does it describe accurately the job as it now needs to be done?
3. Make a list of competencies (skills) needed to do the job.
4. Make a list of questions you need to have answered by the applicant.
5. Make a list of items the applicant needs to know.
6. List the types of prejudices you think you may have against certain applicants. For example, do you react negatively to people who are very quiet or to people who are very talkative? What characteristics do you feel comfortable with and what irritates you? Only when you make yourself aware of these unconscious attitudes can you discount your own prejudice *against* a candidate or even *for* a candidate.

8

ORIENTING AND TRAINING THE NEW WORKER

Today your new workers start work. You can assume they are nervous, want to do well, are worrying about how much they'll know, how they will work out, how they'll get along with others, and if the others will like them. Chances are that much of what you will explain to your new workers will not be remembered. There is too much newness for people to take in all the needed information. One of the worst things you can do on the first day is to leave your workers on their own. It is important that you or someone you trust shows the new workers around and introduces them to colleagues, those they will have to interact with or report to and anyone who reports to them. Tell the others what the new workers' responsibilities will be.

Expectations of performance should be clearly stated on that first day or first few days. They must understand exactly what you want them to do. Be sure they have enough to do to keep them busy, but not so much that they panic at not being able to finish. New employees should be told about transportation, car pools, where the bathroom is, when the breaks are; they should know about any special office procedures, about the running of equipment, even about office parties and outings. They should also know if there is a cafeteria and what the usual procedure is for lunch. Do not leave your workers without arranging for someone to be with them at lunch. If people lunch in the office, have something ready or forewarn the new workers to bring their lunches. It is surprising how often perfectly well-meaning people will forget about the newcomer and go off by themselves, leaving that person alone and upset. See to it that someone is in charge of new people for at least the first week to make them feel welcome; it is critical for the adjustment of new workers that they feel cared for at the beginning and not ignored as being unimportant.

Being Included

We all have different ways of entering a new group. Do you usually remain quiet and isolate yourself for a while until you have figured out what's going on? Or do you join in immediately, making yourself known as quickly as possible, trying to get to know others by asking a lot of questions? Do you attempt to become accepted by performing services, by complimenting people, or do you just do your job and believe that when others are ready they'll come to you? Whatever style of entry you have, identify it for yourself. If you don't like the way you first enter new groups, and you see a new worker exhibit similar behavior, you may find that you resent that worker not because of what he or she does but because he or she reminds you of your own shortcomings. Watch how these new workers enter their new places of work. You may be helpful to them if you are a good observer. Assign one of the senior workers to take charge of those persons to help integrate them into the work group. What you would have wanted to have been done for you may or may not be what is helpful to your new workers, so ask them. Some of them will be able to tell you.

Hazing

Be watchful lest your other workers give the newcomer a hard time, especially if the newcomer is a woman in a male-dominated environment or a minority person in a predominantly white group. Members of a work group may resent new people and close the doors to them, making it difficult for them to gain entry and to perform effectively. Observe these early days. If need be, you may wish to talk to the person who seems to be the informal leader of the group about what to do to ease the new person's acceptance. You may also wish to talk to the new person about how to be included by earning their stripes and passing muster.

Most human groups, whether in primitive tribes or in corporate

America, make newcomers go through some sort of initiation rites. These take the form of jokes and pranks such as making the new person look for a left-handed hammer or striped paint or a bacon stretcher, none of which, of course, exist. Sometimes the new person is given the less desirable work (cleaning up, getting the coffee), or the worst shifts or the poorest work stations. What this does is reveal the pecking order in which the more senior members have special privileges. As a supervisor, you will need to make sure your new worker understands that this is normal practice so that he or she does not feel singled out and discriminated against. Watch out for unduly stressful hazing; if you see it, stop it by discussing it with the group members or with whoever is responsible.

Hazing is a testing period. Will the new workers fit in? Can they take a joke? Will they be loyal to the group and not tell the boss?

If the testing is done to all new people, it is hazing and the result is inclusion—becoming a member of the group. If the testing is done only to specific individuals, it is harassment deliberately designed to keep the new people out—to exclude them from the group. The new workers are accepted when they "can take it, roll with the punches, be one of the boys." Complaining to you, the supervisor, will only help to exclude them further and make matters worse, so it is up to you to keep a sharp eye out for any undue hardship visited upon your new workers. If you receive a complaint, never let anyone know, but use your own observations to stop dysfunctional practices.

I have collected over 500 hazing events in the past couple of years and have found that a large percentage of new workers get hazed and that 10 percent quit as a result. One of the most effective ways to help newcomers over the hazing hurdle is to give them sufficient preparation and support so that they can recognize when a joke is being played on them.[38] If no one shows them how to do a job correctly and they must find out how it is done on their own, they lose valuable time, make unnecessary errors, and have no protection against hazing. You will not be able to stop hazing completely, but you can make it less stressful by keeping track of what is going on.

Hazing

My first day at the job
I'm excited and hope they will like me
Why are they whispering in a corner?

Is it about me?
Did I do something wrong?
They make me nervous

They're looking at me laughing
Aren't my clothes right?
I feel anxious

They went off to lunch
And left me alone
I cried in the bathroom

My boss came and asked if all was well
I said "just fine!"
With pounding heart

My typewriter jammed
Was it done on purpose?
I'm sick to my stomach

At the end of the day
No one said good-bye
I don't want to go back

Norms

All organizations have norms. Norms are the unwritten rules that everyone knows, yet rarely speaks about. For example, in a bank, the dress code may be regulated; in other places the dress code may be informal, however it is not a rule but a norm. The following are some typical norms:

- Talking about personal matters may be all right in one office but not in another.
- Leaving one's desk messy may be a sign of being busy in one office but a sign of sloppiness in another.
- Bringing coffee to your desk may be fine in some places but frowned upon in others.
- Lunch hours and coffee breaks may be regulated in some places but may be loose in others.
- Having access to the supervisor may be formalized in one place but may be spontaneous in others.
- Making personal phone calls may be allowed in one office but not in another.

- Joking or using profanity may be accepted in one place but not in another.
- Asking for help may be encouraged in one place but not in another.
- Handling conflicts may be done directly in one place but not in another.
- Workers wait to be assigned in one place or are expected to be self-starters in another.[39]

These unwritten attitudes about behavior exist in all organizations. What are the norms in your department? Make a list of them. You and other members of your department might compile such a list for newcomers, rather than letting them learn through trial and error. After you have your list of norms, you may wish to check those you see as working well in your department and those you see as being detrimental. You may decide to correct those you feel negatively affect productivity or work climate. As a supervisor, you should be careful that the norms in your department do not clash with the norms of the rest of the organization. For example, at a high-tech company where I was a consultant, all the engineers on one floor were free to come and go during the day, taking a few minutes for coffee breaks at no assigned time. On another floor, the coffee break time was 10:15 to 10:30 with no exceptions. The looser structure was very productive for that particular floor, but when the engineers on the other floor found out about it, they became upset at the seeming unfairness. In other words, conflicting norms created stress for a part of the organization. This problem was resolved by tightening up on the flexibility of one floor and making the other floor somewhat more flexible—some people lost a little and others gained a little. Time and effort were spent on explaining the situation and finding a solution. Even though there was grumbling, the solution was finally accepted.

It is much easier to give *more* to people than to take anything away from them. You have to be careful how much you allow because it will be quickly taken as a right, not as a privilege. Remember that norms are not written down and that they are not formal policies or rules but are in fact fuzzy areas difficult to discern.

Training

You tell us what to do
but you don't show us how
You teach those most like you
for you know they can be taught
You do not teach us
for you have no experience
with those different from yourself

And so we must be self-taught
without help, with no support
not even constructive criticism
so that we can improve
You withhold that too
in order to protect us
protect us from being hurt
which protects us from learning

And so we don't make it
we don't hack it
we don't pass
You can then smugly say
that women just can't take it
that blacks just can't make it
that Hispanics or Asians just don't understand
But I know it's because
you didn't believe we could.

Training

The questions you need to ask yourself about training are (1) What are my expectations from my trainees? (2) By what standard will I gauge their successes? (3) How much error can I live with and for how long a period of time? These points should be shared with the workers you are planning to train so that it will be clear to them what it is that they need to do to please you. Training a new worker will be an opportunity for you to get to know that worker well, and will also help to establish a working relationship.

Perhaps the most critical thing to remember in training anyone is that people learn better from successes than from failures. People need to know what they can improve on, but they also need to know when they are working well and when they are meeting your expectations. People need to be praised.

What do you think new workers are hoping for? They hope that the job has some importance, that they will get along well with their supervisor and with the other workers, that they will do a good job, and that the supervisor will set standards of performance that will challenge them and that they can meet.

Why Train?

There are three main reasons to train: (1) The new workers do not know how to do the job; (2) the workers can do it, but not up to your standards, or (3) the workers do it incorrectly. These three are facts you can observe. Other reasons, however, are more difficult to ascertain: Do the workers *want* to learn to do the job according to your standards? Ask them how they feel about their performance. If they admit to you that they don't know how to do the job, ask them if they would like to learn. If they say yes, train them very specifically. If they insist that they are doing it correctly and you disagree, you have an obstacle to overcome.

Before you can teach people a new way to do things, they must understand that the old way is inadequate. It's worth taking the time to explain the need for change because unwilling workers are difficult, if not impossible, to teach. Some senior workers who are near retirement may be worried about trying new things, while others may enjoy being challenged. It is up to you to find out why they are unwilling and to iron out the difficulties. Another type of person difficult to train is someone who has limited intelligence and is unable to understand the job. That person is underqualified and should be given a job that is less demanding.

If you have a language problem with some workers, it is wrong to jump to the conclusion that they do not understand you because of limited intelligence. They might not understand because you do not speak the same language. You may wish to assign someone to them who knows how to do the job *and* who can speak their language.

Learning

As a supervisor, you are also a teacher and a coach. How workers learn from you and their effectiveness will depend on how well you train them. How do *you* learn best? It is important for you to identify your preferred learning style because that will also be your preferred teaching style. Since other people may have different ways of absorbing knowledge than you do, it is important to identify your ways of learning. For example, do you prefer to *look* at a map to see where you are going or do you prefer to have directions *told* to you? Do you understand better when you read and look at charts or do you absorb more when you listen to lectures or hear cassettes? There is still another way of learning that is not accomplished by seeing or hearing, but by *doing*. Do you prefer to repeat what has been said? Do you learn best by rote? Do you need to *do* whatever it is that has been shown to you for you to remember it? Are you a "hands-on" person? If you are a person who learns best by seeing, your tendency will be to *show* people. If your learning style is through hearing, your tendency will probably be to *tell* people, and if your learning style is by doing, then *your* tendency might be to work *together* with them. One of the things we know is that all three styles will best promote learning if they are used together. People from different cultures will have different learning modes.

STEP 1	STEP 2	STEP 3
I TELL YOU	**YOU TELL ME**	
I SHOW YOU	**WE DO IT**	**YOU DO IT**
I DO IT		
		I WATCH
YOU WATCH	**WE TALK ABOUT IT**	

Should *You* Train Your Workers?

Do you do your own training or do you delegate it? Training is an art. It is a form of teaching, and not everyone is good at it. If you're going to be doing it, you should learn to do it well or teach someone else to take over the task. You have to like to train in order to do it well. If you're impatient and intolerant of others' mistakes, you will have a difficult time being a trainer.

Are you a perfectionist? How much do you expect of yourself? If you expect a great deal and are intolerant of your own mistakes, you might also be intolerant of someone else's. To train people and then let them do it on their own is taking a risk. Whether you are willing to risk errors depends on how costly an error could be to your department. The issue then becomes: How closely should you control? Some people really appreciate it if their supervisor keeps in touch by checking, looking over, helping out, giving suggestions; other people may feel suffocated or insulted by this kind of presence. One way to find out is simply to ask. Most people have a preferred style and use it in all situations. Share it with your workers and ask if they prefer a particular method. If you are obsessive or compulsive about work, you may have a very difficult time letting go. If you are lackadaisical and think, "Oh, well, they'll handle it," you'll have a very difficult time controlling the situation. Find out what your own inclinations are by recalling your past behavior in similar situations and then decide if it is appropriate for the new worker.

In order to be a successful boss, you must know how to train your workers.

1. **Be prepared.** Know something about your workers' previous training and experience. Know enough about their past responsibilities so that you can help them apply their past knowledge to the new things that have to be learned. Combining the known with the unknown will help the learning process. Have their office or workplace equipped and ready for your workers before they arrive, and have some simple task for them to start with so that they will feel like part of the department as soon as possible.
2. **Be caring.** Ask whether the newcomer got to work easily, and by what kind of transportation. Check to see whether you can help with any related problem. Provide information about vacations and sick leave, and offer yourself or someone else as the person to consult with about problems at work or with personal issues that may affect productivity.
3. **Be factual.** Do you have policies and procedures that your workers ought to know about? Are there safety regulations? This is the time for them to find out about lunch hours, rest periods, vacations, and sick leaves. Your workers should know where the pencil sharpeners are and where they can obtain a snack, and they should be taught how to operate the copying machine, if that's what they'll be doing.

   Have the new workers repeat the facts to you so that

you're sure they have a clear picture of their responsibilities. Do they know whom they can ask if they need help? Do they know what procedures to follow in case of emergencies?

4. **Be available.** Do ongoing evaluations. Be sure your new workers know how often you plan to check in with them and what you will be checking so that they are aware of standards and timing and will not be taken by surprise. If your workers know that your checking is a way to determine progress and to be available for help, it will not be seen as a negative action. Some people are more reticent about saying they need help than others. You may want to ask your new workers whether asking for help is difficult for them; in that case, you will have to check up more often. In some cultures, asking for help is a sign of weakness or stupidity; in others, it is a sign of initiative and of showing interest. Be sure that you or someone else is available to your new workers. Anonymous surveys on worker satisfaction can help but only if they are followed up, or else people feel used.

In an attempt to understand how the values of a minority population might affect their expectations and behaviors at work, I gave a questionnaire to white, black, Hispanic, and Asian workers, half of whom were female. As was predictable, all minorities in general had lower expectations as to career advancement and monetary compensation than did the white respondents. Though all ethnic groups were skewed toward the low end of the distribution, Asians were skewed closest to the whites. While most workers prefer to have their wages tied to performance, quite a few whites showed preference for their wages to be tied to seniority, while no minorities showed this preference. This is an important finding because it tells a supervisor that if seniority over performance is chosen as a measure of compensation, whites as a group would benefit and minorities would feel discriminated against.

In response to a question asking if being on time is "important," "somewhat important," "somewhat unimportant," or "unimportant," the white population checked "important," but the minority populated tended to check "somewhat important" more often.

When asked how they feel when they don't understand instructions, whites answered "anxious," but blacks and Hispanics checked "very anxious." Asians responded with feelings somewhere between these two. It is important for supervisors to realize that since not understanding a directive or an instruction would be more anxiety-producing for minority workers, persons in charge should make extra efforts to be clear as to their expectations and not be punitive if they have been misunderstood. When they were asked if they preferred to work with coworkers and immediate supervisors of the same ethnic background, education, religion, sex, age, or values, both whites and minorities wanted to work with those of similar education, religion, and values but did not care about ethnic background, sex, and age. This finding is helpful in determining possible comfort levels in establishing work groups.

What do people want most from their supervisors? White men said they wanted to be informed continuously with respect to their jobs and would like to be asked for their ideas. Women and minorities showed a preference for a supervisor who could build team spirit and would recognize good performance.

What does this finding mean to the supervisor? People often want most what they lack. It could be that while white men feel they get enough recognition, women and minorities either don't get as much or need more, and therefore, wish for it. Either way, a supervisor should be aware which of the workers may need more recognition of performance. That white men want their supervisors to ask them for their ideas means they have an upward orientation, while the white women's and minorities' wish for team building seems to focus more on peers and a horizontal orientation. We can hypothesize that women and minorities wish for more support from peers and prefer collaboration to competition.

More white women than any other group felt that when first hired, they were left on their own to figure out how to perform their new jobs. This made them feel unwelcomed. There may be a tendency to teach white women less well than others, and supervisors should look for any evidence of it, but whether white women's perception of lack of training is real or not, what matters is that they experience it as insufficient. Supervisors need to make sure that *all* workers get the training they need to be comfortable when beginning their new jobs. If in doubt, ask if more help is needed.

As to how workers deal with conflict, I found that white males, Hispanic and black males and females, for the most part, felt comfortable confronting both coworkers and immediate supervisors, while white females and Asians of both sexes had difficulty in doing so. Again, it is important for a supervisor to know that he or she is unlikely to be challenged by white women and Asians and that these two groups of workers will be uncomfortable in conflict situations.

In general, women's answers to the questionnaire showed less comfort than men in asking their supervisors for information concerning their jobs, such as benefits, promotions, raises, company policy. The difference in comfort levels was one of gender much more than one of race or ethnic background.

When asked the circumstances under which they perform best, some very interesting tendencies emerged. Blacks have a tendency to perform better when they are praised, promoted, receive monetary rewards, and have a pleasant work environment. Hispanics have a tendency to work better when they know what is expected of them, participate in decisions that affect them, are learning new skills, and are challenged at work. Asians perform better when they have friendly coworkers, participate in decisions that affect them, and have a boss they respect. Whites perform better when they participate in decisions that affect them, have a boss they like, and have a job that has variety.

The minority distribution to this question also shows that minorities perform better when they have job security, but job security was not as important a factor in whites' job performance.

A recent finding from a study of civilian personnel in a navy yard noted that out of a worker population of 5,500, there have been 132 informal complaints. Of these, 40 percent were black, 40 percent were white men over 40—and the remaining 20 percent were Hispanics and Asians, with more men in that group than women. The majority of the complaints were centered on not being selected for a promotion.[40]

We can infer from this that prejudice against blacks and prejudice against older people might be unconscious factors in determining promotions. However, since white men have the highest expectations of income and position of any group, it is logical to assume that they would complain the most if these expectations were not met. I have no data either to confirm or to deny the reality of the complaints. Again, this should help supervisors to understand better what reward systems would work most effectively with what worker population.

To illustrate the significance of these issues, we went to a computer firm in Orange County, California, that employs recent Indochinese refugees, and asked management to discuss problems that they may have encountered.

Since the company was formed five years ago, it has flourished with a work force composed almost entirely of Indochinese refugees, but like many other firms employing foreigners, it is being exposed to an often puzzling culture.

Employers have discovered that Southeast Asians on the whole are hardworking, meticulous, productive, and above all, loyal employees. But at the same time, they have learned that a foreign language is not all that is difficult for Americans to understand about the new employees. Cultural differences have created communications problems and some misunderstandings in the workplace.

It is common Indochinese practice, for example, to give presents to bosses they like, a frowned-upon practice in the United States. Also, American workers often complained about the offensive cooking odors of traditional Indochinese food when refugees use cafeteria microwave ovens at lunch time.

Company officials say, too, that they are often baffled because Indochinese workers seldom admit they do not understand an instruction, do not speak their minds at company meetings, and do not make eye contact with their supervisors.

The company had to hire cultural consultants and conducted several workshops to smooth the continuing process of assimilating refugees into the industry, admitting that they initially hired the Indochinese workers without regard to the potential language and cultural problems that have since emerged.

Cultural consultants have said that the Indochinese workers feel chagrined when Americans coworkers summon them with an upturned palm or finger, a gesture that in Southeast Asia is used only to call animals. Similarly, they have said, American workers are insulted when Southeast Asian workers ask them the price of the clothes they wear, a question that Americans often consider an invasion of privacy but that the refugees regard as being simply a matter of practical interest.

The management also was concerned that the refugees, because of failure to improve their English, were not being promoted to more leadership roles. However, not until an employee attitudinal study was conducted did they discover the full dimension of the communications gap; namely, that many refugees could not read a single word. It became apparent that they learned their highly repetitive jobs through imitation and made use of a buddy system, whereby one refugee would interpret for many others.

The company conducted a workshop to teach American employees about refugees and the refugee employees about Americans. Included were some "do's" and "don'ts" on such sensitive topics as the use of bathrooms and of culinary preferences.

Since the development of the program, the management has noticed a dramatic difference. The complaints from nonrefugee employees have diminished, and the refugees are making a greater effort to be friendly with American coworkers.

Among some other peculiarities that still characterize the behavior of the Indochinese workers is that they smile both when they are happy and angry. The smile is a mask to hide emotions. To Indochinese, if you show emotion, you are not a refined person. Another problem is their inability to accept compliments gracefully. They often pass the credit on to their coworkers, sometimes to their own detriment.

Indochinese workers also have a tendency not to stand out individually, but to work in groups; they prefer their leader to speak for them and to remain silent at company meetings. They also feel more comfortable speaking in their own language, and those who are uneducated object to women supervisors.

As we can see, cultural differences can have a very significant effect on the well-being of a company and on its business. With many American companies becoming multinational and with the growing number of refugees and other foreigners entering the American work force, these problems are becoming more and more acute. We cannot simply close our eyes to them and expect them to go away. Improving human relations in the workplace must become a matter of great concern for every business enterprise and for everyone dealing with people of various cultural backgrounds.[41]

Possible Pitfalls in Training Your Workers

What are some of the pitfalls that can befall a supervisor as he or she trains? The first pitfall is believing that the job is easy enough so that you just go very quickly through the motions. Remember that whatever is easy for you may be difficult for some people when they try it the first time. Even if you're training people who have done the job before, they may have done it for another person who had different expectations. Don't assume that there is knowledge just because there is experience. It is better to be overly specific, especially in the beginning, than not to say enough and to have errors. The new workers may be so eager to please that they will not ask for details so they can appear to know what they are doing. They will not ask to have things repeated or ask to be shown but will say, "Yes, yes, I know," even though they don't. Be aware that in some cultures, to ask a boss to repeat something means that the boss was not clear enough the first time around and workers will be afraid they may be seen as insulting to the boss. Therefore, patience is your first rule. Check to see if your instructions have been really understood.

The second pitfall is giving too much information at one time. Most people can handle about three different types of steps or instructions at a time. Be sure those steps are mastered before you go on to the next three. Reduce tension by being pleasant and unhurried. If people make mistakes, do not say, "But I just showed you how to do it." Rather, "It's easy to make a mistake at the beginning. Don't worry about it, let's try again." Remember that learning is very tiring, and even though you may not be exhausted from teaching, your employees may be exhausted from the effort of acquiring new knowledge, a new skill, or just by being in a new place. Be sure that there are enough rest periods during your training program.

Finally, the third pitfall is failing to build in feedback measures so that you can be sure your workers know how they are doing at every phase of the training. The job may seem monotonous to you, but it is not necessarily monotonous to your employees. You should express enthusiasm rather than give the impression that you think training is boring.

If you train your new workers well, you will be building the future of your department. Even though some supervisors do not like this part of their responsibility, it is a critical one to which a great deal of thought and care must be given. When you train people, it is important that you describe in detail what your expectations are. Don't just say, "Please type a letter." You might say, "When you type this letter for me, please be sure there are no spelling mistakes or grammatical errors and that the letter is very neat—I don't want to see erasure marks." Or you may say, "This is a draft. I don't mind erasure marks and typeovers; just do it as quickly as you can." You may also add that you expect work to take a bit longer at the beginning but that eventually you expect a certain number of letters or pages of a report completed in a day. You should not put pressure on workers at the beginning, but make sure they know what your expectations will be.

Who were the earliest teachers of your workers? Their parents. So, in a way, you have a temporary parental role. This role can elicit very warm, positive feelings, and your workers may be very dependent on you, or it can evoke very negative feelings because some people don't want to feel once more dependent on another person's judgment.

If you are an older person training members of a younger work force, you may run into counterdependence if the younger people think they know it all and don't want to take instructions from a parentlike figure, especially if they have just recently gained their independence. If you are a younger person instructing an older one, that older worker may have problems taking instructions from a younger boss because it is a reversal of the normal role pattern. If the supervisor is a woman, men may have even more difficulty in taking any instructions from her because they are accustomed to seeing women in subordinate positions. If the supervisor is a minority person, trainees may also be unprepared to listen to and respect someone they have been taught to discount. If you sense an impending problem due to racial, cultural, ethnic, or gender differences, sit down with the workers you are about to train and ask if they have had training from an older/younger, female/minority person before, and if they have any feelings about this. You may want to address the problem head-on by saying that you know that this may be a new experience for them and that they may feel apprehensive, but that you hope they will be able to adapt to the situation.

Most people prefer to be trained by someone who is like them, just as most people prefer training those who are most similar to themselves. Predictable behavior, shared interests, and shared values create a more comfortable atmosphere. When you don't know and don't understand the culture the other person comes from, it is much more difficult to teach or to be taught. Another culture may represent an unknown geographic location, a different educational level, a different value system, or a generation gap. One of the ways to overcome this is to talk to the people about the way they learn best, and about what they consider to be important so that you get a better understanding of their background and points of reference.

Training Your First Secretary

You have really arrived if you have your own secretary. Usually you will share one with other people or, even more likely, use the secretarial pool. If you share a secretary, I suggest you get to know the people who do your typing and praise them if a job is done particularly well or faster than you had expected. You will thus be assured of attentive service in the future.

If there is a secretary who works for you and for one or more people, you will need to find out the approximate amount of time you can count on for yourself by discussing this with the people who share the secretary. There are periods of heavy work, others of lighter loads. Check to see how much the secretary has to do, and always say how quickly you will need a particular piece of work. For example, I ask my secretary, whom I share with other faculty members, whether she can get an assignment out on the same day and am grateful if she can. If I have a project that is not urgent, I always let her know, and she's grateful for the information so that she can manage her time better.

If you have a secretary all to yourself, then you must train this person to be your assistant. Your secretary can screen phone calls and visitors, keep your calendar, remind you of deadlines and appointments, and set up meetings. Your secretary can open your mail and write responses if only routine answers are required.

During the training period, give your secretary samples of your writing, show how you like letters set up, and share your work-related ideas.

Your secretary should know exactly what you expect and that should include knowing when to interrupt you, when it can be delayed, what information you need and where to get it. Your secretary should also be able to establish work priorities, not need to ask questions about details, and show interest in your work and in the organization's goals. Keep this person abreast of what is happening. The more informed your secretary is, the more effective he or she will be. Your secretary can be your ally (although not your confidante), your liaison, your editor, and your research assistant. Do not ask your secretary to do personal errands for you. This person is not your servant, unless this is part of the job description and agreed upon beforehand. Of course, there are always emergencies, but such times are not routine. Delegate as much work as you can. If you cannot trust your secretary to be polite with others, to be efficient and timely, then change secretaries.

The Smiling Secretary

Typing
Filing
Smiling

Opening mail
taking dictation
photocopying papers
pleasantly

answering the phone
greeting visitors
making reservations
cheerfully

emptying ashtrays
watering plants
with pleasure

with a headache
with a bachache
with a sick kid at home

Re-typing
Re-filing
Re-smiling

Exercise

1. Remember your first day at work, and make two lists: (1) all the things you wish had been done for you by your supervisor but were not, and (2) all the things you thought were helpful. This list will give you an indication of how you should prepare yourself for your new workers.

2. Experience in training reveals that what seems simple to one person may seem most difficult to another. Try the following experiment: Teach another person how to tie shoelaces, pretending that the other person has never seen a shoelace or tied a knot in his or her life. Do not demonstrate, just describe how it is done. You will see how difficult it is for someone to perform that task correctly and rapidly. Be aware of how much patience you have, and afterward ask that person to give you feedback on your training methods. Did you praise the effort? Did you get irritated with any slowness in catching on? If so, how did you express it? Did you remain opposite the person or did you stand side-by-side? That is very important in this instance because you are speaking about right and left hands and the way you use them. Always teach from the side of the people you're training rather than by facing them, unless there are no hand motions involved.

3. Make a list of norms, also known as the unwritten rules, of your organization. Which ones help everyone? Which ones do not? Do some norms benefit some particular individuals or groups? What is your authority to make them give up those behaviors? Do you have anyone you can count on to serve as your ally and supporter? Can you have a talk with that person beforehand?

Hold a meeting with your workers. Explain what norms are by giving the following examples:

Going to lunch together is an accepted practice.
Having a messy desk is regarded as a sign of hard work.
Staying late is a way of demonstrating commitment.
Smoking in nonsmoking areas is routine.

Ask your workers to make a list of their norms. (This is easier if they work in groups of four to six because the list then is anonymous.) Post the lists and make decisions about which norms can be kept and which should be modified. If you have disagreements, you may have to be very direct and say what you will tolerate and what you won't.

For example, your workers may determine that one of the norms is to take longer lunch hours. This may or may not be a dysfunctional norm, depending on whether the work gets done and the workers are happy. Another norm may be that safety regulations are not adhered to strictly. That certainly would be a norm that would need changing. But, as a supervisor, you are better off getting commitment through agreement than through an enforced ruling. However, if safety is at stake, you will have to be strict in its implementation.

9

MOTIVATING YOUR WORKERS

You have interviewed and hired new workers. You have oriented, trained, and motivated them to learn. What now? The next step is to motivate them to perform, to capture their loyalty, and to get them to commit themselves. Motivation is getting people to want to do what you want them to do.

There are three sides to motivation: the work, the workers, and the supervisor, as follows:

1. The work must be seen as having some meaning and satisfaction, as being worthwhile, and as playing a significant part of the production as a whole. It is difficult for workers to take pride in their work if the result is indistinguishable in the total output. For example, it may seem more important to tighten a bolt on an airplane part than to put paper clips in a little box, but if putting paper clips in boxes is the job, then the worker must know to what purpose and result.
2. The workers must believe that they have some responsibility for the outcome of whatever they do—whether the making of a product or the rendering of a service. Thus, they must have some measure of autonomy. Also the workplace should be friendly and without undue stress.
3. The supervisor must provide feedback and praise to workers for a job well done and must give suggestions for improving the quality and the speed of the work to be done.[42] Some workers feel rewarded by the work itself—for example, their products have had few or no rejects; others appreciate a

letter praising their performance; still others may like to be taken out for lunch, be given an extra day off, or be given more autonomy or more responsibility. Find out what your workers consider to be a reward.

The goals of most corporations are long-range and general in nature, while employees usually focus on short-term gains such as improved wages and working conditions. Many workers have had years of bad experience and believe that companies exploit people. Of every 100 workers, five to ten have been disappointed by some job-related experience beyond the company's control. This disappointment may have resulted in alienation, making it difficult for managers to build trust and morale.[43]

Motivating employees is a very difficult task and probably one of the more important ones for a supervisor to perform effectively. What motivates people? In order to understand it better, let us divide motivation into three categories: (1) how it relates to one's self, (2) how it relates to one's boss, and (3) how it relates to one's coworkers.

First, let us start with the individual. There are four reasons that may motivate you to work effectively: (a) Work is *a means to and end,* such as a promotion, a raise, or just the weekly paycheck. Your work, at the least, must be performed adequately to ensure that you are not fired. (b) You look at work as the fulfilling of a *responsibility,* believing that it is your duty to do the best you can. A positive attitude about work is generally based on the ethics instilled by family, schools, and culture. (c) Doing your work well gives you a sense of achievement. (d) Working is a way of *mastering* a new skill, acquiring new knowledge, answering a challenge, or being stretched to new heights. Motivation can be any one of these four—a means to an end, fulfilling a responsibility, an achievement, or the mastering of new skills. These four are all related to the individual.

Second, let us look at motivation as it relates to your superior. You are motivated by your boss either because you want to please him or her, or because you're afraid of being punished. *Fear of punishment* may or may not be real; but since it frequently is real, you work hard and well. If you don't, you know you will be reprimanded, demoted, or even fired. In wanting to please a boss, you are motivated to work hard because you like the boss and are looking for a reward. Such a reward is not necessarily a material one; it can be recognition, a word of praise, or an approving look. Bosses who seem to be able to elicit this response are those who care for their employees and who show it.

There are some bosses who are not particularly nice and yet have workers who try extra hard to please them. What is going on? This is a phenomenon called *transference,* which is the attribution of faults or qualities to people in authority that really belong to someone in your past. For example, when someone you don't know enters a room and you get a feeling that you like or dislike that person, you are in fact transferring; you are giving that person attributes that may or may not belong to that person but to someone that person reminds you of. A walk, a gesture, a tone of voice, a very small mannerism may trigger something in you that somehow makes you have a positive or negative feeling about that person. Transference occurs most frequently from subordinates to bosses because they are people in authority and their opinions are valued more than the opinions of peers. If you dislike your boss for no apparent reason or are awed by and admire your boss excessively, you may be involved in a transference.

The only way you can deal with transference is to become aware that it is going on. By definition, transference is an unconscious process, so you should ask yourself who that person is to you and why you are overreacting. I found a good example of the process of transference among the young women employees whom I have worked with and who had crushes on their bosses. After asking them, "Who is this boss to you?" the answer often was, "Well, he's so much like my father." It is necessary to remind yourself that the person in question is not the father, but the boss, and to act appropriately.

Third, let us look at motivation as it relates to your coworkers. Studies have shown that work groups with high group pride and loyalty are more productive and that members of such groups have greater job satisfaction, less absenteeism, and less turnover. Work groups with high group loyalty show more teamwork and more willingness to help each other than those with low group loyalty. It is also interesting to note that plant managers of high production work groups report that their groups perform well even when they, the plant managers, are absent—that is, where supervision is not close and where job assignments are given to the whole group, who then divide the individual tasks among themselves.[44]

The motivating factor here is to be a good team member and so achieve respect from coworkers. The peer pressure that motivates someone in this category is very strong because workers believe that if you do not perform according to your peers' standards, you might be isolated and discounted or ridiculed and ostracized.

The other factor in motivation as related to coworkers is competition, the need to outdo some individual or another team. A good supervisor provides enough competition to motivate workers but not so much that they either give up or enter into frenzied activity that puts speed ahead of quality. It is important to stress the self-defeating aspects of this type of competition. A word of caution about competition. Not all people like competition—particularly the North American style of win/lose. Some cultures stress collaboration and team effort—sacrificing personal gains for the benefit of the group. It might be difficult for a supervisor brought up in the United States to understand the lack of competitiveness shown by some foreign workers. The research that has studied the differences between what motivates males and females has been inconclusive. My own research has shown that contrary to popular opinion, women are as interested as men in pay, status, and opportunity for self-improvement.[45]

It is not always a supervisor's fault if a worker is not motivated. Some people are unreachable and uneducable and cannot be motivated no matter what you do. However, with most employees, it is up to the supervisor to see that a combination of all three categories is used in the process of motivation.

Friendly Coworkers

The hours spent at work are the major portion of any person's day, and thus job satisfaction needs to be derived from these hours. One of the things that research has found is that a great source of satisfaction at work is having friendly coworkers; this takes precedence over pay, opportunity, security, challenge, and so on.[46] People want to have their social needs fulfilled, and work is a logical place for it. Knowing this, a good supervisor will see to it that the employees have opportunities to meet with one another, socialize, and have pleasure from each other's company, at least during longer breaks, as opposed to isolating them by putting each worker into a separate cubicle without opportunities for interaction.

If supervisors want to encourage their workers to form good support groups, then they must be sensitive to the various cultural components in the work force. Most older people would like to have a few older people around them; most women prefer to be with other women some of the time; most minorities want to be able to speak to at least one other minority person. Two blacks will not necessarily have more in common than a white and a black, but often there is some comfort in the company of someone who relates to issues in the same way.

Participative Management

Participative management means that supervisors do not make decisions and announce them but discuss the issues involved either with an individual or a work group and listen to the workers' opinions about how the work should be performed. The supervisors then either make a decision, taking workers' opinions into consideration, or agree to have a joint decision-making session, abiding by the outcome; the danger is that if the supervisors do not pay attention to the suggestions of the workers, the workers will be very upset and feel used. If the supervisors do not plan to follow through with the joint decision, they should take the time to explain their reasons. Many studies have found that workers who have a say in what will ultimately affect them will feel more committed to the outcome than workers who are just told what to do and how to do it.

This, however, may not be true of all cultures. Supervisors must be sensitive to the fact that in some cultures workers will wonder why their supervisors are getting paid more if they can't make decisions by themselves and need to check with their workers. Some people are brought up not to disagree with authority figures and will have a hard time giving an opinion if it is different from that of their bosses; therefore, they will not be truly involved or participate in decision-making. It is also important for supervisors to be aware that in making group decisions, they may be prejudiced toward listening to the more powerful people in the group, often white males, but that minorities and women ought to be paid equal attention to and not devalued because of their gender or color.

Sins of Omission

It is not only what I say
for I am seldom prejudiced
in any obvious way

It is what I don't say
it is the forgetting
the not noticing
the disregarding
the overlooking

It is not only the support not given
it is not knowing
when it is needed

I do not sin by commission anymore
I sin by omission.

The critical thing to remember is that what motivates people is an expectation of some sort of reward; if that reward is expected and then not given, motivation will drop. If motivation is related to yourself, and the reward is mastery but there is no opportunity to learn—motivation will drop. If motivation, as related to your boss, is to please and yet the boss does not recognize good performance—motivation will drop. And, finally, if motivation is related to your coworkers in a competitive situation, and working hard as a group member does not win respect—motivation will drop.

The first thing that you as a supervisor need to do in order to understand how to motivate your workers is to take an interest in them and find out what matters to them. If you have no clues, sit down and talk with them. They will tell you, unless they don't know themselves what it is. A good supervisor can provide motivation where none existed before. For example, you may have a worker whose only satisfaction seems to come from getting a paycheck and getting out as quickly as she can. She is a clockwatcher. If you put her in charge of a project, provided, of course, that she is trained to do it, you may see a very different kind of attitude at work. On the other hand, what you don't know is that she may need to go to the market on her way home, pick up children, and fix dinner for a hungry family, so she needs to rush out as soon as the clock strikes five. It is, therefore, important for supervisors not to make assumptions about the motivation of their workers until they really know what's going on. And again, not everyone can be motivated, so don't blame yourself if you don't succeed with everyone.

One of the more difficult tasks in employee motivation is not only to get them to produce but also to help them reduce costs.

Cost Controls

Most supervisors have not had formal training in how to budget, how to control costs, and how to reduce expenditures. There is constant pressure from upper management to reduce costs, but no one can say exactly how that is to be done and what the priorities are. It is not unusual for a manager to issue a directive for all supervisors to cut costs by a certain amount. This tactic works well if a supervisor is not operating efficiently and thus can improve the unit; however, it penalizes those supervisors who are already very efficient in managing costs, for there is no leeway for them to cut back further.

Some people feel at ease with numbers. Those who are afraid of numbers may shy away from dealing with budgets and cost controls; however, it is an essential part of a supervisor's responsibility. Is it better to hire one more person to work on an old machine or is it best to buy a new machine and forgo the extra worker? The budget may not allow both for another worker *and* for a better machine. How do you decide?

Controlling costs is not only a response to a budget crisis but is also a continuing, ongoing concern of supervisors. Good supervisors must be able to predict how fast supplies will be exhausted so that new ones can be ordered, yet they must not order too much because inventory costs money. A common error may be to try to save on equipment maintenance when, in fact, the consequent breakdown can be more costly.

Human power use becomes complicated for an organization that has peak demands and then leveling-off periods. Do you retain good employees who work at less than capacity, or do you keep firing and rehiring with the consequent cost of training and breaking in new people? Sometimes arrangements can be made with the workers by including them in the problem-solving process. Perhaps the workers will agree to take more time off without pay reduction during some periods and work longer or harder without pay increase during others. Unless there are union regulations forbidding this practice, it is one way of dealing with maintaining a work force without turnover.

As a supervisor, you should look to see where waste is occurring and where there can be tightening of budgets. Studies have shown that about 20 percent of the workers account for 80 percent of the problems in an organization. This means that most of your organization's workers function smoothly, while a few create continuing problems. Another way to see the situation is that 80 percent of your workers may be cost conscious and 20 percent may be wasteful. Studies have also shown that when errors occur, they occur in one particular section of a department. There is no need to harangue those who already do well; focus only on those who need help in reducing costs.

Not only should supervisors look at what the incurred costs are, but they also should see where the maximum profitability can be derived because this is where the cost cutting is needed the least, if at all. For example, giving insufficient or inadequate tools to a high-performing worker may reduce cost but will also reduce profitability.

It is important to train your workers to be cost conscious. They should be aware of how much their materials cost to buy, replace, and maintain, and which are more expensive and need to be especially cared for. When workers are so informed, they can then be helpful in discussing ways in which they themselves can reduce costs.

Supervisors must be aware that they are models and cannot behave in wasteful ways if they expect the workers to be cost conscious. Supervisors should talk about specific methods that can be used to lower costs and not just complain that things are inefficient or wasteful and that workers don't care and are negligent. Again, we need to look at the specifics that will make a difference. When a technique has been identified that will reduce costs, a time period must be set in which it can be applied. A method for an evaluation of results must be agreed upon, so that the effort made has value.

If some workers have made an error and have spent more money than was necessary, it may be that they had not been informed as to the better procedures. Give them the benefit of the doubt and work out a schedule with them as to how they can do it differently.

The best thing a supervisor can do is to have a program for maintaining control over costs. This means that every work area should have a list of resources required, people required, and objectives defined. Supervisors should focus only on those areas where they think there is room for improvement. Sometimes angry workers waste equipment on purpose. They may be upset because of their own tight financial situation and resent the bosses who seem to be throwing money around. Part of their revenge may be in wasting company money. Trying to motivate workers to reduce costs so that the company can make more money will be far more difficult in such a case. But helping them to see that cost reduction would benefit them by improving their work record, work effectiveness, and subsequent performance appraisals might be more effective.

Remember that cost reduction is not a blanket operation that should be everybody's responsibility. Some workers are already operating at peak efficiency. However, cost consciousness is something that all employees should be aware of in a way that is challenging, but not punitive. Just as people like to learn new skills, they can also be taught that cost consciousness is a skill that can be mastered.

Career Planning

Career planning is part of the whole motivational picture. It means you sit down with your workers and discuss where they would like to be going, what skills they will need to acquire, what responsibilities they would like to have, and what their ambitions are. See if they are being realistic and if their wishes are within the company's ability to fulfill. If they are, then you can make a plan with your workers so that they know what steps they need to take, what courses they need to attend, and what skills they need to learn to fulfill their ambitions. Career planning is a dialogue between you and your workers. Unless your company has career planning personnel and workshops on that topic, you may wish to stay in touch with your workers' progress so that they know that someone is on their side in promoting their growth.

Plateauing

The pyramid squeeze is real. As more and more people reach for the top, fewer and fewer can be selected. Some well-prepared, well-motivated, well-functioning, and effective performers will not be promoted. The selection process is not always fair and frequently the people who don't make it because there are too many people for too few jobs will feel depressed and angry, and will lose their motivation. What should you do? It is important for the supervisor to explain the rationale behind their *not* being promoted—explaining, if it is the case, that the difference was very small, that it has nothing to do with them, that perhaps the person selected may not be better qualified—it's just that a choice had to be made, and that it may have been almost the toss of a coin. The object is to get the disappointed employees to understand that they are valued so that they feel good about themselves. The next step is to discuss the problem with them and try to find what will keep them happy on the job. Would that be a lateral move, such as going to another department at the same level? A new title? Another office? These public signs of recognition are meaningful to most people and worth addressing. Plateauing, or remaining in the same position, is a fact of life for a large majority of people who are upwardly mobile, and the supervisor has to deal with the frustration this situation creates. It is important for supervisors to show sensitivity, warmth, and caring. One approach that seems to help is to allow people to air their disappointment or anger so it doesn't simmer.[47]

Plateauing is a word that is usually used for middle managers. The word more often used for workers at the lower levels is "stuck." Some people may make the next step up very late in their careers; others will never make it at all. Some people have no particular desire or ambition to move up and are perfectly content to take home their weekly paycheck and not have any more responsibility. Others may feel they have been discriminated against or that they have not been dealt with fairly, and a supervisor should be sensitive to those who are upwardly mobile but who, because of their numbers, won't have the opportunity. They must be told that the lack of movement is not due to lack of merit or lack of hard work.

What may make it easier for these workers is a realization that their feelings of identity as a worker are not the only identity they have, that their success or failure at work does not make them successful or unsuccessful human beings. It is important for a supervisor to help them see that they can gain some pleasure, satisfaction, and recognition in their lives outside of work and to make them aware that they may need to look elsewhere to reinforce their self-esteem. The people who have not been moved up can still get recognition for their work if they can be made to understand how valuable they are and how much the supervisor and the company appreciate them. Sometimes supervisors can delegate some of their own responsibility to such people so that they are in charge of something and have autonomy in some of the decisions that affect their work.

The Four Work Stages

During the work life of any worker, four major stages can be identified.[48] The first one is the *learning stage* when the worker is concerned with acquiring new skills or knowledge. When workers are mostly concerned with achieving competence, they want to know how to do certain things, they undertake new activities, they are dependent on another person for being their teacher or mentor, and they generally need guidance and support from their supervisors. During a lifetime, if people started work in their early 20s, this stage would occur the decade of their 20s. As the supervisor, you will need to accept their dependence and be their teacher.

The second is the *producing stage* when workers have learned the necessary skills to be competent; they are less concerned with competency and more concerned with autonomy. At this stage, often occurring in their 30s, workers need goals. They want visibility, challenge, and advancement. They look to peers and colleagues for friendship. As the supervisor, you need to give autonomy, to delegate tasks, and to give recognition.

The third stage is the *teaching stage*. This stage occurs when workers are in their 40s, and 50s and they are ready to be mentors and role models to others; they are ready to groom younger people. As the supervisor, you should let them train others. This stage also is often a time when workers reassess their career goals.

The fourth stage is the *leaving stage*. For many workers who have been in a career since their 20s, this is a time when their family takes on a renewed importance. As a supervisor, you will have to be tolerant of signs of withdrawal from their commitment to work and try to provide new challenges, even though they might not be welcome at this time.

For women who either return to work after having had a family or who start to work later in their lives, these stages still exist but in a more encapsulated form. A woman returning to work in her 40s would still go through the learning stage, the producing stage, the teaching stage, and the leaving stage. However, instead of going from the 20s to the 60s, she would go from the 50s to the 60s and accomplish these same goals for herself as would her male counterpart who had started earlier.

Thus a man at 60 may be in the leaving stage, while a woman who is also in her 60s may be in the producing stage and is very excited about a new career. For example, I got my Master of Social Work at 40 and my Ph.D. at 50 and was promoted to full professor in my 50s. As I write this at age 58, I am in a new career, just starting again. The four stages of a worker's life apply to *any* job one learns, does well in, teaches to others and then leaves. These stages can take a year or two for simpler jobs, but it may take between five and ten years for the more demanding one or even a whole lifetime for a career to develop. When one goes through the process of learning, producing, and teaching, and having achieved mastery, there is often not enough challenge left. It is at this time that people tend to leave so that they can begin the cycle of learning, producing, and teaching all over again.

It is important for you, the supervisor, to understand which stage your workers are in so that you will know whether or not they should be given a lot of support and guidance in their learning stage, if they should be left alone and given autonomy in their producing stage, if they should be given the responsibility of training others in their teaching stage, or if they should be used as consultants in their leaving stage. You should also try to assess in what stage you are so that you will know how to respond to your own needs and to make the appropriate demands of your boss.

Exercise

Take a look at the following list of motivational factors and rank them in terms of what is most important to you.

After you have made your selections as to what is most and least important to *you,* make that same selection as you think each of your workers would make it for him- or herself.

Now look at the results in both columns. How close or how far are you from one another's choices? Supervisors who fill out these lists often see themselves as wanting very different things in a job from what their workers want, when, in fact, research has found very little difference. You may want to ask your workers to fill out their own questionnaires. You may wish to compare your answers with those who have filled out this list. You may find that whatever is important to you may also be important to other people. You may also find that older people or nonwhites might give different answers, which may be something you may wish to pursue in a discussion with your workers.

I	My Workers	What is Most Important for Me in My Job
		My work is interesting.
		I have a chance to use my mind.
		I have good job security.
		My job does not involve hard physical work.
		I am well paid.
		I have good chances for a promotion.
		My work offers me variety.
		My boss is concerned about me.
		I can participate in decisions regarding my job.
		My responsibilities are clearly defined.
		I am not supervised too closely.
		I have time for outside interests.
		I have friendly coworkers.
		I am not expected to do work which is not paid for.
		I have the freedom to decide how to do my work.

What is Most Important for Me in My Job
(To be duplicated and given to your workers, if you wish.)

	My work is interesting.
	I have a chance to use my mind.
	I have good job security.
	My job does not involve hard physical work.
	I am well paid.
	I have good chances for a promotion.
	My work offers me variety.
	My boss is concerned about me.
	I can participate in decisions regarding my job.
	My responsibilities are clearly defined.
	I am not supervised too closely.
	I have time for outside interests.
	I have friendly coworkers.
	I am not expected to do work which is not paid for.
	I have the freedom to decide how to do my work.

PART V

BUILDING CONTROLS

10

EVALUATING YOUR WORKERS' PERFORMANCE

We now come to what, for most supervisors, may be the most difficult and at times unpleasant part of their job—evaluating their workers. It can also be the most rewarding. Before you evaluate any of your workers, you should try to understand your feelings.

Begin this chapter by completing the following sentences:

1. The last time my boss evaluated my performance, I felt...(For example, were you anxious? Were you excited? Were you frightened? Were you looking forward to it? What were your feelings about the performance appraisal itself?)
2. When I evaluate one of my subordinates I feel...(What are your feelings about the process, not about that person as a worker, but instead, how do you feel about spending an hour with that individual?)
3. The last time I evaluated one of my subordinates's performance, he or she must have felt...
4. The last time I was evaluated, my boss's feelings about the process were probably... (Again, it is not whether or not the boss thought you were effective, but how you **think** your boss felt about evaluating you.)

This process puts you in the place of your worker and enables you to see how that person feels about your evaluating skills.

At the end of this chapter, there are lists of adjectives that supervisors have used in answering these questions. You may wish to see if any of your feelings are similar to those of others.

Why is performance evaluation so difficult? and why is it so seldom done well? There are four main reasons. First, most of us don't like to sit in judgment of others; when supervisors feel very close to their workers (if the workers are former colleagues), it becomes even more difficult. Second, it is unpleasant to give criticism to others because we believe that we'll be disliked. (Giving a negative performance evaluation can incur a worker's dislike.) Third, it is not always clear what data is used by supervisors to make their judgment, and they often do not know whether their evaluations are correct or not. (They are afraid not to be objective.) Fourth, supervisors may not have been giving continuous feedback about the worker along the way and they are afraid that the evaluation will come as a surprise. (If feedback had been given on an ongoing basis, the review would only confirm expectations.)

Let us start with the first reason: resistance to sitting in judgment of others. Resistance is understandable because most of us have our secret weaknesses and fear that they may be discovered, and because we do not wish to be judged, we also do not like to judge others. However, it is part of the supervisor's job to help improve the performance of workers, and it is not possible to help a worker do a better job unless there is an evaluation of the work being done. Improvement can be based only on data that come from an evaluation process. If you can convince yourself that you are not there to do harm, but to help, then you can use performance evaluation as a tool for increased communication, for more focused training, as part of a career plan for the worker, and as a way for you to find out more about the climate of the workplace and the satisfaction of your worker. Thus information is both given and received. If you try to approach an evaluation as a special time when you and your worker can sit quietly together and talk in ways that the usual bustle of work does not permit, you may even begin to look forward to it; and after a few experiences, so will your workers. Then it will become not a threatening time, but a time of sharing, understanding, growth, and planning.

The second reason—criticizing an employee and fearing to be disliked—comes from the fact that the bearer of bad news is always unwelcome, and you are the one who bears the responsibility of giving the bad news of poor performance and dissatisfaction with a worker, which may include a probationary period, a warning or a demotion, or even a dismissal. No one enjoys the prospect of giving pain to another person. If you take the time to think about how your worker may feel, then you can start a poor performance evaluation by talking about feelings: "You're going to have bad feelings about this; you're going to be upset; you will also be hurt. That, however, is not my intent. My intent is to help you to do your job better." At least then you will be honest in saying that you understand that the process is unpleasant, even painful. The difference between good criticism and poor criticism is its specificity. If you tell a worker that he or she has a poor attitude, there is not much he or she can do except feel hurt or angry. But if you say, "When you come to work in the morning and slam doors and shout at people and throw things around, it is upsetting to me," then you are giving very specific feedback, and the worker may be able to do something about it more readily than if you remain vague and general. Also, the fact that you say how these actions affect you adds a dimension with which the person cannot argue. Your worker can't tell you that you should not be upset; if you are, that is your own reality.

There's no question that when you criticize workers, you may be disliked. Most supervisors have to choose between being respected and being liked. It is not always possible to be both. If you have integrity and do your job well, you will be respected; and that is more important in the world of work than being liked. If being liked is most important to you, you might try to ingratiate yourself, which could reduce your effectiveness as a supervisor. Most men are dissatisfied only if a relationship is actively bad; most women are dissatisfied if it is not good. Because of this difference in basic attitudes, women supervisors must be even more watchful that they do not sacrifice respect for being liked.

Workers don't think much of bosses who do not stand up for what they believe, who do not make their opinions known, who do not have high standards of quality, who let things slip by, who are inconsistent, who overlook safety regulations, and who generally can be walked over.

The third reason is the confusion about what will be evaluated and how. There are two kinds of data available to a supervisor: objective and subjective. Subjective data are personal feelings or opinions. Generally they are not quantitative and often come from a secondary source. An example of subjective data is the opinion of a coworker. The supervisor should be wary of such data because they cannot be readily verified, and if the subordinate denies their validity the supervisor is confused as to whom to believe. For one thing, using these kinds of data might mean that the supervisor would be asked to reveal their source, which can lead to even greater conflict. If the source is not revealed, then the workers have no way to defend themselves. It is better, therefore, to regard all such opinions as hearsay and not rely on them for the purposes of performance review. Have you ever been told by people that they have heard negative things about you and then have them refuse to reveal their sources? This may tend to make you paranoid, unable to trust your coworkers, and concerned about who's spreading rumors about you. Rumors make the workplace very uncomfortable.

Objective data, however, are reports, products, files, customers' complaints or compliments, achievement of objectives, and your own observations.

The fourth reason is the lack of continuous feedback. Workers ought to know on a routine basis how they are doing. Then the performance evaluation becomes just a stepping back and looking at the total performance in order to take the time to think and to plan.

The Incident File

In order to keep track of data, I suggest that you keep an incident file containing brief descriptions of occurrences of when your workers performed well or not well. If you don't keep such a file, you may remember only the most recent events, and what your workers did six months before will be forgotten. The tendency also is to remember negative things. What will stand out may be the time your worker did something poorly. But it is even more useful to single out successes than to notice failures because people will perform better if they are recognized and praised for what they have done well than if they are criticized for what needs improvement. For example, you might notice that two of your workers are having a heated, unpleasant discussion while a third one settles the dispute. Not only should you say to that third worker how much you appreciated the way the situation was handled, but you should write a note to yourself and file it under the worker's name, describing the incident in a short paragraph. It will not take you more than a minute to record each incident. After several months of gathering these kinds of data, when you look at the total file, you will see how many positive and how many negative incidents there have been, and you will be able to balance them more fairly than if you relied only on your memory. Since most of us cannot remember much about someone's performance beyond the three previous months, this file can be an aid to a supervisor's memory. These files should be open to the workers involved to allay any suspicion of "secret dossiers," and workers should be encouraged to put information into their file when they have performed well.

Also, you should keep a file on your own performance to present to your boss when it is your turn to be evaluated.

The Performance Review

We all like some people and dislike others without any apparent reason. The chemistry is wrong; the connection isn't there—you can't put your finger on it; you just don't like that person. The opposite can happen, too. For some reason, you always have fun with a particular person, feeling at ease and comfortable, and the communication flows easily. It may be only human nature to give a better performance rating to someone you like and to be more critical of someone you dislike. That is why it is important for supervisors to recognize their feelings about workers before sitting down to write a performance evaluation. You should always ask yourself the questions, "What do I *feel* about this person? Do I like him? Do I dislike her? Why?" If you don't come up with good reasons why you like or dislike a person, you may be reacting unconsciously to something in that person that may have nothing to do with actual performance.

We have already discussed transference—developing either positive or negative feelings about people based on the fact that they remind us of someone else. Unconsciously. your workers are experiencing transference in relation to you, and you are countertransferring in relation to them. For example, you might have a worker who is very dependent on you, who needs to ask you a lot of questions, who constantly looks to you for approval, who tries very hard to please you and who is afraid to make decisions without checking with you. If you have had little sisters and brothers whom you loved who have always depended on you and you are used to receiving their love in exchange for being available and helpful, you may then have a positive countertransference to that worker. However, that same worker may make different bosses very upset or angry with the lack of self-sufficiency and autonomy because those bosses have always resented their mothers' continuing dependence, and thus also resent the worker's dependency; their countertransference is negative.

Let's take another example. You may have a worker who is very independent, who initiates, who is self-sufficient, who does not seem to need your approval or even your comments. You may like this person for good reason—that independence frees you to do other things. This is a rational response based on the way you like to work—not on transference. Another boss may feel that this worker is too independent and should check in more often because, in the past, a younger brother had always assumed authority without checking, and had gotten his family into embarrassing situations. These examples make it important for you to reflect on why you like or dislike certain behaviors or specific workers. It is only when you are aware of these situations that you can evaluate the *qualities* of a worker instead of evaluating the *person*.

You are almost ready for the performance evaluation itself. You have your data, you have reviewed them, you have made a list of your feelings, and you are aware of them so that they will not prejudice you. Now make a list of the major points you want to cover and jot down what you want as an outcome of this review. You are then ready to arrange for a mutually convenient time. If the review is infrequent, such as twice a year, it should not be less than one hour long; however, if you review your workers more often, the time you allot can be shorter. Also, how much time you spend depends on how much you have to say. If all goes well, the review can take 30 minutes. Of course, it is best not to allow any interruptions; this arrangement shows that you feel the review is important. If you can avoid having visits or phone calls during that time, you will help create a better climate. If you are a supervisor who is on call or must be available for emergencies, you may have to conduct your review somewhere outside the office in order to avoid interruptions and to assign someone else to take over in your absence.

Conducting the Performance Review

A performance review has five major phases: the social phase, the review of objectives phase, the information phase, the planning phase, and the closing phase.

In the social phase, put the worker at ease as best you can. Explain the overall purpose of performance appraisals and say that it is like a routine physical examination where one just needs to do a check as to how things are going. Each organization has its preferred forms to fill out. Don't feel you have done your job if you marked it with only a few check marks. It is only a starting point. You should also say that the review should answer the worker's questions, such as: "How am I doing overall? What are my strengths? What can I build on to improve my performance?" If there are no major problems, you can put your worker at ease by saying, "I see that things are going quite well. Let's look at the particulars." This quickly puts a worker at ease and says that nothing negative is about to happen. The social phase should not take more than a few minutes, for it is a transition from work into the evaluation period, and time is always needed to get a bit settled.

In the review-of-objectives phase, if you're doing a first performance review with a worker, you should together look at your worker's job description, establishing agreement as to whether it is correct. If it is not correct, a new job description that is mutually agreeable should be worked out. If this is not a first review, then you should review the goals and objectives that were set the last time to see if they have been fulfilled. Thus, the review phase is concerned with the work that was done, its quality, and the length of time it has taken. The review phase deals with past expectations. It is important that you and your worker agree as to what these expectations were or are going to be.

In the information phase, you look at the data together. Did the worker meet the objectives that both of you had set and agreed on? Which of your worker's specific strengths made that possible? Be sure to recognize not only the results but also the effort. Look at your incidents file, and praise your worker for good work. If your worker failed to meet those objectives or failed to perform according to the job description, ask that person to explain why the objectives fell short. Using that person's strengths to build on, ask the worker to tell you how that goal could be reached in the future.

Some words of caution: Performance appraisals fail at the point when supervisors are afraid to be specific and direct in informing a worker about not meeting performance levels and standards that both parties had agreed on in the first place. There is no need to dwell on the person's failure, but there is a need to state shortcomings, to agree on the fact that there is a shortcoming, and to find ways to avoid falling short of the objectives again. You need not fear challenging or stretching people to reach a greater level of productivity; this is done by building on their specific strengths, skills, knowledge, and abilities. This also leaves the responsibility of finding ways to improve in the hands of the worker.

If workers do not agree with your assessment and think they are doing well despite your evidence to the contrary, then it is important to step back again and take a look at the review and at your expectations. It is critical at this point to be as specific as you can be. In other words, you cannot just tell workers they have bad characters. They can do nothing about their characters, which is a generalization, but they can do something about a description of their behavior, such as coming in late, slamming doors, throwing papers around, and yelling at coworkers. Specific examples such as these are possible indications of personality problems, and they can be noted as behavior that needs to be changed. It is during the information phase that you need to give feedback. The following are some rules to remember:

1. Be descriptive and not evaluative in your feedback. This means that when you describe a behavior, you are not judging the person. "You are lazy" is a judgment; "You work more slowly than the others" is a description.
2. Be specific and not general in the examples you give. "You take unfair advantage" is general; "You take 30 minutes for a 15-minute coffee break" is specific.
3. Be direct in your criticism toward a behavior your worker can do something about. You cannot expect people to be smarter if they have limited intelligence or expect them to be quick if they ponder and are somewhat plodding. These are personality characteristics that probably cannot be changed. If there are positive characteristics that you can mention, do so.
4. Be sure that your workers have heard your message clearly.

Have them repeat what you have said to them, especially if it is unpleasant. Sometimes even compliments are not heard, so if you praise your workers, ask them to explain in their own words what they think you said.

5. Be aware that *you* may have a need to "unload"; be sure that you're not meeting your needs but the workers' need to receive all the information from you that will aid their improvement.
6. Be careful with the question "Why?" If you ask why they do a task one way, instead of in a more efficient way, that is okay, but be careful about asking "why" when it has to do with psychology or with childhood events. For example, it is okay to ask workers why they come to work late, because if it is a personal problem, you may be helpful. It is not okay to discuss why they are the kinds of people who always seem to be late, or what influence their parents may have had in the matter.
7. Be attentive to your workers' needs, values, and emotions. Some workers may remain passive and appear to accept whatever you say. You may get no feedback from them that reveals how they are reacting to your performance appraisal. This may be very disturbing to new supervisors who would like to know how well they are doing and whether they are reaching their worker. Some cultures frown on workers who disagree with their superiors, and people from those backgrounds may disagree without your knowing it. Some people from Asian cultures are very deferential to persons in authority and consider contradicting to be very rude. They also avoid confrontation. For example, Indonesians may say "ingin," which means "yes," but this answer does not always mean they agree to do a job. All it means is "I understand," or even "I hear you talking."[49] The only thing you can do in such a case is to ask your workers to tell you how they plan to do things differently. In this way, at least, you can get them to talk about their performance.

People from other cultures may also be quite argumentative, and they will have an answer to whatever you say to prove you're wrong. That can be equally disturbing because you don't seem to get agreement on anything. According to brochures given to international business people, some French people, for example, enjoy conflict and debate. They will interrupt conversations with countless arguments and will often voice disagreements.[50] In situations such as this, you should put your foot down and be clear about the expectations you require them to meet. Your workers should know that they do not have an option to fail to perform to your standards.

Before you give negative criticism, ask yourself the following six questions:[51]

1. Is the person able to receive this criticism right now? Your worker may be going through tough times and may be fragile. You may want to say that you have some difficult things to discuss and ask whether or not this is a good time to do it.
2. Are you willing to stick around long enough to pick up the pieces? You cannot give strong negative criticism and leave without knowing how the person feels. Your workers may feel destroyed and unable to function without talking further about some of their reactions. They may need to be reassured that you are not evaluating them as total persons who are not adequate, but that you are looking at one specific piece of work or a particular behavior. It may be necessary for you to mention other tasks that you feel have been done well.
3. How many times has the worker heard this criticism before? If you feel that you have been repeating yourself, then saying it once more is obviously not going to make a difference. What you should focus on is not the criticism, but why, having heard the criticism before, the person is still unable to respond to it. Is there something else that should be said or done since what you have been saying and doing up to now have evidently not been working? Get the worker to help you do what is needed.
4. Can the person do anything about it? Your workers should be able to say what they believe they can do in order to improve.
5. Are any of your own problems causing you to make this criticism? It is possible for a supervisor to feel threatened by employees, to feel disliked by them, and unconsciously to

want to punish them. Be sure you are not responding to your emotions instead of to your reason. We often most dislike those people who have the faults we dislike in ourselves.

6. Are you sure that what this person needs is another criticism? You will know the answer to that question by trying to put yourself in that person's place and thinking how you would feel with this specific criticism directed at you.

Being truthful with yourself and facing realities will make it easier to be honest with and helpful to your workers. If workers have no idea how to improve their performance, then you should help by making suggestions, but it is important to make sure that the suggestions the workers accept are feasible. To know whether this is happening, ask your employees to repeat what they think they ought to be doing differently and to give you some idea as to how soon they feel they can start making that difference. You now have the opportunity to set a time for the achievement of that goal, which takes you into the planning phase.

In the planning phase, if you have covered the review and the information phases correctly, the planning phase builds logically on what you have just decided concerning whether or not objectives have been met. Now the discussions should center on what to do, how to improve, and other aspects of the job that both of you have to work out together.

In the closing phase, you should summarize how the employee is doing overall. You should review the specific, mutually agreed upon objectives and performance standards, establish a deadline for accomplishing these goals, and set an approximate date when you will again formally sit down and review the work. Setting a deadline is important so that both of you know what is expected and by when. That time period may be the same afternoon, the next day, a week later, a month, or six months away. Before the date set, you may want to check on the work in progress.

The sentence "Let me know if you have problems" is not always understood the same way by everyone. For some, it means the door really *is* open for them to come to you if there are problems; to others, it is only a polite phrase, and their acting on it would be a sign of weakness and incompetence. Make sure your workers understand that you welcome their asking for help. In this closing phase, you should ask once more if your workers really know which *specific* skills, knowledge, efforts, and abilities they need to address.

"You're doing fine" is a meaningless statement unless you are ready to come up with specifics and have taken the time to identify the behavior that is "fine." No one feels good about "doing fine," but people feel good about being appreciated for a specific piece of work that the supervisor observed. Thus, you should know what you consider good and bad performance, and your worker should know that, too.

Also in this phase, the two of you should agree on objectives and goals to be met by the next performance evaluation. These agreements should be written down and a copy made for each of you and for the file so that when you both meet next time, they become the basis for your review.

Many supervisors believe that if they are easygoing, they will be liked, but this is not always true. Studies have shown that workers prefer to be challenged, to learn, to sharpen their skills, and to increase their knowledge. Often many of us secretly hope that someone else will push us with specific goals and time limits, especially when we are unwilling to do so for ourselves. Setting *realistic* goals will stretch your workers without making them feel hopeless about being able to reach them. Remember that you should have precise objectives that are measurable, ones with targets achievable within a specified period of time. When you talk about standards, you should define the conditions that will exist if the job is to be considered well done and your workers should understand what they must accomplish to merit an excellent performance evaluation.

You can end your evaluation as you would end an interview. Shift your position in your chair, put papers aside, and ask your workers how they felt about the review; whether they felt comfortable, whether they have any more questions, and whether they know what is expected. In other words, you now discuss the process both of you have gone through. You may even want to share some of your own feelings about being relieved at how it went or disappointed that it did not go as well as you had hoped. Don't rush through this process. Look over your notes to see what your objectives were and to see if there is anything that still needs to be said. The worker should wait for you to look over your notes.

You may at some point (not at every performance review but when appropriate) ask the workers if their career objectives are being met, if their job expectations are being fulfilled, and if they know where they are going and if they are taking the steps necessary to achieve their objectives. You may also at this time ask your workers what expectations they have of you as their boss, if you are meeting these expectations, and if you are being as helpful to them as they feel you ought to be. Thus, you can get some feedback about your own performance in terms of your relationship with your workers. Don't be defensive—just listen carefully. Whatever workers say, it is their perception of you, and you cannot argue with it.

The Boss

I can only lead you well
if you tell me how to best lead you.

I can make the best decisions
only if you keep me informed.

I can prescribe best
if you tell me the consequences.

I need to know
my impact on you.

But I go beyond representing you
beyond being your reflection.

I point out the way to new visions
and to new paths for you to take.

Even if your company has set specific times for performance reviews once or twice a year, you may decide to have your own interim review to help your workers. If your company has a form, be cautious; filling out these forms can become very mechanical. The point of a performance review is to establish trust and *mutual* exchange; you can achieve this goal if you each talk approximately 50 percent of the time. If you hear yourself doing most of the talking, then something is amiss.

Be sure to discuss the performance reviews of your workers with your own boss so that he or she is kept informed and will support you in difficult situations.

Dangers

Do you allow a worker's recent negative occurrence to cloud months of good work? Do you take the easy way out and rate a worker very high, even though it is not deserved? These are two of the tendencies some supervisors have. Be sure to give the worker a copy of the developmental plan that you have made up for your next performance review. Surveys have found that subordinates consistently have a tendency to overestimate their overall performances. This, of course, presents the problem that if workers believe they are doing a better overall job than their supervisors believe they are doing, they will often be in disagreement and feel disappointed. There are two reasons that workers continue to overestimate their performance in spite of the performance feedback they receive. First, the feedback may not be specific enough to eliminate their misperception because workers perceive the feedback given to be less specific than did their superiors. Second, giving negative feedback is unpleasant. Thus, supervisors, while presenting a low performance rating to subordinates, then proceed to elaborate and try to explain away the lower rating in order to improve the interpersonal climate of the appraisal session. Also, a superior's explanations given for poor performance may not be acceptable to subordinates, leading them to deny or downplay their lower ratings. Subordinates tend to attribute poor performance to factors outside themselves, factors such as the working conditions, the quality of tools, the quality of a sales district, and so on. Supervisors tend to attribute poor performance to internal factors, such as a lack of ability or a lack of effort; so if the supervisors communicate reasons for performance that do not agree with the subordinate's reasons, the subordinate may deny the poor performance feedback.

Research shows that the way subordinates react to performance appraisals fits into their total perception of the work experience. Supervisors interested in improving their effectiveness during performance reviews should look at general issues of supervision throughout the year.[52]

One of the issues the supervisor may encounter is the workers' unwillingness to be open, especially if the performance review is tied to raises and promotions. Even when it is not formally tied to these, workers may perceive it as being so, and a negative word tends to make the workers defensive about their record and fearful that an admission of weakness or error would lead to lack of rewards, such as no pay increases. A supervisor should very clearly say whether the performance appraisal is related to pay increases or promotion.

Again, cultural differences will play an important part in the possibility of open exchanges. Be aware that openness and candor are white North American values not necessarily shared by others. Spontaneity is not considered desirable by everyone. There is an Arab saying: "Turn your tongue in your mouth seven times before you speak." Think about these cultural influences, but remember you are dealing with an individual who may not necessarily reflect ethnic or racial patterns.

Recognition for Good Work

Through the setting of objectives, the supervisor lets workers know what is expected of them and what the criteria are for rewards. Motivation is developed through the workers' knowing, first, what the expectations are, and second, what the rewards will be if the expectations are fulfilled. By being rewarded for performance, workers learn that the organization knows what it is doing and that their supervisor is observant in recognizing merit. This system of reward is important in maintaining high standards.

When pay is based mainly on length of service and cost-of-living increases and there is little regard for performance, the motivational aspects of pay are diminished. Workers will do only enough work to avoid being reprimanded or threatened or fired. Rewards such as time off, bonuses, pay increases, and promotions cost the company money. A supervisor who does not have money available to reward performance must use a different set of rewards, such as praise, added responsibility, or public recognition. These are important motivators. The supervisor should use these types of rewards for good performance so that workers will learn to expect a positive reaction from management. One possible reward is added responsibility. This does not mean just adding more work to the regular load, but giving tasks where workers can have more autonomy in making decisions and will be held responsible for results with less supervision—showing that they can be trusted. These tasks should be regarded as rewards because they help subordinates to increase their skills and to challenge themselves. The more you treat a trusted, well-performing worker as an equal, the more that person will feel recognized. Effective supervision is not necessarily close supervision. The more you can trust a worker, the less supervising you need do.[53]

Most evaluation forms consist of some type of rating scale and a space for the supervisor's comments. Superior performance earns workers a very high or even the highest rating on the scale-rating system. However, this system often introduces problems for a supervisor who wants to single out a worker for outstanding performance. In many organizations, evaluations are inflated, and every worker receives a very high rating. The superior worker becomes just one of the crowd, and the rating of excellent loses its meaning. High ratings can also create a different problem when a person who has received a very high rating is then not rewarded with a promotion, a desired transfer, or some other expected benefit. The supervisor's evaluation thus means little, and the worker's motivation may in fact decline.

With such problems in mind, the supervisor should adjust the comments to differentiate performance among the workers who have similar ratings. Giving an outstanding rating that has not really been earned is just as damaging as failing to give an outstanding rating that has been earned. You can expect each worker to be aware of the performance of others in the department; such awareness can lead workers to form opinions about what constitutes a fair evaluation. Morale and credibility can be damaged when people receive ratings that are too high, too low, or out of line with the work that they have performed. You must maintain your credibility with those you review because your reputation for giving accurate appraisals enhances the value of an outstanding evaluation as well as the credibility for a poor one. Remember that your performance evaluations become part of the permanent file of your workers.

If you really want to reward an outstanding performance, you may want to write a special letter to your superior about this worker, and give a copy of the letter to that worker. This letter can be part of the pleasure shared with the worker's family. You may wish to remind your worker that an outstanding evaluation is not a guarantee that personnel action will take place. If you give all your employees very high ratings uniformly, you may have to account for this action to your own boss during the time *your* performance is being evaluated. The easy way out, especially for new supervisors, is to inflate evaluations because, as we have seen, they find negative criticism very difficult to give. However, be careful not to give everybody a poor one. If you keep a good incident file, your evaluations should be accurate most of the time.[54]

Feelings about Performance Evaluations

Look at the sentences you completed at the beginning of this chapter about how you felt at your last performance review or at the first one you ever did. Compare your feelings to the following list of other supervisors' feelings about performance evaluations:

1. The last time my boss evaluated my performance, I felt...
   anxious
   my palms were sweaty
   frustrated
   wished it were over
   nervous
   felt I'm in the way—my boss is too busy
   afterward I felt relieved that I'm okay
   disappointed, he was too critical
   issues were avoided
   felt unrecognized
   happy
   angry—my strong points were overlooked and my weaknesses were focused on
2. The last time I evaluated one of my subordinates, I felt...
   reluctant to state negatives
   frustrated by difficult forms
   concerned about being able to balance the positive and negative
   nervous about their reaction
   confused about facts versus impressions
   awkward
   good
   bearer of good news
   one-way street—the worker is passive, and I don't like to play judge

3. The last time I evaluated one of my subordinates's performance, he or she must have felt...
   powerless
   apprehensive
   bored because of waste of time
   frustrated by artificiality of the forms
   criticized
   surprised by information
   worried the relationship would worsen after the review

It is interesting to note that on all counts, the supervisors who completed these sentences had more negative feelings about the process than positive ones.[55]

Exercise

This exercise will help you prepare for an evaluation review. You should plan the review by doing the following:

1. Review the job description of your worker, making the necessary changes in order to be able to discuss them.
2. Make a list of all the objective data that you have about your worker.
3. Make a list of subjective data you have, listing the sources.
4. Write the feelings you have toward the performance of the worker.
5. Write the feelings you have about the personality of the worker in order to become aware of them.
6. Make a list of the points you want to cover.
7. Write down what you hope the outcome of your evaluation to be.
8. List the strengths of the worker, giving specific instances where these were exhibited.
9. List the specific weaknesses of the worker and where they have come up.
10. List the specific steps by which you believe improvement can be made.
11. List the standards you expect from the person performing this job, in terms of quality and quantity.

12. Ascertain what your role can be in order to improve the performance of the worker.

Just as you prepared *yourself* for a performance review, ask your workers to prepare for their performance reviews, too. Ask them to do the following:

1. List what the workers consider to be the most important parts of their jobs, such as production, quality, customer service, new ideas, and so on.
2. List the problems they feel that prevent them from doing as good a job as they wish they could.
3. List any ideas they might have about what could be done to solve the problems.[56]

11

DEALING WITH ALL KINDS OF WORKERS

Problems occur at work because of poor work produced or inadequate service rendered, because of personality difficulties of the workers, or because of their different cultural backgrounds. The problems are either within the workers or about their work. A worker may have a difficult personality and create a poor work climate by not getting along with peers, yet may perform adequately; or the work might be of poor quality or not done on time, yet the worker may be a very pleasant person. The first thing for the supervisor to do is to identify if the problem lies within the worker or if it concerns the worker's output.

Output is easier to quantify because you can measure it against a standard.

Personality Differences

Personality problems are most difficult to pinpoint and take more effort to solve. Sometimes a worker's difficult personality will affect the quality of the work, but not necessarily. Even though personality problems may not interfere with the workers' doing their jobs properly, they may have negative consequences on fellow workers' jobs, causing a distressful environment. Problems may be caused by personal difficulties such as abuse of alcohol and drugs, marital conflicts, abrasive personalities, chronic tardiness, or absenteeism. Some workers seem apathetic and indifferent, while others are always joking and goofing off.

Some problems not related to personality are beyond your workers' control. For example, your workers may not have received the necessary guidance to do the job or may lack the needed skills or training. Some workers may have been given a job beyond their capabilities. The environment may not be conducive for workers to try harder if earned rewards are not given or if harassment by coworkers is allowed. And what *you* consider as appropriate behavior may not be understood by workers coming from different environments. Chatting with others on the job may be frowned upon by your boss, but it may be the essential ingredient that will make your workers happy.

After you have first identified whether the problem lies with the worker or with the work, you should then identify whether it is due to individual problems within a worker's control, to the worker's cultural background, or to the structure of the work environment. How do you know? You should ask questions, you should observe, and you should gather information. Do you feel that you have adequately explained what is needed and what standards must be met? Do you feel that you have trained your workers adequately, yet they are still not able to perform well enough?

The question you should ask yourself is whether your workers *cannot* do better or whether your workers *will not*. To answer that question, you should talk to them and discuss the problem to discover what prevents them from doing better. Here are some general strategies for dealing with problem workers and some suggestions for handling specific problems.

If workers make mistakes because of lack of information or lack of skill due to poor training, it is the supervisor's responsibility to change that situation. However, if workers make mistakes because of carelessness or negligence or even willfully poor performance, the only responsibility the supervisor has is to find the causes and then discuss the problems with the worker in order to work out the solutions.

Culture-based difficulties are the hardest to deal with because they are part of ingrained value systems. You should know what is important to your workers, and they should know what is important to you.

Let us first look at personality types. Workers who are very systematic are consistent and organized; they may be plodding, very detailed, slow, or overly reliant on procedures. Other workers may be intuitive, original, and able to spot new needs, or to create new ideas. Others may be impulsive and start tasks they do not finish; they may be unfocused, unaware of details, and disorganized.

Some jobs need attention to detail, others need creativity and still others need a combination of both. It is important for you to match the job to the personality type of your workers. You may be more comfortable or less comfortable with people who have certain characteristics. It is important that you be aware of your personal responses so that you don't punish workers who are very different from yourself but who fit the requirements of the job.

Special Problems: Alcohol and Drug Abuse

Let us look at some specific issues such as abuse of alcohol and drugs, which is a major problem in today's work force in the United States. As a recent article states, "Alcohol is still the most abused drug and its impact on industry cannot be minimized, but the new explosion of illegal drugs caught industry unprepared. Many supervisors who downed a couple of martinis at lunch were hesitant to discipline an employee for smoking a joint instead. Bosses who knew how a drunk worker acted had no idea how to identify a pill-popper."[57]

The cost to the American economy is enormous—nearly $26 billion, including $16.6 billion in lost productivity. Employees who use drugs on the job are one-third less productive than those who do not, are three times as likely to be injured, and are absent far more often. "Stoned, strung-out, and coked-up" workers affect the morale of offices and scare away customers.

More than 4,500 companies, including most of the 500 largest, have established employee assistance programs for drug and alcohol abusers. A computer profile of typical recreational drug users in today's work force showed that they were born between 1948 and 1965, were late three times more often than fellow employees, requested early dismissal or time off during work 2.2 times more often than nonusers, had 2.5 times as many absences of eight days or more, used three times the normal level of sick benefits, were five times more likely to file workers' compensation claims, and were involved in accidents 3.6 times more often than other employees.[58]

We can see from the preceding information that a supervisor

must be very sensitive to signs of alcohol or drug abuse among the work force. Supervisors should note changes of mood or sudden drops in productivity and question the worker. For some companies, it is less expensive to rehabilitate workers with drug problems than to hire and train new ones. Find out what your company's preferences are and act accordingly. If there are no counseling services for workers in your organization, you may need to have a list of counselors to whom you can send your workers for help. It is not a problem that you, an untrained person in that field, can deal with alone because it is not an issue of willpower with abusers, but rather an issue of a habit that needs to be treated medically and psychologically.

Family Problems

We know that a worker who has just had a fight with a spouse or has a sick child in the hospital will not be performing well. According to statistics, almost half of your employees at some point will be going through a divorce. These are stressful periods, and a supervisor can be helpful by making time available for workers to see a lawyer or to appear in court. Very few people can forget personal distress and concentrate fully on work. Those who cannot concentrate on their work need a sympathetic supervisor who will help them through the difficult times by being willing to listen to them and to find out ways that can be helpful to the workers. For example, some workers may be willing to lose pay for the opportunity to leave a few hours early each day to visit a sick family member in the hospital, or they may be willing to work nights in order to come in later in the mornings. Even if flexible working hours are not part of your organization, in special cases you may be able to be flexible with your workers. This may create a problem if others want similar privileges and become resentful if they don't get them. You should stand firm and say that you will respond to specific needs. Whatever action you take, remember to discuss it with your own boss beforehand.

The Abrasive Personality

Persons with abrasive personalities who are also poor workers do not present a problem since the choice to dismiss is more easily taken. But what about the high performers with difficult personalities? These people may be intimidating to others. They may be aggressive, sarcastic, arrogant, argumentative, and generally difficult to get along with, creating a tense work atmosphere wherever they are. Persons with abrasive personalities who are also good performers are very often extremely ambitious, always pushing themselves toward impossible aspirations but never being able to achieve them. When they fall short of the perfection they expect from themselves, they are frustrated, angry, or upset. Self-control for such people is very important. Such persons often overorganize and cope with imperfections by overcontrolling, by not delegating, and by refusing to take any responsibility for problems they create in interpersonal relationships.[59]

What can you as a supervisor do? First, understand that abrasive and provocative behavior arises from a person's extremely vulnerable self-image. Such people hunger for affection and are eager for contact. Do not become angry. Instead, initiate frequent discussions with them, describe their abrasive behavior and how it affects you and others. Point out that you recognize their desire to achieve and that you want to help. If your workers are willing to listen to you, you may even enter into a mutual agreement to point out the abrasiveness every time it happens since they are not always aware of it.

If your caring and gentle counseling does not work, then these people must be firmly told that their behavior affects the workplace and is therefore unsatisfactory and that they may need professional help. You should explain further that their being referred either to a company counselor or to an outside psychologist means that you feel they are so competent or skilled that you don't want to lose them. You want to do everything you can so that they can mature and assume greater responsibility. Being sent to a psychologist, a psychiatrist, or a counselor should not be seen as a punishment but as a step forward, representing your belief that they will come through all right.

Pay attention to workers with charming personalities. Not all are self-centered, but many are. Notice that the more exhibitionistic these people are, the more they need approval and the less thoughtfulness they may extend to others. How often do these people use the pronoun "I"? This may indicate that they have problems working as part of the team.

Whiz Kids

Whiz kids are another type of problem employee supervisors have to deal with. These are people who suffer from incurable egotism. They can throw into confusion everyone who is below their phenomenal work rate, but however good they are, their speed will hardly compensate for the loss of effectiveness of your other workers. They constantly shatter work records and production standards. They might even threaten your position as boss. Whiz kids have no respect for rank except in aspiring to it. They might bombard you with more ideas than you can handle and will expect you to be as instantly reactive and as mentally agile as *they* appear to be. Whiz kids often have meteoric rises, sweeping all obstacles before them, with very little appreciation of all the frustrations and political factors that executives have to grapple with or the problems posed by human issues and budget restrictions.

Since every organization depends on bright ideas for survival, you will want to find a way to use the whiz kids in your organization, but your first consideration is to ensure that they don't ride roughshod over the sensibilities of your existing team. Give them special projects, especially tasks that show tangible results, because they are hungry for achievements that demonstrate to themselves that they are making a real contribution. Give them important tasks that may be even beyond their capabilities; since they are often intolerant of others who don't demonstrate the same degree of intellectual imagination, they might need to be taken down a peg or two.[60]

The Unreachable Person

An unreachable person is someone with whom you feel communication is impossible, almost as if you are talking to a stone wall. No matter what you say or do, if you don't elicit a reaction, you won't know if you have been understood or even heard. There are symptoms of unreachability: deliberate avoidance of eye contact, eyes shifting rapidly, or a vacant stare. Fidgeting or rigid body posture are also signals. The person may appear to be absorbed in other activities or allow phone calls and other interruptions to disrupt your conversation. Other symptoms include repeated yawning, frequent looking at a watch, giving "yes" responses automatically, or not responding to the topic under discussion or to the question posed. Repeating the same phrase or comments over and over or seeming to be in a hurry to go on to the next topic are other signals.

You can use the following five basic methods of getting through to the unreachable person:

1. The **direct approach,** which requires you to confront the issue. For example, you might say, "I do not feel you hear me, and I don't know what else to do." Express your feelings; try saying, "It upsets me when you don't pay attention to me."
2. The **preventive approach,** which takes this form: "I know you have had trouble listening to me in the past, but would you try this once to hear a different point of view?"
3. The **therapeutic approach,** which requires you to say, "You seem to have difficulty focusing on the discussion and often retreat behind a wall. This makes you unreachable. Are you aware of it?"
4. The **punitive approach,** which requires posing an ultimatum such as, "If you can't discuss the issue without interruptions or without changing topics, I will have to decide without your input."
5. The **indirect approach,** which can take three routes: writing a letter (some people communicate better through the written word than through a face-to-face exchange), using a third party who has the confidence of the person, or disregarding him or her.

It is important to know when to stop putting effort, time, and energy into a hopeless situation. Some people are just not reachable or educable if they cannot or will not cooperate. These people often show up at training programs (to which they have usually been sent) because they have demonstrated little interpersonal ability and are seen as rigid people, with little understanding of human problems. After you have tried the five approaches, give up—it is not your problem anymore, it's theirs.[61]

The Problem Workers' Review

Your review session with your problem worker has four phases. The first phase is *describing the behavior* or the standards that they are not adequately meeting. These workers must know *exactly* what they are doing, what is not acceptable or what part of the work is not meeting objectives, and how the poor performance affects other parts of the company's output. In describing the behavior, it is *you* who should offer the information.

The second phase is called *eliciting feelings*. This is where you gather information. You try to find out from your workers how they regard the problem, how they feel about it, and if there are any causes the workers may know that prevent them from doing the best possible job. Get the workers' side of the story.

The third phase is *negotiating change*. This is where you and your workers have spelled out the particular problem and have reached an understanding of what some of the reasons are for the problem and negotiate an improvement. You and your workers can now try to solve the problem, but they must be convinced that it can be done. Be sure expectations and checkpoints are clear. For example, be specific by explaining that you expect work turned in to have less-than-five-percent error rate, or that the work is to be completed by a specific deadline, or that there be no fighting with coworkers for the next week, and so on.

The fourth phase is the *contract*. If at all possible, it is good to have your negotiated decision written down and a copy given your workers. The contract includes your schedule for checking on progress and may include the necessary steps to measure progress. The workers must know specifically what you consider good outcome.

Following are 11 guidelines for this type of interview:

1. Keep it private, never reprimand workers in front of others.
2. Take one point at a time. When supervisors start giving negative feedback, there is often a tendency to overcriticize and let loose with all the complaints they have had for the past weeks or even months. Too much criticism can be harmful because subordinates can feel attacked and lose perspective about which problems concern you most and thus will not know where to begin correcting their behavior.
3. Criticize constructively and specifically. If you tell workers to be more careful, they may not be clear as to what you are talking about. However, if you spell out the details that have been left undone or the extra costs that have been

incurred because of their errors, subordinates can better understand.

4. Be consistent. Do not develop a pattern of ignoring a single violation of a rule, watching violations accumulating, and then finally exploding. Take care of each violation as it occurs.
5. Do not use the word "always" in your criticisms. For example, if you say, "You're always forgetting to punch the time card," the worker may adamantly disagree that this is not *always* the case, and will probably be correct.
6. Use praise. Even though you mention workers' strengths during an interview where you also mention weaknesses, they will probably remember the negatives. It is important to say when your workers have pleased you. Some supervisors think that praise should be given first, some say it should be given last; it is not clear which method is better, so use your judgment but be sure to use praise at some point.
7. Do not joke. A light touch may seem pretty heavy when laced with criticism, and your workers might think you are ridiculing them.
8. Be careful when criticizing. Some workers tend to personalize more than others. (It is often thought that women personalize more than men.) Criticism leveled at people's work may be taken as a direct criticism of the people themselves. For example, if one were to tell me that I did not teach well today, I might think of myself as a bad teacher in every respect, as opposed to my not having done a good job between 10 and 11 this morning. So be sure, then, to limit your criticism to a specific work issue and not to the workers themselves.
9. Use comparisons carefully. It is not helpful to compare one worker to another. Most people compete best when they are competing against themselves. Unfavorable comparisons may also produce hostility within the work group.
10. Do not underestimate your power over your workers. Even if you think of yourself as a warm, kind, compassionate, easygoing person, your workers see you as someone who has an enormous amount of power over them.
11. Don't expect to be liked or to be popular when you criticize.

Your job is not to make friends, but to be respected and to get the work done.

The most important objective is to make your workers aware that their problems make a difference in the total company output and that they are an important part of the organization because what they do affects everyone.

Stages of Disciplinary Action

The stages of disciplinary action must be a written code to ensure fair treatment of the workers and to protect them from impulsive or unduly harsh punishment for wrongdoings. Avoid sarcasm, loss of temper, humiliating remarks, profanity, threats, bluffs, favortism, extremely harsh penalties, inconsistent enforcement, or delaying tactics.

Following are the four stages of disciplinary action:

1. **First offense:** oral warning. Workers must understand what has gone wrong and be told of the stages of disciplinary action. Make a note to yourself of the time, place, and circumstances of the warning.
2. **Second offense:** informing workers in writing that the error is a violation of rules or standards and that another infraction will result in loss of pay or job. A copy of the warning is given to the worker, a copy is put in the personnel file, and a copy is kept by the supervisor issuing the warning. If there is a union, that body should also receive a copy. Be sure your own boss knows it too.
3. **Third offense:** disciplinary layoff. Workers are suspended without pay for a period of time consistent with the seriousness of the offense. This period can range anywhere from one to five working days. And again, be sure that all this is documented.
4. **Fourth offense:** demotion, transfer, or discharge. By now, it is presumed that workers have been given the opportunity to improve and that failure to do so indicates that the interest of the company is best served by taking them off their jobs, by giving them a different or lesser job, by transferring them, or by firing them. Here is a word of warning about transferring workers to another department. It is easier for some supervisors to transfer people, creating

problems for other departments, than to fire them. You are not helping your company by transferring workers who are inadequate. If the problem is related to a specific job and you feel the workers will be better with a different kind of job, or if you have a relationship problem with your workers and feel another boss can do better, then you can make the transfer. Be sure that all relevant facts are known by the next supervisor who will be dealing with these workers.

There are several things you need to ask yourself before discharging someone:

1. What is the past record of the worker?
2. Do I have all the facts that apply to the situation?
3. Has the worker been given a reasonable chance to improve?
4. Has the worker been given fair warning of the seriousness of the error?
5. What actions have been taken in similar cases?
6. What effects will this action have on the rest of the department?
7. Should I consult anyone else before taking action?[62]

To summarize this, you could ask two basic questions: What is desired by you as a supervisor and what is possible for your worker to accomplish?

Before you fire any workers, ask yourself how you can be most helpful to them at this time. Can you help by asking questions, clarifying, comforting, giving information, explaining, giving advice, listening, challenging, confronting, giving permission, solving problems, brainstorming, planning strategy, or taking action for others, with others, on behalf of others?

Ask your workers if what you are doing is helpful and if they understand what you are trying to do.

Firing

Firing may be the most unpleasant task a supervisor faces in the course of a career. Some people think they need a drink before they do it; others are so shaken that they have to take some time off afterward. I know supervisors who have spent sleepless nights trying to find a way of softening the blow. There is no way. Even though the firing may not be your decision but your supervisor's decision and may be caused by economic cutbacks, you as the bearer of bad news will be seen as the responsible party. It will be easier for you to sympathize with the workers you are firing if it is not your decision. However, workers will often feel that you did not use your influence or try hard enough to keep them on the job.

If you decide to fire for inadequate performance, it may appear easier because you are more convinced of the correctness of your action. But it will in fact be just as hard because of the responsibility you bear in making a decision that affects a person's livelihood. A doctor's prescription, a lawyer's advice, an arbitrator's decision, or an executive's policy all affect people's lives. You as a supervisor are now in a position to do the same. Yes, it is a tremendous responsibility, but it is one you must take on and deal with fairly.

Do not keep ineffective workers. It demoralizes your work force and lowers your productivity. Just because you feel sorry for ineffective workers is not a good reason to keep them on the job. It is sad and painful to fire older workers or needy workers with families in hard economic times when you are not sure they will find another job. You can try to help your less effective workers by giving them extra training, by trying to look for ways they can improve, and by finding out if they can fit anywhere else better; but after you have attempted everything, there comes a time when you have to dismiss them.

When you have given several warnings and the workers know that they have not performed up to standards, you must give them a firing notice. The interview should be short. You would like to avoid having your workers break down in front of you, and they may need to leave and be alone. Some workers need to vent their anger during the exit interview; you will then be the recipient of the expression of their frustration. There is no need for you to answer back; listen and acknowledge that this is very difficult for them, that they must have a lot of anger and pain, but that you have no choice in the matter other than to act the way you are acting.

If the responsibility is theirs and their inefficiency was really within their control, you can add the fact that you hope they will learn from the experience so that it will not happen to them again. The workers must be told very clearly the reason they are being fired so that it can be a learning experience. If you cannot give this worker a good reference, this person should know not to use your name and be warned that, if called, you will state the facts. Find out what your company policy is on giving referrals. Many companies now prefer to give only dates of employment for fear of being sued.

Sometimes you may need to fire workers because of the bad feelings they create in your department. For instance, if one person is responsible for dissension, there must be something specific that you can point to. This is the most difficult of all situations, for if you want to fire someone because of that person's personality and destructive relationships with others, you may need to show cause. Find out the policies in your particular organization before acting.

If you're frightened before your first firing, role-play this with a family member or a friend who should try to be as difficult and as tough in the situation as possible to give you some practice so that you are not taken off guard if there are threats, outbursts, or signs of losing control, all of which may happen. If you fear for your safety, ask your supervisor to be with you—do not take chances. It is a good idea to have a friendly witness in any difficult disciplinary action. If your supervisor is unavailable, find a colleague who is at least at your level. Never do a role-play with a coworker of the worker about to be fired.

Not all dismissals are traumatic. Some workers are even relieved, especially if you have put off doing the firing and the situation has deteriorated. Your worker may have known what is coming and be glad the decision has finally been made.

Firing a worker will often upset other workers. Coworkers, no matter how substandard the performance might have been, may have sympathy toward the fired person and may see you as being callous. That's all right; you may also gain their respect for doing what they know is necessary.

The important thing is to know your company's policy on severance. Is out-placement assistance available? Check with company lawyers, accountants, or counselors before confronting the worker. Remember that fear of firing is normal. If you don't have some fear of firing workers, it may mean that you feel distant from them—and it may show a lack of compassion. Some anxiety is not only normal but also healthy.

Dealing with Grievances

Every organization should have a written policy about its grievance procedures, which ensures a sympathetic hearing and fair treatment.

The first step is a complaint to you, the supervisor. If it can't be resolved at that level, then the worker can go one level up to your boss without fear of reprisal. At that level, the grievance should be presented in written form. If satisfaction is not obtained, the next step is to go to top management, and if that doesn't work, then the final step is arbitration.

To avoid having to file a formal grievance, the strategy for the supervisor is to take care of small complaints quickly as they develop—this step will avoid larger ones later on. In order to identify the complaints, it is important to talk to subordinates often and to stay in close touch with them. If they can trust you, they will be able to complain without fear. As a supervisor, your hope is that your workers are productive, happy, and open with you—both to complain and to compliment. Keep the channels open, and you will rarely need to worry about grievances.

There is another category of workers which may create problems for a supervisor—not because they are problem workers but because they are very different from the supervisor. The problem depends not so much on who they are but on who the supervisor is. We are talking about fitting in comfortably with others.

Disabled Workers

Many people are uncomfortable with physically or mentally disabled people. In reviewing hiring decisions, studies have shown that employers choose the person who has been disabled later in life or whose disability is least threatening to them personally. The reason for this is that people can identify more easily with an individual who has been recently disabled, who was until recently more like themselves.[63] Disciplining a disabled worker is often a problem because of the supervisor's guilt about being healthy. It is important to treat a disabled person as you would anyone else as long as the expectations are appropriate to the handicap. The important thing is for the supervisor to be clear as to how much the worker can be expected to do. Disabled persons are as much a part of the team as anyone else. If team members need to perform some of their duties, they can reciprocate by doing extra things for others, too.

People who are handicapped mentally pose a different type of problem because they are not always able to be clear themselves about how much they can do. The disability may be one such as dyslexia, which is an inability to read and/or write accurately but which does not indicate low intelligence. In fact, many brilliant people are dyslexic. In comparison, there are mild forms of mental retardation where people can adequately perform some very easy and routine tasks, but such people may have too limited intelligence to initiate ideas or improve on their own. Trial and error will usually provide a sensitive supervisor with information needed. In other words, observe and test.

Young Workers

If you are an older supervisor and you have a very young work force, it is important for you to understand some of the value shifts that have occurred between the time of your youth and today. The younger hourly worker does not necessarily accept the authority of a plant manager or a union steward as a matter of course. But they do expect to get increased leisure time, child care, maternity and paternity leave, a pleasant work atmosphere, and consideration for their family obligations. Put another way, today's young workers are examining the quality of their work life and insisting that it be improved. A study by a large public utility found that the average age of their workers who had less than three years experience was about 26, while the average age of their workers with more than three years experience was 46. This suggests a high turnover in entry-level jobs, which will continue unless companies start to make those beginning jobs more desirable.

Unions are not immune to this trend. Currently, young members make up 25 percent to 35 percent of all union memberships. One of every four union members is under 30 and more than one-third of the workers in the rubber industry are under 25. The United Steel Workers Union reports that most steel union members are under 30. Forty percent of the union members in the auto industry have had less than five years of service. Of General Motors'

200,000 UAW members, about 35 percent of the rank-and-file workers are under the age of 30, and that is typical throughout the industry. The new breed of young workers, on average, is better educated than the older workers on the job. In 1980, only one in 16 adult workers had less than eight years of schooling, and seven of every 10 adult workers had completed at least four years of high school. Considering a labor force of about 100 million in the 1980s, these ratios are translated into about seven million workers with less than eight years of schooling, but 70 million workers with a high school education and two million workers who have completed at least four years of college. This certainly represents a major change in the educational background of workers.

The work-related point here is that the better-educated workers have a different self-image, a stronger sense of self-respect, a wish to be treated more like individuals, much less tolerance for authoritarianism and organizational restraints, and a different and higher level of expectations concerning what they want to put into a job and what they want to get out of it.

There is evidence that young people want to participate in some way in the decisions that affect them and their jobs. This is exciting news for a supervisor and a company that hopes to improve and expand; it is threatening news to those who prefer to stand still. The way to deal with these workers is to go out and listen to them, ask questions, and find out what they need in order to perform more effectively. Some of the goals the new young workers in a plant might have are better machine maintenance, better tools, cleanliness of toilets and eating areas, a fair promotion system, more helpful supervisors who can recognize and reward good worker performance. Money is rarely the basic issue among the young workers.[64]

While older workers are more accepting of circumstances, many younger workers believe that society really can be improved. Younger workers have more material goods than their fathers ever had, and they want more. Television has shown them what rich people have, suggested that it is readily accessible, and they want some of these things, too.

If you listen carefully to what young people have to say, you will find that they often make sense. The only problem with your asking many questions is that you may encourage workers to believe that a change will certainly occur. You must be very careful not to promise or even to imply such a promise; just because you are asking for opinions does not mean you have the power to institute change. In fact, if you accumulate information of this nature that you will not be able to act on, it is important for you to comment to your work force about it so that they won't blame you for soliciting their input and then not using it.

Older Workers or Workers About to Retire

If you are a young supervisor and have an older work force, you will face some of the values and issues you have faced with your own parents so that whatever conflict you may have felt with your family you may again feel with your older workers. If you are an older supervisor dealing with a younger work force and if you have been disapproving of your own children, this disapproval may be carried into the relationship with younger workers. The same thing can occur when a supervisor is younger and has workers who are older. If you have been fighting with your father because of the way he rigidly wants things done or the way he adheres to the rules, and you have workers who behave in a similar way, it might frustrate you much more than if family relationships were not similar. Be aware of what's happening. You may not be able to change you initial reaction, but you *can* change your behavior.

There may be demands that older workers learn new technology and adapt to different situations. Many cannot or will not adapt because they value the way things have always been done. They do not understand the benefit of changing, and they may feel pressure and stress about change. There may be a period where they feel uncomfortably deskilled while they're learning something new. They may fear being shown up or ridiculed by younger people, and thus feel that they are inadequate and failures. As a young supervisor, you need to be sensitive and compassionate. The chances are that they think they have a supervisor who is too young to understand either them or the requirements of their job.

You may have more to learn than you realize from your older work force. There are tried and true ways of doing things—so don't necessarily change everything just because you have learned some new techniques or have taken a course or earned a degree, even when you're convinced that your way is best. In order to keep a satisfied work force, you should be willing to compromise and to use someone else's ideas in order to show respect and not ride roughshod over your workers' feelings. You can make changes gradually and have them accepted without challenge. It is essential for you not to rush them.

Culturally or Ethnically or Racially Different Workers

Many of us have been raised with a specific value system we hold dear and believe is the best. But you may have a different value system from that of your work force. Comfort lies with the known, the predictable. If your workers' backgrounds are not familiar to you, you may feel inadequate because you cannot predict their behavior. You may become judgmental in order to protect yourself and assume that your workers are wrong and you are right. Be careful not to evaluate people as poor workers just because they make you feel uncomfortable.

If you are a spontaneous person whose friendly overtures to Asian workers are met with aloofness, it is not necessarily because they are cold—it is because distance in Asian cultures is a sign of respect. To be friendly to you would be seen as being disrespectful to the boss.

Knowing and Knowledge

What children know
is soon forgotten
when replaced by learning

What women know
is discounted
in a man's world

What black people know
is devalued
in a white society

When knowing
is replaced by knowledge
we lose touch
with the truth

Other-Gender Workers

If you're a man and you're supervising women, or if you're a woman and supervising men, you will find some differences in the culturally different value systems that have been part of the socialization process of the opposite gender. If people's value systems are unfamiliar to you, all you can do is talk to them and learn about them. Ask questions and listen carefully. If you, as a supervisor, acquire good listening skills in order to understand your work force and what their needs are, you can then supervise them effectively, rather than acting in every situation according to your own values, needs, and preferences.

Men and women are raised differently today with different expectations that start at the cradle. When parents are asked to make comments about a baby dressed in a pink dress, they might say that she is cuddly, cute, feminine, charming, and fragile, while the *same baby* dressed in little blue pants may elicit comments such as, "You can tell he's a tough little boy, look at his muscles, he'll be an athlete, a real winner." Thus, parents have feelings that they turn into expectations, and the child will be rewarded for fulfilling them. Research has shown that when a little girl cries, the mother assumes the reason to be pain and will run to her more quickly than to a little boy because his cries are interpreted as anger. Infant boys learn to fend for themselves for longer periods when distressed than little girls do.[65]

How this affects a child's future behavior is not clear, but that it does affect it is evident. In what way has your own socialization influenced your behavior? In what way will it make you more or less tolerant of the behavior and values of the opposite sex? If you supervise people of a gender different from yours, you need to answer these questions for yourself.

Temporary Workers

Given skyrocketing operating costs, organizations are seeking ways to reduce what they budget for personnel. One way is to use more specialized temporary workers, often referred to as "temps." They enable an organization to delay adding permanent workers or to obtain unique expertise needed only for a brief period of time.

These workers fall into two categories: those with specialized or professional skills, and those with relatively simpler skills, such as clerical, maintenance, or manual skills. Temporary workers with highly specialized or professional skills can be used for temporarily expanded operations, one-time projects, start-up operations of new facilities, and the like. Highly skilled temporary workers can also help train permanent workers in the performance of tasks while these permanent employees are being trained. They can provide the skills and talents needed but not possessed by permanent workers. The budgeting drawback is that temporarily hired specialized people usually charge high fees.

Organizations involved in the process of technological conversions may also use temporaries. The use of clerical temporaries is probably more common than the use of temporary professionals. Clerical temporaries are more frequently used during peak work periods, vacation periods, periods of extended employee absence, or during relocation of facilities. Although temporary workers may like to work at top efficiency, their loyalty probably rests with the employing organization that has recruited, selected, and hired them.[66] Temporaries usually require less orientation and preparation prior to becoming productive on the job. The supervisor's task then becomes one of acquainting the temporary with the company's customs, procedures, and policies that are important to getting the job done.

Such instruction is important. It is important for you to know the skills, abilities, and past experiences of temporary workers before they arrive on the job. This will help you plan the degree and amount of orientation and instruction needed to make the person fully productive. Speak with respect about your temporary workers, and avoid disparaging comments such as, "They are *only* temporary employees!" Prepare your permanent workers for the arrival of the temporaries. You may want to assure them that the need for the temporary worker is not an indication that the regulars have been performing under par. Discuss any suggestions or concerns your permanent workers may have regarding the use of a temporary.

Clarify your expectations to the temporaries—they are hired to do a specific job. Document the performance of temporary workers as you would any other worker because your personnel department will probably want to know whether the agency that has sent them is a reliable agency that has a roster of good people. Performance evaluations may also be requested by the sponsoring agency for its records. The temporary worker often brings specialized skills and abilities to your department through training and the experience gained from assignments in other organizations. If the temporary workers are more efficient and proficient in certain activities, you will have to resist the temptation to compare their work with that of your permanent ones.

Pregnant Workers

Twenty-one states have laws or guidelines that extend some form of legal coverage to employed pregnant women. You should know the regulations of your state and the policies of your company.

Do not make assumptions about the lack of work commitment of pregnant women. Most will probably want to return to work later and assume their full responsibilities. What you will have to do as a supervisor is to make budgetary decisions on whether you should use a temporary worker to replace your worker on maternity leave, or whether you should distribute her work among your other workers. The second choice may present problems of overloading workers, without compensation—so be sure that there is some reward like overtime or time off for those who have helped out until her return, or at least give recognition for the extra effort.

Regulations require you to keep a job open for a woman on maternity leave. The last month before her leave may be difficult because she may tire more quickly; the first weeks of her return may be equally difficult because she probably has been up late at night with an infant.

I believe that organizations should provide a small room with a couch for exhausted workers who may wish to take a short nap during their lunch hour. The more sympathetic you are in helping to make the transition to motherhood, the easier that transition will be for your workers. However, within a reasonable period of time, you can expect your worker to be back at the original productivity level. Don't overlook fathers. Paternity leaves are much talked about, and you may get requests for them. Many people believe that paternity leaves are as legitimate as maternity leaves. Even if one of your male workers does not take a leave, you can expect him also to be more tired because of being up with a new baby all night. He may come in later or leave early in order to help with the household chores. You can negotiate with him for a temorary cut in salary or can expect that when things settle down, he will be willing to work later for a while to make up for lost time. Again, if you're sympathetic, you'll have grateful workers who will work harder when they are able to.

If you schedule a maternity leave for yourself, be sure to train someone to do your job. Your replacement can be a colleague or a person hired from outside the company. Be careful about accepting your boss's offer just to manage without you. If you're not needed while you're gone, you may not be needed when you want to return.

Your substitute should be completely trained by your eighth month in case your baby arrives early. Once your baby has arrived, set aside a time of day when your substitute can call you at home, instead of having countless calls that interrupt you during the day.[67]

Supervisor's Guide for Workers Who May Be Suffering from a Personal Problem[68]

Human beings tend to behave in habitual ways. An individual's work pattern has generally been established in the first two years of employment. Workers with occasional "normal" variations will maintain this behavior pattern throughout their tenure except when some personal problems or major change in life-style occurs.

Workers suffering from alcoholism, emotional, behavioral, or other personal problems can be identified by unsatisfactory job performance. When a previously satisfactory worker develops a pattern of a deteriorating or erratic job performance, something of significance has occurred to alter that worker's behavior.

Deteriorating or erratic job performance because of preoccupation with personal problems is noticeable. It is manifested in a variety of ways, such as increased absenteeism, substandard quality and quantity of work, higher accident rates and frequent compensation claims, safety violations, and impairment of relationships with coworkers and supervisors. Although every problem worker will behave differently, *the key to early identification of such a worker lies in the supervisor's keeping a file with descriptions of the events.*

It is the supervisor's responsibility to identify an individual as needing assistance beyond what the supervisor can provide based on one or more of the following:

1. Poor attendance
2. Inability to report to work on time and to maintain a regular work schedule
3. Dramatic lessening of worker's efficiency in job performance
4. Frequent absence from the assigned work area
5. On-the-job performance that jeopardizes the safety and health of other workers
6. Abnormal number of early quitting times
7. Development of absentee pattern
8. Unusual or belligerent attitude toward fellow workers
9. Reporting to work in unfit physical condition

In the event that one or more of the above factors is present and you have probable cause to believe the situation may be problem-related, you should, after consultation with the department supervisor, offer the worker a referral to an appropriate agency or counseling service.

Under no circumstances should you confront individuals with the statement that they are alcoholics or drug addicts and so on. *It is not the position of the supervisor to impose this type of judgment on any individual.*

The following are some do's and dont's for supervisors:

1. DON'T try to diagnose workers' problems.
2. DON'T discuss drinking or a similar problem with them unless it occurs on the job.
3. DON'T moralize. Restrict criticism to job performance or attendance.
4. DON'T be misled by workers' sympathy-evoking tactics, at which they may be experts.
5. DON'T cover up for friends. Your misguided kindness can lead to a serious delay in having real help reaching them.
6. DO remember that personal problems get worse, never better, without treatment or assistance.
7. DO make it clear that you are concerned only with job performance. Unless job performance improves, the worker's job is in jeopardy.

8. DO explain that workers must decide for themselves whether or not to seek assistance.

The following are tips on how to deal with troubled workers:

1. Establish the levels of work performance that you expect. Determine what is acceptable and unacceptable to you.
2. Record all absenteeism, poor job performance, and related matters. Specific behavioral criteria are necessary for you to evaluate the situation.
3. Keep your own supervisor advised regarding details of the situation and of your intended course of action.
4. Set up a private interview with the troubled workers and allow ample time for it.
5. Plan in advance what you intend to cover. Make notes for reference during the interview. In your planning, tailor your approach to your knowledge of workers and their personality traits.
6. Keep the interview impersonal. Be firm and friendly. Don't require abject submission or agreement; you want the person to change behavior, not just to say yes.
7. Don't accuse or recriminate. Stick to a discussion of the behavior that must change; your objective is to correct workers' observable behavior, not their personality.
8. State the problem clearly, as you understand it. Be specific; don't exaggerate; avoid unsupportable generalizations.
9. Stick to the subject. Don't apologize for the interview or find excuses for the worker's behavior. Avoid "softening up" by praising. Don't let yourself get trapped into lengthy discussions on a different topic.
10. Use examples that you can relate to standards of performance and behavior.
11. Maintain a helpful attitude. Work sincerely with the workers to plan for a change.
12. Listen to a worker's side of the story. Don't jump to conclusions. Look for mitigating circumstances.
13. Respect a worker's dignity and right to a viewpoint.
14. Stay calm. Don't bluff or threaten. Don't argue. You're there to solve a problem.
15. Share the blame gracefully if you're at fault yourself.

16. Be aboveboard. Don't harass. Don't entrap.
17. Work together toward a solution to the problem. State minimum standards for change required.
18. Set a deadline for specific measurable change.
19. Take adequate notes during the interview.
20. Summarize the discussion.
21. Express confidence in the worker's ability to improve. Make clear that this confidence has been implicit in your decision to have the interview, and in the plan you have worked out.
22. Set a time for a progress review.

As soon as a pattern of erratic, deteriorating, or unsatisfactory job performance occurs, discuss the situation with the worker. Reemphasize what you and the company expect in terms of performance and specify a reasonable period of time for the worker to demonstrate improvement.

Exercise

If you think you have a problem worker, fill out the following checklist. It will give you an indication of the severity of the problem. Then use the tips given in this chapter.

SUPERVISOR'S CHECKLIST[69]

EMPLOYEE NAME ____________________ **SS#** __________

Place an X-mark next to each characteristic you have noted in the above-named employee.

1. *Absenteeism*

_______a. Multiple instances of leaving work area without authorization

_______b. Excessive sick leave

_______c. Frequent Monday and/or Friday absences

_______d. Excessive tardiness, especially on Monday mornings or in returning from lunch

_______e. Leaving work early

_______f. Peculiar and increasingly improbable excuses for absence _______g. Higher absenteeism rate than other employees

2. *On-the-Job Absenteeism*
   _______a. Frequent absence from assigned work area
   _______b. Frequent trips to water fountain or rest room
   _______c. Long coffee breaks
3. *High Accident Rate*
   _______a. On-the-job behavior jeopardizing the safety and health of self or other employees
   _______b. Accidents on the job
   _______c. Accidents off the job (but affecting job performance)
4. *Difficulty in Concentration*
   _______a. Work requires greater effort
   _______b. Jobs take more time
5. *Confusion*
   _______a. Difficulty in recalling instructions, details, and so on
   _______b. Increasing difficulty in handling assignments
   _______c. Difficulty in recalling own mistakes
6. *Spasmodic Work Patterns*
   _______a. Alternate periods of high and low productivity
7. *Generally Lowered Job Efficiency*
   _______a. Missed deadlines
   _______b. Mistakes due to inattention or poor judgment
   _______c. Wasting material
   _______d. Making bad decisions
   _______e. Improbable excuses for poor job performance
8. *Poor Employee Relationships On the Job*
   _______a. Belligerent attitude toward fellow employees
   _______b. Overreaction to real or imagined criticism
   _______c. Wide swings in morale
   _______d. Borrowing money from coworkers
   _______e. Complaints from coworkers
   _______f. Unreasonable resentments

_______g. Avoidance of coworkers
_______h. Inappropriate number of calls during work
_______i. Other _______________________________

9. *Personal Health and Hygiene*
_______a. Reporting to work in unfit physical condition.
_______b. Frequent physical complaints
_______c. Deterioration of personal appearance

PART VI

BUILDING LEADERSHIP

12

TEAM BUILDING AND GROUP SKILLS

Although most of us have been raised in families with a mother, a father, and one or two brothers or sisters, some people today have been brought up in single-parent families or with a frequently absent parent. The family is the first group that children belong to; they learn about group life from the way their family group functioned. A child who has been raised in a family with a very authoritarian father will feel and act differently in groups than one who has been raised with a single working mother who was often absent. The single child will have a very different experience than one with many siblings. The older child who is used to taking on leadership roles and making decisions will be a very different group member from the baby of the family for whom decisions were always made and whose opinion was frequently considered of little value.

Think about your own family as a group and reflect on its dynamics. What was your position in it? Who was in charge? Did it work? Who rebelled? How? Who compromised? Who gave in? And how did you feel about all of these events? Then think through how you usually behave when in a group. Do you talk or do you remain silent? Do you initiate ideas? Do you support others? Do you confront others when you disagree? Do you translate ideas into actions and make suggestions for methods? Do you sit sulking and feeling frustrated at the stupidity of others? Do you doodle during a meeting you think is useless and too long? Do people pay attention when you talk, or do you have to say something three times until you are finally listened to? Do people make eye contact with you? With whom do you have eye contact? Ask yourself these questions, and you will begin to see your own pattern as a group member.

Just as you follow a pattern when you function in a group, so do your workers. Start observing how your team of workers functions. Who is the leader? Who are the followers? Do the followers go along reluctantly or willingly? Is there competition for control of your team? Do you think people are afraid to speak up, to contradict, or to give suggestions? Do some people seem invisible, sitting there as if they were not there at all? Are there others who seem to talk too much? Is the discussion on target, or does it ramble? Is there one person who seems to be very critical or even hostile, and is that person feared? Is disagreement handled comfortably, or is it considered a threat to group harmony? Do people seem to like one another and share some basic values and goals? And if they don't, are they tolerant of the differences? As you look for answers to these questions, you will become more skilled at observing group dynamics and understanding the people who are working for you. This will help you lead group meetings more effectively.

Meetings

As you enter a new job, you should find out what people are used to, as far as meetings are concerned—how often they are held, how long they last, who calls them, who sets the agenda, and how people feel about them. Some regard meetings as opportunities to socialize; to others they offer the pleasure of accomplishing a task with coworkers; and to others they are a burden and a waste of time. Some people see them as chances to make themselves prominent. Some people enjoy being in groups, others do not. Even if your organization does not have meetings, it is important for you to institute them because meetings are one way of keeping tabs on the relationships among your workers.

You should provide a forum for them to discuss ideas, needs, and expectations. Depending on the agenda you set, you can conduct problem-solving sessions on cost effectiveness, or you can hold sessions to develop innovative ways of doing a routine job, or you can discuss new techniques. Because people are social beings, they like to meet with one another and hear about what is going on. Studies have found that people are more productive when they have an opportunity to communicate with others. It is good for people to meet together when they are in the same field and also outside it, because they bring different perspectives and novel suggestions.[70] Some supervisors have meetings only to reiterate company goals or concerns and to make people feel part of a team. This may be a sufficient reason. Many companies have them for this sole purpose, because no major decisions need to be made within the work group. If that is the case, keep them short and do not schedule them too frequently.

A good way to start your first meeting is by asking people to voice some of their concerns and give ideas as to what they wish would be done. They should also say what is going well and what they want to see continued. This is the appropriate time for you to talk about some of your thoughts, or, if you feel it is too early because you're a new supervisor, you may just say you are gathering ideas and want to hear from others before formulating your own. This is a legitimate reason to hold a first meeting. Be careful not to be too quick to give suggestions, to make demands, or to criticize. Give yourself time to observe.

Running a Meeting

Even though meetings may be held at regularly scheduled times, reminders are important, and people should be given plenty of notice before a meeting is held. If there is an agenda, it should be shared prior to the meeting. If people have the opportunity to think about a topic, they will be better prepared to discuss it. It is important for you to start the meeting on time even though not everyone is there so that you will create a precedent of punctuality. It is also important that you tell people when it will be over, and then end it at that time.

Begin by presenting your agenda and asking if anyone has anything to add to it. The agenda can be posted on a bulletin board or printed and distributed, with items listed by priority, especially if it appears that there will be insufficient time to deal with everything. If you need to cover *all* the items and time is limited, you may wish to put a time limit on the discussion for each item. For instance, item 2 can be discussed for ten minutes, item 3 for

20 minutes, and item 4 can probably be dealt with in five minutes. If, during the meeting, you see people fidgeting, you may decide to take a five-minute break. I find it helpful to have coffee and decaffeinated drinks available.

If the meeting is to be long and your work force is tired, cheese and crackers or fruit are nice additions to a meeting. I do not recommend Danish pastries and doughnuts. Even though they give people a quick surge of energy, there is also a faster loss of energy in the long run.

If you wish to have notes taken, you may want to delegate this task—unless you want to do it yourself for your own information. You can make procedural rules. For example, you could say, "If I see that we are not discussing the topic, I want to feel free to get people back on track." Or you may say, "If I see that we are taking longer than necessary to discuss an item, I will feel free to stop the person speaking." You can also say that you don't expect people to agree with you and that you believe disagreement is healthy, for open discussion creates the opportunity for new ideas to be expressed; but that if it is evident that a particular topic generates hostile exchanges that are not fruitful, you will stop it and go on to another topic. You will make some decisions on your own; you will delegate other decisions, and still others will be made by consensus. Your workers should know in which decisions they will have input and how much, and in which decisions they will not.

Long Boring Meetings

Long meeting
long and boring
people talking on and on
my eyelids feel heavy
my eyes are closing
in spite of myself

I wiggle my toes
fidget in my chair
draw doodles
chew gum
trying to stay awake

My head is nodding
it falls forward
I startle
have I been asleep?

Maybe no one noticed. . . .

What Kind of Group Do You Have?

Each group has its norms. You should find out the norms of your group, especially if the group existed before you became supervisor. If it is a new group, then the norms will develop along the way, and you should observe how they evolve. The following are some norms you may wish to pay attention to:

Are people friendly?
Does everyone participate?
Do people understand the issues?
Are people free to disagree or are they afraid to?
Do people say yes whether or not they mean it?
Are they able to criticize each other's ideas or do they personalize and criticize each other?
Can feelings be expressed openly?
Are you the only leader or is leadership shared?
Is the group able to talk about the way they work?
Are they only task-oriented and unwilling to look at how they function as a group or do they discuss only how they are working as a group and do not accomplish the task?

One of the more important things to remember about any group meeting is that decisions that have been made need implementing. To accomplish this before the meeting breaks up, assignments must be made as to who should perform what task and by when. Meetings that end with "Yes, it's a good idea, let's do it," will not result in action unless a particular member or members are assigned to accomplish specific tasks. If the group members have come to a decision and it is not going to be implemented in the immediate future, that decision will need to be recorded for future action so that the group does not have to go through the whole process again. Groups that have rotating membership very often fall into the trap of deciding the same thing over and over again. This rehashing may be fruitful because it builds a consensus. Decisions will only be implemented if there is commitment. Commitment comes from the opportunity of having participated in the decision-making process, which affects the workers or their work. It is important for the supervisor to periodically review the past recommendations of any such group.

Again, we must be wary of cultural differences. Deference to authority may be so strong in some members of a group that they will not be able to be effective team members but will agree only to whatever others have decided, especially if it means agreeing with the boss. For others, being in a group situation may revive old competitive attitudes that they experienced in their families. They will revert to ineffective behavior, attempt to gain control of the group, and become angrier than the situation warrants when their ideas are not implemented or when they are contradicted.

As a supervisor and group leader, you should anticipate and confront this dysfunctional behavior by requesting opinions from the silent members and by telling your belligerent members that their fighting for control is not helpful. If this seems too strong a measure in a group situation where it might upset your angry worker, you may wish to speak to that person in private about the behavior you feel blocks the successful accomplishment of the task. You may wish to solicit this worker in running the meeting more effectively so that this person becomes your ally and not one who sabotages your efforts.

A good working team is one that is creative, has energy, and has a sense of fun. If you see that the same people are doing the same things year after year, find out if this situation is really satisfactory. If organizational rewards go to those who do the most routine jobs instead of those who are risk-takers with innovative ideas, perhaps your company has reached a level that is too stable for its own good.

In order to have a creative organization, it is important to include different types of people. People of different genders, races, ethnic origins, cultures, ages, and educational levels should be mixed as much as possible. Not only should these people coexist, but their channels of communication should also be open. Encourage contact with outside sources so that people do not become inbred. Don't rely on stereotypes such as "This is the way we've always done it,'' but be sure to listen to new ideas.[71] If you, the supervisor, are not open to new ways, your workers won't listen to new ideas either. You can help your staff to examine new attitudes, ideas, beliefs, and values—if you are willing to do that yourself.

It is important for you to reward your workers for being cooperative, lending supplies to one another, helping coworkers, and replacing one another when necessary. This spirit of cooperation creates an atmosphere that is pleasant to work in rather than a hostile one where workers do just their own jobs and pay no attention to anyone else. People respond to helpfulness from others in very positive ways. Again, you as a supervisor can set the mood and the model by behaving cooperatively yourself.

It is up to you to help your workers feel that they are a team, a unit in the department, and not just single entities working separately from one another. If there are no jobs your workers have in common, you may wish to institute a group project or a group outing to give them opportunities to get to know each other outside of the work setting.

The Chance to Reciprocate

If every one of us
who looks good
makes the rest of us
look better
And if the rising tide
lifts all ships

Why do we still compete
instead of helping each other?
Need we keep others down
in order to elevate ourselves?

If I help you today
I will be helped tomorrow
because the world
is not made up of bastards
but of people who would like
the chance to reciprocate

Intergroup Dynamics

Suppose that you have more than one unit you are supervising or that a colleague of yours is also supervising a unit. To work well with one group is difficult, but to make several groups work together effectively is even more so. In this situation, you may wish to instill some competition because many people are challenged to excel by comparing themselves or their unit to other units. The problem with intergroup competition is that sometimes the company's goals are lost and the people compete in ways that do not promote the company's objectives.

If, for example, two units are assigned to produce parts of a product but, because of their feelings of intense competition, one team sabotages the efforts of the other, obviously the second team will come out as best; but the company will have lost time and money. It is important for a supervisor not to show favoritism either to individual employees or to units, departments, or groups. Even the fairest supervisor is often seen as being unfair by the people or groups who have not come up to standard; and rather than take the responsibility for their performance, they will blame their shortcomings on their supervisor's lack of judgment. As long as you can hold back your own prejudices—which are directed not only to individuals but to groups—then your preference does not need to be an obstacle.

If you have groups that are very competitive, and if intergroup conflict seems to be emerging, there are some things you can do. One is to establish forced lines of communication by creating work groups with members from each team. Studies have found that the more interaction among people and the more they come to know one another, the better they can accept each other. It is only when people have no access to information about the other teams' members that destructive myths are created about "the others."

As each group forms an identity, members become more attached to their own group. The consciousness that this is "my group" also carries with it a tendency to think better of one's group members than of those of other groups. One also becomes loyal to one's group, has a higher regard for its ideas and output, and disparages the ideas and output of other groups. This, of course, may increase the distance and arguments between groups.

A supervisor can help groups look for points of similarity—there may be more similarities than many people believe. If you need to negotiate differences, see what good points exist in each group, and try to arrive at a compromise using the best features of both. If conflicts are strong, you may wish to include members of the various units in a new problem-solving group to develop ways of working together. Then these members will have loyalty not only to their old group but also to the interrelating group to which they now belong.

The following are stumbling blocks to effective intergroup work:[72]

1. When a group forms, it acquires an identity to which members become attached even before they have much of an awareness of it. This identity gets stronger as the group continues and especially if it feels successful.
2. Thus, consciousness that "this is my group" also carries with it a tendency to think better of "my" group than of other groups of approximately the same status.
3. This leads to the feeling that the ideas of "my" group are better than the ideas of the other groups and should be defended as such. These are reinforced by feelings of loyalty to one's own group and its members.
4. The inclination to defend one's own group's ideas as better leads members to listen selectively. When listening to the other group's ideas, members listen for weaknesses in order to criticize. When listening to ideas of their own group, members listen for points that reinforce the desirability of their own group's position.
5. Thus, the tendency is to increase argument, widen the distance between groups, decrease the likelihood of collaboration, and intensify competitiveness. (A desire to push one's own group's ideas at the expense of other groups.)
6. When representatives handle the relations between groups where collaboration on work is necessary, the following phenomena tend to appear:
   a) *If* the groups have been together long enough so that members know one another's talents, the most task-oriented people tend to be selected. The reason is that these people are seen as best able to articulate the

substance (content) of their group's ideas. But little attention is usually paid to negotiating or interpersonal skills. Very often task-oriented people—who focus most strongly on content—are weak interpersonally or not very conscious of the impact of interpersonal exchange. Thus, representatives chosen on such a basis tend to argue harder, dig in their heels, increase competitiveness, and produce more polarization.

b) Representatives feel greater loyalty to their group exactly because they have been selected to represent its point of view. Therefore, they are more resistant to compromise for fear of "selling out" or of being seen as selling out.

Just as most people have hidden agendas, so do most groups want things that they do not reveal publicly. It is important for a supervisor to try to find out what it is that the various workers and groups may have as hidden agendas. What do they really want for themselves? Is it higher status, recognition, winning in the competition, more allocation of resources, preferential treatment, more time off for different pursuits, or time to do more research? Some groups have such a good time together they will look for any excuse to meet, which may not always be productive for the organization.

How Groups Develop

All groups go through predictable phases.[73] In phase one, people need to get to know and observe one another, forming first impressions. This is the *dependence* phase of group life. People tend to depend on a leader to tell them what they should be doing. The issue here is membership—who will be included and who will be excluded.

As a supervisor in phase one, accept the fact that people will look to you for direction. This means setting the agenda, setting priorities and time limits, and deciding on how to proceed. As a group leader, you are the model and set the norms of behavior. Unless you exert too much control, this phase does not last a long time.

In phase two, the group goes through *counterdependence*. Members begin to struggle for control over the group either overtly by challenging the leader or covertly by sabotaging the leader. The issue here is who is in charge and who follows. As a supervisor in phase two, you will notice one or more of the following behaviors: disagreement with you—strong or subtle; noncommitment to the task you suggest; procrastination or sidetracking; delay in getting the meeting under way; apathy, which is a form of passive rebellion. These behaviors are merely ways to challenge your leadership and competence. Don't take it personally—most groups go through this phase in one form or another. If you persevere, giving your people enough autonomy yet remaining the person in charge, your group will move into the next phase.

In phase three, the group achieves *independence,* which means that it has established norms and can work effectively. There is less need for strong leadership. People are resources for one another, and thus group members develop mutual affection. Here the issue of the group is—who is friendly with whom and who is distant. As a supervisor in phase three, you should become less in charge, control less, and be sure that everyone participates.

The last phase is *interdependence*. During this phase, people are performing at their peak; they can be both task oriented and concerned about people; the leader becomes a member; there are no issues over who is in, who is out, who is up, or who is down. Group members feel a great deal of intimacy, as if they were members of a family, and look forward to meeting and working together. This is a very productive time in a group.[74] There is a lot of pleasure in being members of such a group, and they enjoy it.

Observation Guide

Listen closely and watch the members of your group to pick up any nonverbal behavior. The following questions will help you to know what to look for:

1. **Participation:** Did everyone participate? Were some excluded? Was an effort made to draw people out? Did a few dominate? Did anyone withdraw?
2. **Leadership:** Did a leader emerge or was leadership shared? Was the group ever devoid of leadership? If so, what happened? Did a leadership struggle exist?

3. **Roles:** Who initiated ideas? Were they supported and by whom? Did anyone block suggestions? Who helped push for decisions? When ideas and suggestions were presented to the group, who picked them up, or were they immediately dropped? Who helped to establish and maintain good working relationships among the members of the group?
4. **Decision-Making:** Did the group suggest a lot of ideas before beginning to decide, or did it begin deciding after only one idea? Who agreed to the decisions made? Who helped influence the decisions of others? Were attempts made to summarize and pull together various ideas? What issues did the group seem to resolve? Not resolve?
5. **Communication:** Did people feel free to talk? Was there any interrupting or cutting people off? Did people listen to one another? Was there clarification of points made? Whom did people look at when they talked—specific people or no one in particular?
6. **Sensitivity:** Were members sensitive to the needs and concerns of each other? What feelings did you see being expressed either verbally or nonverbally?
7. **Openness:** Were people frank and open with each other? Did they share with the group their true feelings and concerns? Were differences confronted openly and honestly? If openness was not the norm, how did it affect the group?

Exercise

Diagnose the various members of your team in terms of their group behaviors. Make note of what you see as their strengths and weaknesses in functioning as members of a team by answering, "X is good at..." or "Y could improve on..." For example, Mary may be good at generating ideas, but she is poor at listening to anyone else's ideas. You will conduct better meetings once you understand the dynamics inherent in all groups.

13

POWER POLITICS

By now you should know how to interview, orient, train, delegate, manage your time, deal with stress, run meetings, and make decisions. You also know about the generation gap, sexual issues, and race relations. What else do you still need to know? You should understand about power, leadership, and influence. You also need to know about office politics. Why? Because, whether you want to or not, you are part of a game that is being played out every day at your place of work.

Everyone has a hidden agenda of personal expectations and needs. Your boss wants you to make him or her look good, your subordinates have their expectations, and you have your own needs; and these may or may not be in conflict. Whatever the case, you must try to figure out what you want, as well as what everyone else wants. You must do a hidden agenda analysis. Because people keep their agendas secret, you have to rely on minimal clues in order to know what others won't tell. If you ignore office politics, you can be blamed for what is not under your control and not be rewarded for your accomplishments. If you want to get into the game, it doesn't help to say, ''I don't like to play politics''—you must know the rules and play by them. Once you're in the game, you can change the rules, but by then you may be like most people who are satisfied just to go along and not rock the boat.

To do a hidden agenda analysis, assume that people have likes and dislikes, strengths and vulnerabilities, secrets and hidden fears. You will also want to know the special needs of the various units or departments.

Your chart may look like this:

My Boss

Likes	Dislikes
1. His colleague Joe	1. His boss
2. Harry's secretary	2. Sloppy work
3. To play golf on weekends	3. Travel
4. Long lunches	4. Dealing with conflict

Strengths	Vulnerabilities
1. Delegates well	1. Drinks too much
2. Is trusting	2. Is lazy

Secret Hopes	Hidden Fears
1. To get promoted	1. To be seen as incompetent
2. To have more time outside of work	

Needs for His Department

1. Better cooperation from other departments
2. Clearer quality controls

If you take a look at this list, you will immediately see that you have a good chance of getting your boss's job, if that is what you want as your next career step. If he dislikes his boss, you can assume the feelings are mutual. Because your boss delegates well, you can take on more of his responsibilities, which he will welcome since he's lazy. Your strategy would be to be most competent in his weak areas. However, you also want to make your boss look good, so you must decide how much or how little you want his boss to notice you. Be very careful with your diagnosis—we're treading in very sensitive areas.

All departments have needs that are often in conflict. Each boss wants the largest share of the budget, the equipment, and the personnel. How this gets juggled and who allocates what to whom and on what basis are parts of what you must begin to understand. You won't find these written anywhere; you'll have to observe who calls the meetings, who attends, who sets the agenda, who has eye contact with whom, who interrupts whom, whose work gets done first, and who seems to be listened to and is respected. Do people talk behind the backs of others, and what is said?

You will soon begin to get an idea of who is *really* powerful and who has *real* influence. It may not be the person with the title and the large corner office. It is important to know who has power in your organization because it is the powerful people who can help you to get the resources you require, the information you need, and the promotion you want.

It is up to you to become known to your superiors, especially if you are of a different gender, race, age, or ethnic background. The "different" people tend to be ignored and have their work underrated. Since familiarity breeds promotions, work on projects with the powerful people; volunteer to help in community services or charitable organizations they are involved in; find ways to be seen and known by them. Remember that whatever you feel or think about your boss, your subordinates may feel and think about you. They will work with you in ways they think will enhance their chances at more interesting work and better pay.

There are many definitions of power, most of them quite abstract. I would like to propose a model in which you, the supervisor, are the center. You are then both the victim of the power others have over you *and* the wielder of power over others. Thus, we will discuss power from two points of view—who has power over you and whom you have power over.

Who Has Power Over You?

People such as your boss have *direct* power over you. They can give you what you want or take it away just as teachers have direct power over students through the process of grading.

Other people who have *indirect* power over you are your boss's boss, the company president, and policymakers in government. Their decisions will affect your life but are not aimed at you as an individual. For example, a loan officer at a bank from which I wish to borrow money may or may not have power over others but can certainly make a difference in my life. If people have direct power over you, you can try to influence them. However, if your company president makes a policy decision that may affect you, such as a change in the benefit structure, that person has only indirect power over you, and there is nothing you can do individually to change that policy, as illustrated on the chart below:

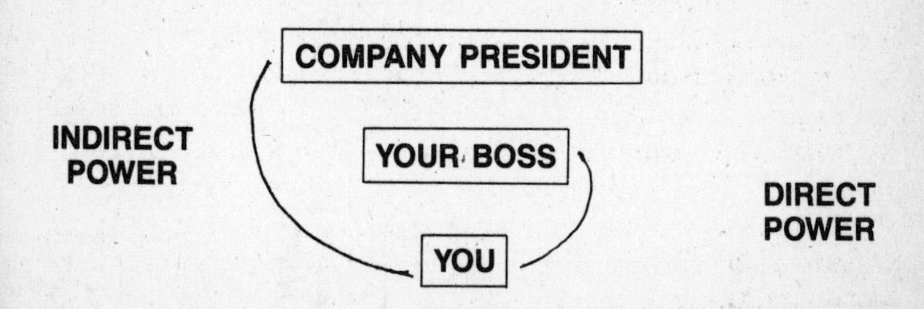

Your colleagues or other supervisors at your level have neither direct nor indirect power over you; but they can make your life easier or more difficult depending on whether they cooperate with you or compete against you. Other departments can also influence how well you get your work done. You have a reciprocal relationship with them, as shown below:

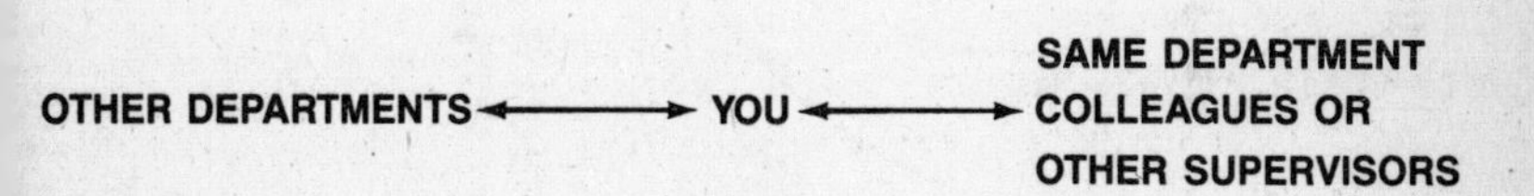

You have direct power over your subordinates because you make the decisions that affect their lives.

1. What you want from your workers is *performance.*
2. What you want from your colleagues or other supervisors is *cooperation.*
3. What you want from your boss is *information* and *autonomy.*
4. What you give your workers is good *training,* clear *standards* they can meet, and *fair treatment.*
5. What you give your colleagues is *cooperation.*
6. What you give your boss is *performance.*

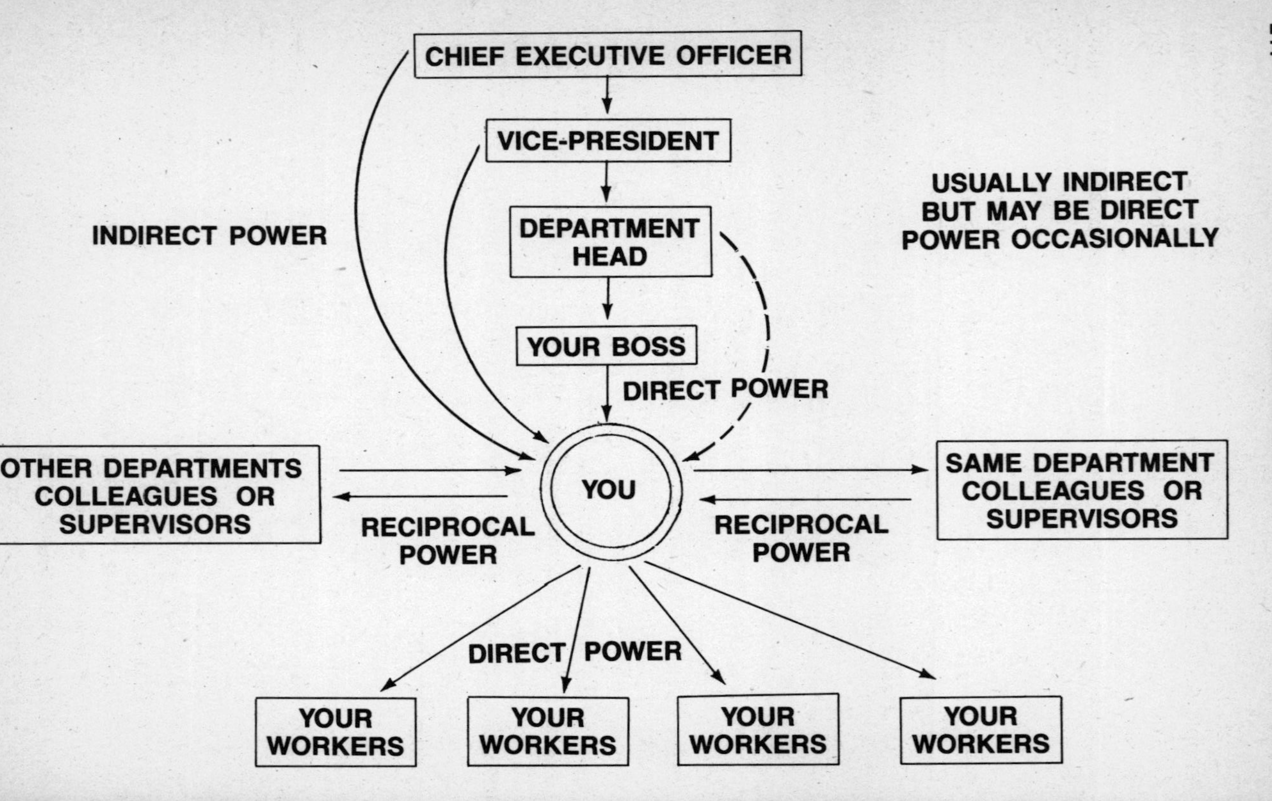
CHIEF EXECUTIVE OFFICER
VICE-PRESIDENT
DEPARTMENT HEAD
YOUR BOSS
INDIRECT POWER
USUALLY INDIRECT BUT MAY BE DIRECT POWER OCCASIONALLY
DIRECT POWER
OTHER DEPARTMENTS COLLEAGUES OR SUPERVISORS
YOU
SAME DEPARTMENT COLLEAGUES OR SUPERVISORS
RECIPROCAL POWER
RECIPROCAL POWER
DIRECT POWER
YOUR WORKERS
YOUR WORKERS
YOUR WORKERS
YOUR WORKERS

In all of these relationships, there is a power dimension. If people don't perform according to standards, they will be demoted or fired; if they perform well, they may be given bonuses or a promotion.

With other supervisors, if there is no reciprocity in an equal relationship, there may be sabotage; if there is cooperation, each one makes the other look better.

The only power that lower-level persons have over someone who has direct power over them is either trying to change things by complaining to the higher-ups or trying to make a supervisor look bad by not helping to achieve department goals. One secretary cannot complain to the senior manager about working conditions and expect results, but the whole secretarial pool may be able to effect a change.

Besides direct and indirect power, there is also a type of power not usually written about, and that is *attributed power.*

Power You Attribute to Others

Attributed power is unwarranted power that individuals *believe* someone possesses or will permit that person to exercise. Attributed power can be direct or indirect. It is indirect when one does not actually know the person, such as a healer seen on television, or an impressive lecturer. It is direct when one attributes power to a friend or colleague whom one respects, fears, or wants to please. It can seriously limit your authority when you give your power to someone you fear.

How can we tell when we are wrongly attributing power? You ask yourself, "What can these people do for me or against me: What can they give, withhold, or take away?" If you don't come up with specific answers, you may well be attributing power where none exists.

Let us take the example of a colleague of mine who is always slightly disparaging of me. Whenever I make a presentation, he notices the points I could have made but didn't; if I receive very high evaluations from my students, he inquires whether I gave them very high grades that semester; and whenever I speak about women's issues, he rolls his eyes up and shrugs his shoulders. He does not make me feel very good.

You might think that the normal behavior for me would be to

avoid him and ignore him. Instead, I find myself seeking eye contact with him or sending him my latest article, hoping to get a favorable reaction from him. What is going on? I'm attributing power to this colleague not because he has any power over me but because I have trouble with people disapproving of me or belittling me. I don't get angry; instead I try to "fix it" by doing better.

As long as I am not aware of my behavior, that behavior controls me, and I continue to act in those ways. My writing about this situation at this moment helps me to become aware of these dynamics, and from now on I will be able to deal with this colleague more appropriately because I have recognized that he is not in a position of power. In the future I will be able to stop attributing power to him.

One could easily argue here, and not wrongly so, that what is really going on is transference. In other words, I attributed to him qualities and faults that I found in people who had authority over me and who were judgmental of me in the past. His being judmental gave him a parental role toward me, and I added on other attributes that parents have, which are the attributes of power over a child. Only when I can recognize this situation can I stop attributing power to others who in fact may not have any.

Caring

There is still another way we are influenced in our behaviors, and that is through the act of *caring*. When we care so much about what another person may feel or think, we allow this to influence us. For example, if we care about a child, that child's cry can make us get up in the middle of the night. A friend's need may take priority over a task that we have to accomplish. Caring is an important aspect of the power we willingly give away.

Research has shown that women are more relationship-oriented than men.[75] If women care more what others feel and think than men do, they will then allow others more frequently to influence their behavior and thus give their power away more often. The belief that women are more dependent than men are and that they long for this dependence (the Cinderella complex)[76] may be due to the fact that they care so much about what others feel or think, they will do anything to please and be cared for in return. They trade power for being cared for and for being liked.

Power You Have over Others

Here again, there is both indirect and direct power. For example, as a board member of a national organization, I help formulate policies that will affect the membership—this is indirect power. As a university professor, I have direct power over my students because I grade them. But what will make people attribute power to me? I need to look powerful, feel powerful, and act powerful.

Looking Powerful

Why do some people look, feel, and act more powerful than others? One reason is physical attributes and the other is the socialization process. If I were to ask you to describe a physically powerful man, the chances are you would envision him as a tall man with broad shoulders and good musculature. If I asked you to imagine how a powerful woman might look, you probably would not describe somebody 5′2″, weighing 100 pounds. The truth is that powerful people look big, no matter what their actual size is. However, we know that women's bodies on the average are smaller than men's, as are their weight and stature. This stereotype reflects a prejudice against regarding a woman as powerful. Note that the majority of dictators in recent history have been shorter than average height. One can question whether they needed to overcompensate for their small stature.

Another physical attribute is voice. A deep, loud, booming voice commands attention more easily and quickly then a small, high-pitched, thin, weak voice. Many women have not learned to speak loudly enough to be heard well in a large room, and are thus unable to make their presences known and their words heard.

In the animal world, power and dominance are exhibited through physical expression. The more dominant male stands over the less dominant males and females, who show their submission by either flattening themselves on the ground or by rolling over belly up. We women have learned how to make ourselves small, make ourselves invisible, and take up little room so as not to threaten a more dominant male. We have not learned the opposite behaviors, which are standing very straight, looking people in the eye, expanding our chests, projecting our voices, for fear that such behavior might be misconstrued as aggressive, sexual, overbearing, or threatening. Most people in the Western world are so used to seeing men and women of color in subordinate positions that they also don't attribute power to them.

Body language, even better than words, expresses how powerful a person may feel within. The way one walks into a room is indicative of self-concept. For example, a wide, forceful stride gives a specific message; whereas a woman on high heels with a narrow skirt will have a mincing walk, giving very different cues. If she wears a tight dress or one with a slit, she has to worry about tucking it in and may not concentrate on taking a comfortable position in the chair and taking up as much room as she would like. As a rule, men and women who are taller make more money than men and women who are shorter. If there is a correlation, it behooves shorter women to take up as much room as possible by extending their legs, sitting on arms of chairs, and moving about, instead of sitting in a corner or standing immobile.

Another physical attribute of power is touch initiation. Doctors may touch patients, not the other way around. Police officers might touch whomever they are arresting, not the other way around. A professor might touch a student, not the other way around. And men might initiate touch toward women, not the other way around. Visualize the following scene: The male boss walks in and passes his secretary's desk while she is typing. He pats her on the head in a fatherly manner and makes a comment on the good report she did the day before.

Now visualize this scene: The same boss is sitting at a large desk, and his secretary comes up behind him, pats him on his head and says she appreciated the report he did the day before. You are probably smiling at the second scenario and not at the first. The reason you are smiling is because it is so incongruous to imagine the second scene. It is incongruous because it is a role reversal of the usual power hierarchy. The boss may touch a secretary, but she may not reciprocate. One of the things women need to learn is how to initiate touch without communicating something sexual. It is not easy because touch by men is construed as dominance, whereas it is seen as warmth when it comes from a woman.

Touch initiation can be a power move. The boss who puts his arm around his secretary is patronizing her and sends a very definite message that he is in charge. She cannot put her arm around him without risking being seen as sexual. It is important for women to start initiating touch toward others, to stand tall, and to speak more loudly and in a more commanding fashion.

I have tested this when I speak in public. I usually do not stand behind a podium with a microphone attached to it because I am not quite 5′3″. I ask for a lavaliere microphone, which hangs around my neck and I stand *next* to the podium so that I am fully visible. In addition, I frequently wear a bright red suit or some very visible combination of colors. I also walk about on the stage when I speak. The few times I have asked the people in the audience how tall they thought I was, they have always guessed several inches taller than my real height.

Perceptions

When I first got hired
They said it was through Affirmative Action
When I read my report
They said I had a nice voice
When I voiced my opinion
They said I looked cute
When I discussed the budget
They said I had great legs
When I chaired the committee
They said they liked my dress
When I reorganized the department
They said I had lovely eyes
When I became their manager
They said I slept with the boss

Feeling Powerful

Not feeling powerful is the result of our socialization process. Everything in a child's world points to males in authority positions and females in subservient and nurturing ones, whether in literature, in children's schoolbooks, on TV, on the radio, or in real life. All of these images have been so much a part of our growing up that we don't even notice the gender difference and the stereotyping that we constantly have been exposed to. As we become aware of it, we begin to see the inequalities around us, but it takes time, effort, and awakening of consciousness even to notice. As long as we don't pay attention and are unaware of stereotyping, we see it as normal, don't question it, and thus keep repeating the same behavior.

Confronting inequalities is very difficult for women not only because it conflicts with the way they have been brought up but also because it violates male expectations about the way women should behave. It is equally difficult for men to change the patterns of their expectations of what is usual and thus normal. However, there are also men who are shy and nonassertive. The same advice applies to them.

For example, a woman will frequently fail to ask, upon being offered a job, whether her salary is commensurate with that of the men doing the same kind of work. If she finds out that men earn more in the same position, she may feel that to confront the issue will jeopardize her job. She may well be right; however, she *can* ask if there is a reason that her male counterparts are earning more. A typical answer is that he is the head of a family. She can then retort with, "Oh, then you pay more if a person has dependents?" If the answer is yes, she can then produce her own list of dependents: for example, an aging mother, a handicapped brother for whom she is responsible, small children, or older ones needing to go to college. It is possible that such a list would make the employer see how ludicrous that criterion for salary differentials really is.

Many women tend to have lower self-esteem and lower aspirations in terms of salary and job positions than men do. Physical attributes as well as socialization patterns create for men a feeling of entitlement to power and a feeling of nonentitlement for women. Women must thus be educated to know they have the right to aspire to power; it is a learned behavior that comes later in life to women than to men. We know that children tend to fulfill the expectations of their parents. If infant boys are seen as tough and aggressive and infant girls are seen as tender and fragile, these children will grow up fulfilling their parental prophecies. This is why it is so difficult for many women to be both powerful and tender—they think they must be one way or the other. It is equally hard for men to be both compassionate and assertive. They too believe that a choice must be made. We can hope that, with time, both men and women will have the possibility to use a full range of behaviors, thus becoming androgynous.*[77]

Acting Powerful

If not feeling powerful is due in part to female socialization, what stops many women from acting powerful is due in part to male socialization. "Acting" presupposes a relationship; by oneself, one can *feel* either powerful or powerless, but one must *act* in conjunction with another person. Acting is relational; one acts upon an environment through the use of people. A woman may *feel* powerful but be unable to *act* powerfully if the people in her environment are resisting her. If white men have been brought up to experience that their abilities and efforts result in the attainment of goals in the majority of cases, they will then feel in control. Control is internal; one feels a sense of power to influence events. In other words, if men work hard and are competent, they're sure they'll reach their goals.

For minorities and for women who have experienced the discrepancy between ability or effort and attainment of goals, they logically conclude that control is external or is in the hands of others.[78] As we know, there is some truth to the concept of self-fulfilling prophecies. If one believes in one's capacity to make a difference, one has a better chance of achieving this. However, we must not make the error of giving the responsibility to women and minorities for their fate, for if they believe that their lack of opportunity or achievement is due to their inadequacy as individuals, as opposed to racial and sexual discrimination, they will blame and demean themselves instead of working to improve the environment by either educating individuals and groups or by forming a coalition of many in order to effect change. One of the surest ways to act powerfully is to be willing to make decisions and be willing to take risks.

Any decision you make is a risk. Any action you take is a risk. The risk is that you may judge poorly, or even that you may judge well; but the result may not be what you intended. Even if your judgment is

**Androgyny* is the term used when each gender can exhibit behaviors usually connected to the other. For example, men could cry; women could show anger.

correct and the results as you expected, your workers may not be satisfied.

Not to make a decision or not to take action is a decision and an action. It is a decision to leave things as they are.

There has been much written about decision-making, suggesting that one should weigh all the alternatives, choose a solution, and then predict the consequences of the decision. However, I have found that most decisions are based on gut feelings, on hunches, or on intuition. Many people don't consciously go through the steps of a decision-making process, but after gathering information, they will often say, "This feels right to me."

Decisions are often made at a level of consciousness that is not the rational, logical level, but the intuitive level. For example, Akito Morita, the president of Sony, said, "When we developed the first Walkman, a lot of our salespeople said, a small machine like that would not sell. But I had a *hunch* it would sell . . . The sale and product-planning people were all laughing, but now we have sold 4,500,000 units of the Sony Walkman."[79]

I believe that we unconsciously store away a lot of information for possible future use. We are not often aware of how much we know, but, when necessary, we make a decision that feels right without really knowing how we got there. Listen to your instincts; there is useful information there. Your intuition is a good guide.

This does not mean that you should not use all the available resources to help you decide, but a manager never has enough information to make a foolproof decision, so at some point with insufficient data, take a risk, decide, and then act.

The people who are most successful are the people who are frequent risk-takers. If you want security and safety, that's fine, but you will remain where you are—which, by the way, is also just fine. It is not written anywhere that everyone should be moving up all the time. Allow yourself to stay put if that's what feels right, which again is your own decision.

Can You Measure Power?

Can I give you my power? Can you take it away? Can I get more by giving you more? Can you give it to me if I don't want it? Can I get it if you don't give it to me? The answer to all these questions is yes. As we have seen with transference, I can be given power without wanting it. If I am a manager and I delegate well to my employees who then become more powerful, I then give them my power, yet I become more powerful myself.

Empowerment

First:
There must be power
which we feel

Next:
There must be power
which we wield

Then:
There can be power
which we share

I can give away my power if I feel weak, vulnerable, and dependent, and you can take it from me if I allow you to make me feel that way. If you have formal power, you can, in fact, divest me of titles, resources, opportunities, or responsibilities.

So what we see is that power is not a finite quantity; it is infinitely expandable and infinitely retractable. Power is intangible; you cannot touch it, but you can see it when it is used by others, and you can feel it when you use it yourself.

A question one can ask oneself is whether power is a property or a relationship. It can be both. As we have seen earlier, if it is "feeling powerful," it is a property; but if it is "acting powerful," it is a relationship.

Women, Men, and Power

There are differences between how women and men perceive power in others and how they use power themselves.

Women tend to attribute more power to more people than do men. Also, more women use expertise as a power base. Because credibility has been an issue for women who have attempted to enter male-dominated work or have tried to climb corporate ladders, they have had to prove their competence by having to acquire more expertise than their male counterparts. As a result, many women often have felt inadequate until they have earned one more degree, attended one more seminar, or read one more book.

As women gain more power, a shift in power is bound to occur. Some men will be displaced and replaced. Men can deal with other men as potential competitors, but they tend to have a harder time dealing with women. When I see three or four men sitting at a table in the faculty dining room, it would never occur to me to ask what they were plotting. However, when I sit together with a few women, we have frequently been approached with that question. Somehow, in the context of a work environment, women in a group seem to pose a threat to some men.

One study of promotional patterns within a corporation found that supervisors gave the highest ratings to older, less aggressive women who didn't rock the boat, but gave lower ratings to the younger, more aggressive women who were blocked at the lower echelons. However, the older women were not the kinds of executives whom senior management wanted for high-level jobs, so neither group of women could advance.[80] This is not surprising if we understand the socialization patterns of men. Women are socialized in ways that directly fit into the male patterns by having been taught *not* to rock the boat. The double bind for women is that if they are ambitious, they are a threat and won't be promoted, and if they aren't ambitious, they are not good management potential.

It is not possible for women to meet everyone's expectations of what they should be like, look like, act like, and sound like. It is indeed difficult for women to be powerful if acting powerful is not only unacceptable but also is punished by ostracism or ridicule.

The only thing women can do is to keep challenging other's expectations of what behavior is acceptable in a male and not acceptable in a female. It is only by making the unconscious conscious that women will change attitudes.[81] Assertiveness is in the eyes of the beholder.

I Know What I Know

I wish I knew then
what I know now
For I didn't know then

how much I knew
Now I know
what I know
Now I know
that I know

Following are 16 ways to increase your power, visibility, and opportunities in an organization:[82]

1. Seek out opportunities to work on important and difficult assignments and projects.
2. Know the organizational goals of top management, and focus your activities on helping to reach them.
3. Participate in problem-solving task forces.
4. Help your boss to meet responsibilities.
5. Be a good "group" person and get along with peers and subordinates.
6. Align personal goals with organizational goals.
7. Align yourself with the powerful, the movers, and the successful.
8. Go after positions that have few rules, have a variety of tasks, are nonroutine, a position where rewards are given for unusual performance and innovation.
9. Participate in programs, conferences, and meetings.
10. Focus upward and outward from your work unit.
11. Locate yourself physically close to top management.
12. Publicize yourself and your activities. Send out memos.
13. Seek out and have as much contact with top management as possible.
14. Advance your subordinates.
15. Recognize the value of lateral moves as well as upward promotions.
16. Be positive and give others credit and opportunity.

A word of caution is in order here. If you are a woman or a minority person and you are being promoted, as you rise in the hierarchy, your tendency will be to get co-opted. What this means is that you will be so glad finally to have made it that you may not be willing to risk the hard-won membership in the "club of white men'' by helping the lower-level people, for fear that once again you will be seen as ''one of them.''

Becoming aware of this tendency will help prevent your falling into the trap of being a ''queen bee'' if you are a woman, or of being considered a black who does not help black brothers or sisters.

Note that we never hear of ''king drones'' because there are fewer expectations of help from white men.

If you are a minority person in a subordinate position and if your superior of the same gender or race is not helpful—perhaps even deliberately obstructionist—try to understand that your boss may not feel secure enough to take better care of you. If that is the case, there is not much you can do about it except to know that there is nothing personal in this.

Exercise

To understand power politics, answer the following questions.

1. Ask yourself, to whom do you attribute power?
2. Does that person have real power over you? Is it direct or indirect?
3. Over whom do you have power?
4. Are other people besides your subordinates attributing power to you? If yes, why? If no, why not?
5. Make a hidden agenda analysis of the three people who most affect your work or your life.
6. Do you look powerful? How? If not, how can you change that?
7. Do you feel powerful? How? If not, how can you change that?
8. Do you act powerful? How? If not, how can you change that?

LAST WORDS

This book ends as you begin your new job. When you encounter problems, which you will, reread the appropriate chapters. The information will make more sense if you can apply it to a situation you are experiencing.

Remember that you are not alone. Find family, friends, colleagues, and superiors who are willing to help you solve your problems. Sit down with one, two, or three people and say, "I need you as consultants. Can you give me 30 minutes (or an hour) of your time. This is my problem . . ."

And then, listen. Don't interrupt with "Yes, but . . ." Pay attention. You may even want to role-play your situation with their help. You are not imposing on them. People like to be used as experts. Would you mind if someone asked you for your expert opinion? Probably not. They won't mind either and may even feel complimented that you trust them and value their suggestions.

If you are an established supervisor and have been on the job for a while, do you want to stay put or do you wish to move up? Either decision is legitimate. "Up" is not the only way to happiness. You may be happy with things as they are. Allow yourself to feel that way. If not, plan strategies. Get to know your boss and your boss's boss. Let them know that you want more responsibilities.

As you move up, the major difference between being a supervisor and being a manager is that as a supervisor, you still will need to know how to perform the work your workers perform, you will be in daily contact with them. As a manager, you will work with supervisors and formulate policies that the supervisors will have to implement. The supervisor is thought by many to be the critical link in any organization. And here is a last piece of advice: Treat others as you would wish to be treated, taking into consideration cultural differences. Be a sensitive and caring supervisor with high standards and integrity. Good Luck!

Where Is the End of the Line?

Some of us know
where we are going
but most of us
don't know
when we have arrived

NOTES

1. Barnett, Rosalind, Wellesley, MA, Wellesley College Center for Research on Women, June 1980.
2. Schaeffer, Ruth Gilbert and Junger, Allen, ''Who Is Top Management?'' Report No. 821, New York: Conference Board, 1982.
3. Cassidy, Robert, ''How We're Viewed by the Men We Boss,'' *Savvy,* July 1982, pp. 15–18.
4. Mirides, Ellyn and Cote, Andre, ''Women in Management: Strategies for Removing the Barriers,'' *Personnel Administrator,* April 1980.
5. Schmidt, Warren and Posner, Barry, ''Managerial Values and Expectations,'' *Savvy,* December 1982.
6. Josefowitz, Natasha, ''Hazing at the Workplace,'' unpublished research, 1983.
7. Baron, Alma and Abrahamson, Ken, ''Will He or Won't He Work with a Female Manager?'' *Management Review,* November 1981, pp. 48–53.
8. Carlson, Barbara, ''Managing the Boss is Easier Than You Might Think,'' *New England Business,* Vol. 4, No. 114, September 6, 1982. (This article quotes Bob Mezoff's seminar on ''How to Manage Your Boss.'')
9. Josefowitz, Natasha, ''The Clonal Effect in Organizations,'' *Management Review,* September 1979, pp. 20–23.
10. Mai, Dalton, et al., ''The Effects of Manager's Sex on the Assignment to a Challenging or a Dull Task and Reasons for

the Choice,'' *Academy of Management Journal,* Vol. 24, No. 3, September 1981, pp. 603–612.
11. Cohen, Allen R., et al. (with the collaboration of Natasha Josefowitz), *Effective Behavior in Organizations,* revised edition, Homewood, IL: Richard D. Irwin, Inc., 1984.
12. Scheflen, Albert E., *Body Language and the Social Order,* Englewood Cliffs, NJ: Prentice Hall, 1972.
13. Dawley, Harold H., Jr., *Friendship,* Englewood Cliffs, NJ: Prentice Hall, 1980.
14. Rogers, Carl and Farson, Richard E., *Active Listening,* University of Chicago, Industrial Relations Center, in Cohen et al., *Effective Behavior in Organizations,* Homewood, IL: Richard D. Irwin, Inc., 1976.
15. Fernandez, John P., *Racism and Sexism in Corporate Life,* Lexington, MA: Lexington Books, 1981.
16. Katz, Judith, ''The Sociopolitical Nature of Counseling,'' *Counseling Psychologist,* in press.
17. Sue, Derald W., *Counseling the Culturally Different,* John Wiley, 1981.
18. Bartolomé, Fernando and Evans, Paul A. Lee, ''Must Success Cost So Much?'' *Harvard Business Review,* March–April, 1980.
19. Ibid.
20. Gabarro, John J. and Kotter, John P., ''Managing Your Boss,'' *Harvard Business Review.* January–February, 1980.
21. Josefowitz, Natasha, *Sex and Power: Workplace Issues,* 30-minute video tape with instructor's manual—available at Regional Training Center, 11772 Sorrento Valley Road, Suite 212, San Diego, CA 92121
22. Center for Compliance Information, *Sex Discrimination in the Workplace,* Aspen, CO: Aspen Publications, 1978, p. 75.
23. Saint James, Diane, ''Coping with Sexual Harassment,'' *Supervisory Management,* 28 October 1983, pp. 2–9.
24. Josefowitz, Natasha, ''Sexual Relationships at Work: Attraction, Transference, Coercion, or Strategy,'' *Personnel Administrator,* March 1982, p. 91.
25. Karp, H. B., ''Working with Resistance,'' *Training and Development Journal,* March 1984, pp. 69–73.
26. Lakein, Alan, *How to Get Control of Your Time and Life,* New York: Signet Books, 1973.

27. Mintzberg, Henry, "The Manager's Job: Folklore and Fact," *Harvard Business Review,* July–August 1975.
28. Guest, Robert H., "Of Time and the Foreman," *Personnel,* May 1956.
29. Stewart, Rosemary, *Managers and Their Jobs,* London, England; Macmillan, 1967.
30. Fernandez, John P., *Racism and Sexism in Corporate Life,* Lexington, MA: Lexington Books, 1981.
31. Gary, Lawrence E. and Leashore, Bogart R., "High Risk Status of Black Men," *Social Work,* Vol. 27, No. 1, January 1982, pp. 54–58.
32. Korn, Ferry International. Study made at the University of California, Los Angeles, Graduate School of Management, *The Wall Street Journal,* November 1, 1982.
33. Schwartz, Jackie, *Letting Go of Stress,* New York: Pinnacle Books, 1982.
34. Palmer, Judith, "How to Make a Woman Lose Effectiveness in an Organization," reprinted by permission.
35. Benson, Howard, *The Relaxation Response,* New York: William Morrow, 1975.
36. The Women's Career Program, Northeastern University, Evaluation report, Natasha Josefowitz and Herman Gadon, 1978. Grant provided from the Fund for the Improvement of Post Secondary Education (FIPSE), U.S. Department of Health, Education, and Welfare, Boston: Northeastern University, 1978.
37. "New Views of Reentry Women," *Women's Network,* Vols. 1 and 2, August 1983.
38. Josefowitz, Natasha, "Hazing at the Workplace," *USA Today,* Oct 12, 1983.
39. Josefowitz, Natasha, *Paths to Power: A Woman's Guide from First Job to Top Executive*. Reading, MA: Addison-Wesley, 1980.
40. Josefowitz, Natasha, unpublished research, Naval Air Rework Facility, North Island Naval Station, San Diego, May 1984.
41. Edwards, Tanya, "Managing Culturally Different Employees in the United States," unpublished master's thesis, San Diego State University, May 1984.
42. Hackman, Richard J., et al., "A New Strategy for Job Enrichment," *California Management Review,* Summer 1975, Vol. 17, No. 4, pp. 57–59.

43. Skinner, Wickham, "Big Hat, No Cattle: Managing Human Resources," *Harvard Business Review,* September–October 1981, pp. 106–114.
44. Likert, Rensis, "Motivation: The Core of Management," in *The Nature and Scope of Management,* Maneck F. Wadia, ed., Chicago: Scott, Foresman, 1966.
45. Hyams, Nanci Barbara and Josefowitz, Natasha, "Perceptions of Rewards as a Function of Gender," paper presented at the Academy of Management, Boston: August 1984.
46. Yankelovich, Daniel, *The New Morality: A Profile of American Youth in the 1970s.* New York: McGraw-Hill, 1974.
47. Bardwick, Judith M., "Plateauing and Productivity," *Sloan Management Review,* Spring 1983, pp. 67–73.
48. Baird, Lloyd and Kram, Kathy, "Career Dynamics: Managing the Superior/Subordinate Relationships," *Organizational Dynamics,* Spring 1983. pp. 46–64.
49. Schmidt, Klaus D., *Doing Business in Indonesia,* Report No. 624, Business Intelligence Program SRI International, 1979.
50. *Doing Business in France,* Report No. 601, SRI, 1978.
51. Simon, Sydney B., *Negative Criticism,* Niles, IL: Argus Communications, 1978.
52. Ilgen, Daniel R., et al., "Supervisor and Subordinate Reactions to Performance Appraisal Sessions," *Organizational Behavior and Human Performance,* 28, 1981, pp. 311–330 (copyright 1981 by Academic Press).
53. Thompson, Ken and Pitts, Robert E., "The Great Balancing Act," *Supervisory Management,* May 1979, Vol. 24, pp. 22–30.
54. Halatin, T. J., "Evaluating the Superior Employee," *Supervisory Management,* December 1981, pp. 17–20.
55. These were answers given by the employees of a large state university, including grounds personnel, kitchen staff, utility workers, general maintenance workers of buildings, cleaning crews, and so on.
56. Boyd, Bradford B., *Management-Minded Supervision,* New York: McGraw Hill, 1968.
57. "Taking Drugs on the Job." *Newsweek,* August 22, 1983, p. 52.
58. Ibid.
59. Levinson, Harry. "The Abrasive Personality," *Harvard Business Review,* May–June 1978, pp. 86–94.

60. Oates, David. "How to Survive a Whiz Kid," *International Management,* May 1982, pp. 69–70.
61. Josefowitz, Natasha. "Getting Through to the Unreachable Person," *Management Review,* March 1982, pp. 48–50.
62. Ettore, Barbara, "Fear of Firing," *Savvy,* September 1983, pp. 85–90.
63. Ricklefs, Roger, "Seminar Enlightens Managers on Best Way to Hire and Handle Disabled Employees," *The Wall Street Journal,* May 27, 1981, Section II, p. 31(E).
64. DeForest, Mariah E., "New Young Employees: Lemons or Lemonade?" *Personnel Administrator,* July 1979, pp. 79–84.
65. Rubin Jeff, et al., "The Eye of the Beholder: Parents' View on Sex of Newborn," *American Journal of Orthopsychiatry,* 1974, pp. 44–47.
66. Knotts, Rose E., "What to Do about Temps," *Supervisory Management,* April 1982, pp. 39–41.
67. Wheatley, Meg and Schorr-Hirsch, Maurice, *Managing Your Maternity Leave,* Boston: Houghton-Mifflin, 1983.
68. Heidel, Stephen H., *Supervisor's Training Manual,* Western Employee Assistance Program, reprinted by permission.
69. Ibid.
70. Pelz, Donald C. and Andrews, Frank M., *Scientists in Organizations: Productive Climate for Research and Development,* Institute for Social Research. University of Michigan, Ann Arbor, 1976.
71. Adapted from Dier, William G., *Team Building: Issues and Alternatives,* Reading, MA: Addison-Wesley, 1977.
72. Cohen, Allen R., et al. (with the collaboration of Natasha Josefowitz), *Effective Behavior in Organizations,* revised edition, Homewood, IL: Richard D. Irwin, Inc., 1984.
73. Schutz, William C., *Elements of Encounter,* Big Sur, CA: Joy Press, 1973.
74. Josefowitz, Natasha, *Paths to Power: A Woman's Guide from First Job to Top Executive,* Reading, MA: Addison-Wesley, 1980.
75. Bardwick, Judith, *In Transition,* New York: Holt, Rinehart & Winston, 1979.
76. Dowling, Colette, *The Cinderella Complex,* New York: Pocket Books, 1981.
77. Sargent, Alice, *The Androgynous Manager,* New York: AMACOM, 1982.

78. Sue, Derald W., *Counseling the Culturally Different,* New York: John Wiley, 1981. p. 65.
79. Range, Peter Ross, interview with Akito Morita, ''A Candid Conversation with the Founding Wizard of Sony about All Those Miraculous Machines and Why Japan Produces Them and American Doesn't.'' *Playboy,* August 1982.
80. Harlen, Anne and Weiss, Carol, ''Moving Up: Women in Managerial Careers,'' final report, Wellesley, MA: Wellesley College Center for Research on Women, September 1981.
81. Josefowitz, Natasha, ''Women and Power: A New Model,'' in *Beyond Sex Roles* by Alice G. Sargent, revised, St. Paul, MN: West Publishing, 1984.
82. Roberts, Connie, ''Management Styles,'' unpublished master's thesis, San Diego State University, Fall 1983.

INDEX